Also by William McInnes

A Man's Got to Have a Hobby

Cricket Kings

That'd be Right

Worse Things Happen at Sea (with Sarah Watt)

Best wishes

WILLIAM McINNES

the making of
modern australia

hachette
AUSTRALIA

hachette
AUSTRALIA

First published in Australia and New Zealand in 2010
by Hachette Australia
(an imprint of Hachette Australia Pty Limited)
Level 17, 207 Kent Street, Sydney NSW 2000
www.hachette.com.au

This edition published in 2012

10 9 8 7 6 5 4 3 2 1

National Library of Australia
Cataloguing-in-Publication data

McInnes, William, 1963-
The making of modern Australia

978 0 7336 2780 4 (pbk.)

Collective memory–Australia.
Australia–History–20th century.
Australia–Social life and customs–20th century.

302.0994

The interviews in this book are reproduced with the participants' permission.

*Aboriginal and Torres Strait Islanders are advised that this book contains photographs of people
who are deceased or may be deceased.*

Cover and internal design by Christabella Designs
Cover image courtesy of Getty Images
Back cover author photograph by Lorrie Graham
Digital production by Bookhouse, Sydney
Printed in Australia by Griffin Press, Adelaide, an Accredited ISO AS/NZS 14001:2004
Environmental Management Systems printer

In memory of Bob Watt and Ian Leggett,
two men who helped make modern Australia

Contents

The Australian Heart

The Australian Dream

The
Making
of Modern
Australia

History as a Caged Cockatoo

One family holiday in western New South Wales, when we stopped at a small country town for lunch at an Apex park, it seemed no different from all the other country towns we had visited. The same cenotaphs with the names of those who gave their lives in service to their country. Just names, perhaps names nobody reads. But they were all lives of sons, brothers, friends and husbands, and they all had stories. Some of those names may have belonged to good people and bad people; their deaths may have been good or ill. And why the lives were lost, I wondered whether that would ever really be known.

During this holiday I was extraordinarily moved by the sense of time and achievement since European settlement. I felt proud of the accomplishments of our shared history. Of the Royal Flying Doctor Service and the work of Flynn of the Inland.

At the bottom of a 400-metre mine shaft in Broken Hill, I listened with my children to the history of three old miners as we walked through the disused mine. Where once the economy of this nation was ripped from the earth, now a group of tourists listened to the histories of these battered and noble Australians.

'You need mates down here, you know,' said Bob Murphy. 'And a mate is basically someone you trust. You may not understand them; they might not look like you; you may not even know them that well. They may talk different to you. But if you trust them and they can trust you, then they're mates.'

Never to me has that concept been better described.

And then on the rolling dunes of Lake Mungo I laughed while my children and a few other kids roared with excitement as they rolled down the silk-soft sandhills. Perhaps other Australian children, Indigenous children, had done these same things here thousands of years ago.

History is many things.

In 2006 the federal education minister Julie Bishop wanted us all to know more about history. Especially that floating group known as young Australians. 'Young Australians should study the past to understand the present, so that they can make informed decisions for the future.'

Fair enough, but history comes in all shapes and sizes. A year later the page had turned upon the government of which Ms Bishop had been a member, presenting a new minister with the opportunity to speak about history and identity and Australia.

There's the history that gets people all hot and bothered. From the supposed fibs of Manning Clark, to Geoffrey Blainey, the roads to Damascus of Robert Manne and even the revisionist teacup rattling of Keith Windschuttle. These are people who are historians. Their business is history.

But there are other histories. The year that Julie Bishop made her remarks about Australia's history I was earning a dollar dressed up as John Curtin. Acting in a TV drama about Australia's fourteenth prime minister. Pretending to be a man who gave his life in service to this country, I walked around an old RAAF base in my lunch break complaining loudly in my best disgruntled customer's voice into a mobile phone about a holiday I was trying to book.

My beratings got the better of some of the crew, who pelted me with a few hardboiled eggs and the advice, 'Shut up and get over it, Mr Prime Minister.'

Ms Bishop would appreciate this: first, a Labor PM, even a pretend one, being pelted with eggs; and also the fact that our history was being told in the form of entertainment, broadcast out across the nation and beyond. She is, after all, member for the seat of Curtin.

Curtin's story belongs to us all. But is it a prescribed history that we should be taught? History is many things.

We are a nation born from an imperial colony and we were bequeathed a great deal of baggage from the British that we may or may not come to terms with. But who were those children who rolled down the dunes at Lake Mungo many decades ago? Should we not share the stories of those Australians, too? Or does history have a simple and efficient start date that fits in with a curriculum? Is it a tale only told within the sweep of grand events? And great figures?

History is many things.

Sometimes it is silent. In that Apex park was a birdcage. A great white cockatoo clung to the wire and croaked hello to anyone who came near it. My daughter stood staring at the bird. She didn't touch her lunch. It was time to go. I called and she looked torn. The bird called to her again. She turned and waved softly to the bird in the cage. She cried for a while in the car. The bird was alone. She didn't want to leave it.

'It just does that because it's been taught to,' I said.

'It talked to me,' she insisted.

History is many things. A different tale told with the same characters, it can be like a caged bird. Taught to mimic words as a trick. But my daughter is right. History, like that bird, will always try to talk to you. The least we can do is listen.

This is not a complete history of modern Australia; it can't be, for the Australia I know and write about is an evolving work. Rather, it is a collection of parts of some lives that may have contributed to making and shaping this country since the end of the Second World War. That is all. Nothing more, nothing less.

The
Australian
Child

1

Just Come Back by the Time it's Dark

Some years ago, I sat on the verandah of a house in Woy Woy, a small seaside hamlet on the New South Wales Central Coast. I sat with my brother, Vaughan. The sun went down and turned the sky and the water and all things we saw that peculiar mix of salmon pink and a golden colour that is timeless and makes you think of landscapes in art galleries – only this landscape was huge and moved and made sounds. The odd waterbird or motorboat. The calls of children. The sounds of the water. Voices of people floating through the air. Makes you happy just to sit and watch. Which is good because that is exactly what we did.

A small jetty extended out into the bay and tiny boats bobbed on the water, reflecting the cottonwool clouds above. We didn't really say anything, my brother and I, for there wasn't any need. It was one of those moments in life where all you need to do is be.

And then Vaughan laughed a little. I kept looking out at what lay before me; if he wanted to enjoy himself and laugh, then that

---

Page 5: *Bob Moore, aged four, at the bathroom window of the family home in Isisford, central Queensland, in the 1950s.*

was his business. Still, after a while I wondered what it was that had taken his fancy.

At the end of the jetty our wives fished and chatted. I didn't think he'd be laughing to himself about them. Further around the bay a man was working on a boat's engine but he seemed to be in no hurry and had everything under control, so he couldn't have caught Vaughan's eye. A silver double-level train let out a low hoot and pulled in to the station on the furthermost point of the bay. It wasn't that either.

I couldn't see what it might be, so I looked around the bay again.

'It's them,' my brother said slowly, gesturing with his left hand in a lazy wave towards two little figures by the water's edge. My son and his youngest daughter. They had been outside for as long as we had been sitting on the verandah, which must have been quite some time.

They were both hard at work. Heads and eyes down, hands held out in front of them like they are a pair of diviners searching for some mystic presence. Then one or the other, or both at the same time, would yelp and dance and pounce. They were after skinks. They had been after skinks all afternoon. Up and down the little foreshore and around by the mangroves they had been on the lookout for skinks – tiny little lizards with shiny backs.

They had been at it for so long that they and their cries had blended in among the scene before us so completely it was as if they were part of the landscape. As if you couldn't imagine seeing the bay without them, like the bay without the water.

I looked down at them. They chattered skinks.

'It got away, the skink got away,' my son said.

'Was it there?' his cousin asked.

'It was there, it got away.'

'You said that about that root,' she said.

'The root? The root didn't get away, it's a root.'

'You said the skink was a root.'

'It was, but the skink got away, that's what skinks do.'

'You sure it was a skink?'

'Yes, it wasn't a root.'

'A skink root.'

'It got away, it was big. And a root can't get away.'

'Yeah.' She didn't sound convinced.

Vaughan laughed again. I joined him. 'A skink root,' I said.

My brother tilted his head slightly and pushed his glasses back up his nose. 'That,' he said slowly, 'is great. Kids just being kids.'

I looked at the skink hunters and back to my brother, then asked him what he meant.

'Kids just being kids. Just being. Not thinking about anything else except skinks and roots and whatever it is they're doing. It's . . .' He searched for the words. 'It's like an afternoon stretching forever. Being a kid is like that. It's great.'

I turned back to the skink hunters and thought of my brother, a man who was successful in his chosen field and worked a pretty relentless and punishing schedule. Work was never far from his mind. But on the verandah, time was in a slow, happy state.

'Childhood should be like that. It's great to live and think that things just go on. It's a shame that it ends, but it does, and childhood's a beautiful thing.'

When I ask him if he talks like that at his rugby club, he gives me a bit of advice, along the lines of procreation, as to what I should do with myself – in a friendly, big brother sort of way.

Our wives have packed in the fishing and walk past the skink hunters and up to the verandah. Vaughan's daughter looks at them a bit anxiously, then mutters something to my son. He looks up, a little worried.

'Do we have to come in now?' he asks no one in particular.

'Just come back by the time it's dark,' my sister-in-law replies before she heads into the house.

The skink hunters look to each other. 'Yes!' says my niece happily as she slaps my son on the back.

'He got away!' yelps my son.

Vaughan and I laugh again.

'Just come back by the time it's dark.'

It's an echo of our childhoods. Our parents would yell it out as general advice as to what was expected of us. I remember my mother pushing me outside the house as I attempted to mooch in front of the television one afternoon after school. I was told to go outside and find something to do, and to be back before it got dark.

'"Just come back by the time it's dark" should be on a T-shirt,' says Vaughan. Then he thinks a little. 'No, it's too good for a T-shirt. It's just good it's said.'

We watch the skink hunters as the light fades. 'You know it'll be dark in about ten to fifteen,' I say.

'Ten or fifteen is as good as forever for those two,' he replies.

We watch a bit more, then my brother calls out to the skink hunters, 'How many skinks have you got?'

There's a pause, then my son yells back, 'We got, we got . . .' He mutters to his cousin before he turns back to the verandah, 'No skinks. We've got no skinks.'

'But we got some roots,' says his cousin. And they go about with their heads down and their hands splayed in the fading light.

That was some time ago, not long, I thought, but just some time. I made notes and looked at the date. It was eight years ago. My son and his cousin have grown through their childhood and into their teenage years. They don't hunt skinks anymore. And as they grow older I suppose afternoons don't stretch as long as those from not that long ago. Not as long as that afternoon in Woy Woy.

Where, I wonder, did those eight years go? Well, I wouldn't be the first parent to wonder that.

Childhood is something you only have once and if you are lucky enough to enjoy the one you do get, the realisation of how sweet and fine it is strikes you, as it did my brother and me on that verandah. But perhaps we in Australia or, more precisely, people like my brother and me, don't expect a childhood, generally, to be anything other than fun. After all, we grew up in Australia, where for many of us a happy childhood is the norm, not a privilege.

I remember one night around the dinner table my father offering the observation that I didn't know how lucky I was to be growing up in a country like Australia. Why was that, I asked him. 'Because Australia is about the only place that would put up with a bloody drongo like you,' he said by way of reply.

It must be noted that this was the day I had gashed my forehead and brow trying to remove a plaster mould of my head. Inspired by a documentary about ancient Rome at school I had taken a fancy to the various Caesars and attempted to make a bust of my head. When I told my mother it was for homework she was quite content to let me go on my way. She even boasted to my father while I slapped plaster of Paris around my head that I was 'off doing homework, been at it all afternoon'.

'So Cabbagehead has come good then?' my father had said a little doubtfully.

I, Cabbagehead – as opposed to I, Claudius – had no real idea what I was doing, but enjoyed myself enough up until the point that I had difficulty seeing and breathing. I used a hammer to try to break the plaster mould, which had only half set in places, so succeeded only in hitting my head with the hammer.

Then I had the brainwave that if I thrust my head against something the offending mould would shatter and I would be free. I managed to work out that if I held my head back at what seemed an acute angle I could have partial vision out of my right eye and could line up a suitable object to run towards. Aiming to head-butt what I thought would be the pole of the Hills hoist, the weight of the half-set plaster orb tilted my head back to such an extent that my target disappeared and all I could see was a pleasant-looking bit of late afternoon sky. It turned out I missed the clothesline completely and bounced off the incinerator into a pile of timber and fencing my father had arranged in the backyard.

This was all done in front of my parents and a couple of their friends as they chatted by the barbecue over a cup of tea. Someone screamed, I think it was one of my parents' friends. It was an unfamiliar yell, so I turned blindly in a vain attempt to see who it might be. That's why I missed the Hills hoist.

'He's still got his uniform on,' said the other friend.

'Yes,' said my mum, 'it's homework for school, I think it might be something on the New Guinea Mud Men.' She was trying her best to give me the benefit of the doubt.

'Jesus wept,' was all my father could come up with. I thought he might have a point.

Despite my more than occasional idiocy – 'Well, at least he has a go,' was my father's way of coming to terms with my arsing around – Australia was a place, he always believed, where anybody could have a go at anything and childhood was as good a time as any to chance your hand.

It seemed it had always been that way. At the end of the Second World War there weren't many places like Australia. The old world had almost exhausted itself during the war and no sooner had the conflict ceased than a new one was being brewed up between the

'Free World' and that of the Communist regimes behind Winston Churchill's famous Iron Curtain.

When Churchill used this term in one of his speeches in 1946, ushering in the Cold War, Australia was a land of seven and a half million people with space, peace and opportunity. Over the next twenty years, give or take, the population would grow to eleven and a half million – in part thanks to a massive immigration program, but mainly due to a boom in the number of babies born during that era.

And with great originality these children, and the adults they grew up to be, were called the Baby Boomers. Two of those Baby Boomers were Bob Moore and Loretta Pendergast, who became

Loretta Pendergast, aged four, in 1950.

childhood sweethearts while growing up in rural Queensland, although Bob Moore prefers his other title. 'Mum always called me her "Peace Baby". I was conceived just after the Japanese surrendered, I'm not sure exactly, there was a few weeks' delay – Dad must have been working out in the bush somewhere or something. Late August, it was, and I was born in June 1946.'

Bob Moore may have been a 'Peace Baby' but his parents had little chance to have much peace and quiet on the home front. Considering themselves loyal Australians, they were hearty followers of the national cry of 'populate or perish'. At the rate at which the Moore family populated, there was little chance of them perishing.

'We had five boys and a girl in our family and that was a fairly normal-sized family. Six of us. Nowadays, two and three are big numbers, aren't they? Just different times altogether!' says Bob.

Bob and Loretta had typical Australian bush childhoods, with knockabout adventures and learning life's necessities on the job. But all this was par for the course, or in Bob Moore's words, different times altogether.

Loretta says, 'When Dad went to work in the bush he'd take me. Kangaroo shooting, shearers' cook and drover. I'd spend the school holidays out there and Dad taught me to shoot and to drive a jeep.'

Bob shakes his head and Loretta laughs and carries on. 'One day, Dad said, "Oh, I think we'll build a shed in the backyard and we'll go out and get this timber." So we did, and I started driving. When it came to getting my driver's licence I went up to the police station and, as I walked in, the policeman wrote out the licence and he said, "I may as well give you a truck licence, too, because I've seen you driving a truck around the back streets." So I ended up with both!'

Loretta was so adept that she taught her husband to drive. 'I was a very fortunate young man, learning to drive on a left-hand-drive

On their way home from visiting the Warrego River in Charleville, Queensland, in 1951.
Left to right: *Loretta's father, Frank Pendergast, Dennis Sheard, Loretta, and Vicki Sheard* (back right).

Loretta at the wheel of her parents' left-hand-drive jeep as a teenager, 1963.

jeep with no brakes,' says Bob with raised eyebrows as Loretta shakes her head.

Growing up was much the same story for Bob – working with his father out in the bush on school holidays and learning about the vagaries of life. His favourite memory is helping to build woolsheds, knocking around with his father and his workmates, and basically learning what it was to be a part of a group working together and to be a man, although sometimes there were a few hoops he had to jump through.

Bob would help to prepare the smoko, when the men could grab a cup of tea and almost invariably light up a cigarette. The fire would be ready and it would only take a few moments to start boiling the water, but the men took the chance to introduce Bob to the school of Taking the Mickey. 'They would say, "Boy, hasn't that kettle boiled yet? Hurry up, hurry up!"

*Bob, aged two, playing at a weir on the Murrumbidgee River, Easter, 1949.
His father, Richard Moore, rests in the background.*

'Every day I tried to get it faster and faster till I had flames floating six foot in the air and they'd still say it was too slow. I didn't wake up till many years later that they were winding me up, but I learned how to boil a billy pretty fast. Wonderful days, wonderful days.

'We had whole open spaces; there was no problem with just going out on your own as a youngster, catching crayfish or hunting for bird's nests, eggs and things like that. There were no restrictions, you could walk anywhere in the bush.'

Loretta with her cousins Les Schumann and Lyn Sheard, in her Uncle Tom's boat during the Charleville flood, 1954.

The bush was as big as your dreams, but it wasn't the only place that seemed to stretch forever; even in the suburbs of the major cities that sense of a never-ending backyard wasn't far away. Les Dixon grew up in suburban Perth about the same time as Bob and Loretta, and he remembers that same sense of freedom.

'You know, we could go anywhere we liked – that was the good thing about those days, parents didn't have to worry about where kids went. We just roamed everywhere. We walked, we rode bikes we found down in the rubbish tip and put together, and things like that. I think kids in my time were more inventive in being able to build things, make things to amuse themselves, rather than having everything bought for them.

'We'd build billycarts out of old soap boxes and the old man's brace and bit drill – no electric drills or anything like that – and take them up the hill. We found old pram wheels at the tip. My brother actually went on to become quite inventive, he made a living out of inventing things,' Les says, and nods his head.

Almost all of the Baby Boomers' parents had lived through two major social, economic and political upheavals – the global economic wreck known as the Great Depression and then the chaos of the Second World War. Even though Australia was a growing nation with a burgeoning economy, the general uncertainty these events brought with them and the ensuing Cold War meant that ideals and values important to the Boomers' parents were passed on to their children: the concepts of thrift and hard work, austerity and respect for authority.

'Well, we had to work for our keep, so to speak,' says Les Dixon. 'To get pocket money we had to chop wood, do gardening, clean up after the dog, make our beds.' But it was worth it. 'We used to get two shillings a week pocket money, my brother and I. It went a long way. We could go to the movies, buy a bottle of Coke, a packet of P.K. chewing gum to put in the Coke to make it fizz up, and a Phantom comic.'

Les Dixon sighs a bit and again nods his head in appreciation of the fine things that a childhood can bring. But as fine as they were, the idea of discipline was never far away, and although Les describes his stepfather as one of the greatest influences on his life, he expected a high standard of order and behaviour from children.

Les' stepfather was a bookmaker at the trots and was, in Les' words, 'pretty well-off and we were never short of anything. He was an all-round nice guy. My brother and I would never say a bad word about him. He put us through college and everything like that.'

Les Dixon, aged five, and his brother, Gary, aged three, playing bookies in 1946.

If Les and his brother Gary stepped out of line, his stepfather, as head of the house, would hand out the discipline. 'We'd get a belting, but looking back it wasn't anything we didn't deserve. Once I got belted for setting the back fence on fire.'

A group of kids had been chasing Les and Gary and so, with a bit of too-quick thinking, Les grabbed a can of petrol, poured it over his back fence and set it alight. The resulting fire stopped the gang, but not his stepfather. 'Yeah, we got a belting. A smack across the backside with the belt. But apart from anything else, he asked me if I realised what I could have done to myself. It was a lesson he did teach me.'

Les Dixon's stepfather was, if nothing else, a thoughtful man, and he found other ways to exact punishment on this errant young fellow. He would tell Les to wait for him in the bathroom and, of course, the longer Les waited, the more his fear grew, until it was far worse than the eventual punishment. His stepfather would come in and say, 'Right, off you go and don't do it again.'

When the boys were older their stepfather used another form of punishment for not toeing the line. 'He realised the best way to get control of us was to say no pocket money, even if we had done our chores.' It was a lesson spread across many families over the generations.

'My mates would come around and say, "Les, coming to the movies?" and I would say, "Oh, I don't think I want to see this show today," and I'd go into my room and cry my eyes out. I'd have rather got ten smacks than miss out on that time with my mates.'

Usually it was the father's job to be the disciplinarian, but the process was warmed up with a chilling warning from many a mother: 'You just wait till your father gets home.'

Catchphrases seem to be handed down from fathers to sons when they have their own children by way of some sort of secret father network. The promise of doom descending upon them is enough to make a child's blood turn stone cold. 'Do I have to get out of my chair?' 'Am I going to have to stop the car?' 'You can forget about your dinner.' 'What did you do to your mother?' 'That's the last we'll see of you tonight.' And the most scary of all: 'I'll deal with you later. You can count on that.'

It's funny to remember them, and even funnier when you catch yourself saying the same things to your own children.

As well as 'populate or perish', another popular and rather ambitious slogan from the Australian government was, 'The child makes the best migrant.' In the latter years of the Second World War, after the threat of invasion had dissipated, Dr H.C. 'Nugget' Coombs, the Director-General of the Department of Post-war Reconstruction, wrote in a memo, 'The Minister thinks we should plan for immigration of large numbers of children after the cessation of hostilities.'

The target was set at an incredible 50,000 children. Instead, around 3,500 deprived and abandoned children arrived from England via child migration agencies between 1947 and 1967. The idea was that they would be easier to manage than adults, cheaper to accommodate and had long working lives ahead of them.

And of course they would love Australia. The land of sunshine, and fresh air and a boundless future. The newsreels of the time showed them walking down the gangplanks of immigrant ships hand in hand, dressed in the best clothes they could muster, smiling for the cameras and the faceless officials who encouraged them to be happy for the press.

Rose Kruger was one of these children. Her father died at the age of thirty-five, leaving his wife with five young children and seemingly little option for their care. Her mother put the children into an orphanage in Scotland and from there Rose journeyed to Australia. She has a simple, unadorned manner and tells her story in a matter-of-fact way, with her blue eyes shining.

'Someone came one day and asked who'd like to go to Australia for a holiday. Being little kids just after the war, I think I was only eight years of age then, we all put our hands up.' A trace of a smile flickers across her face at the foolish innocence of children. 'It was like asking a kid if they'd like an ice-cream.'

Arriving in Perth in 1947, she was taken to an orphanage in the suburb of Subiaco, not far from where Les Dixon and his brother enjoyed a rambunctious childhood. She sits in her kitchen, with a heart-shaped pendant around her neck, and says, 'That's where I spent the next nine years.'

These homes were subsidised by the government but run by church and voluntary organisations. The orphanage in Subiaco was run by the Catholic order, the Sisters of Mercy. 'We were told that we had no family, we had no one, we were here in Australia and that's it. Forget about what happened over there, this is your life.'

The children, Rose Kruger says, were made aware that they had come from the 'slums of England' and had come out 'with not a rag on our backs'. Now, children, who would like a holiday in Australia?

The Sisters of Mercy were the children's carers, but to Rose Kruger the name had a certain irony. The nuns were dressed in black clothes that fell right down to the floor and each one was armed with a leather strap that was kept in a pocket but used constantly.

'Sisters of Mercy? No mercy.' As she speaks there are the faint traces of a Scottish accent, an accent that linked her to the other side of the world. 'Three times a day in church and you fell out of your bed onto your knees, and you fell into your bed on your knees. Very, very little schooling. We were really put to work at the age of nine, scrubbing and polishing the floors. We'd get up at six o'clock in the morning, we worked in the laundry, in the foundling home looking after little children. It was a pretty tough life.' She nods slightly. 'We were ruled by prayer and the strap.'

Rose was bewildered by the nuns' behaviour, but amazingly, she tries to understand their position. 'I think they were just frustrated,' she says. Her spirit of generosity is quite startling, and she goes on, 'Like any normal kid I think we played up to get attention. But no one gave you a hug. Your birthday came and your birthday went and nobody wished you a happy birthday.'

As for Christmas, Rose and the other children fared little better. 'Never had a toy, never had a book. Christmas time we'd walk around singing carols and then we'd go into midnight mass and after that we'd be given a cup of hot chocolate. And a biscuit and a parcel. You'd open the parcel and were told to leave it at the end of your bed. And when you woke up the next morning the parcel was gone. That was Christmas in the orphanage.'

There is a shadow of a smile and she tries again to explain: 'One Christmas I remember vividly, I opened my parcel and there was a dress there, it would have fitted my grandmother, had I had one. The nuns must have got pleasure out of wrapping the parcels but they were gone the next morning.'

Sometimes larking about and nicking a treat would lead to punishment, although of a much harsher nature than handed out to larrikins like Les Dixon. 'One of the girls gave me a lemon so I crept into the kitchen to pinch some sugar and I got caught. I went before the Reverend Mother, the top nun, and I got the cane – and because I wouldn't tell her who gave me the lemon I got another lot of the cane. All for a lemon.'

Rose's childhood didn't conform to the sepia happy-snaps of sandcastles on the beach and backyards and open spaces.

Almost all Baby Boomers were taught to respect their elders and every Monday, schoolrooms and parade grounds echoed to the school oath. 'I love God and my country, I honour the flag, I will serve the Queen and cheerfully obey my parents, teachers and the laws.'

For all the space and freedom of the bush, things got pretty crowded inside the classroom for Bob Moore. 'There were always sixty kids in the class and right from grade one to grade eight, we were sorted into the smart half and the worst half of the class.'

And where did Bob rate in the classroom?

'I got into twenty-ninth place once,' he says rather proudly, 'but that was as good as it got. From then on it was thirty or thirty-one, I could never get into that top half.'

Like most childhoods there is always at least one character from the classroom who lingers in the memory. For Bob Moore it was a new arrival from the city. 'One year, it was about grade four, we had a new boy who started from the special school in Brisbane.

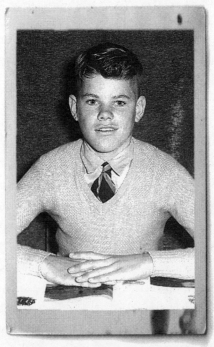

Bob Moore, in his high school uniform, 1960.

So he had some sort of learning difficulty. And in the first exam he beat four kids in my class. And the look on his face. He wasn't the bottom of the class.'

Not all his memories are good. 'The discipline in the state school system was severe,' he says. 'Somebody got the cane every day. I got the cane just for getting sums wrong. And I remember in grade eight I got sent back to grade four for the day because I got more than two sums wrong.'

There's a rueful shake of his head and an intake of breath before Bob continues, 'My younger brother was in that class and I had to sit there all day.'

Loretta adds, 'And he's never let you forget it!'

'Never let me forget. I can remember it like it was yesterday. I wasn't the only one it happened to and it certainly got your attention, I suppose, but it never made me any better at doing square roots by long division. I still have to use a calculator.'

In Yarraville, a working-class suburb in Melbourne, young Geoff Stirling would walk into a classroom that was changing with the waves of immigrants in Australia.

'I walked to school and after a year or two there were other children who had come over after the Second World War, immigrants who lived in a hostel not far from where we lived. So I had exposure to a lot of different cultures. English, Yugoslavs and others that I wasn't aware of – but school was a pretty regimented affair.'

The children would have marching contests into the schoolroom after the flag-raising ceremony and the singing of the national anthem. A recording of a marching tune would helpfully play over the loudspeaker. 'Colonel Bogey' and other tunes that set the beat for the hobnailed tread of military boots did the same to the pad of school shoes.

'The children,' remembers Geoff, 'knew the words from their fathers and would sometimes sing along, lines of little children's voices singing the songs of war.'

Some of the newer Australians could also recognise the tunes, having heard them as troops had marched through their former homes. What they made of it all one can only imagine.

Geoff recalls: 'The marching competitions were ordered with the tallest children up at the front, the smallest children at the back. Schooling then was very much about measuring. Measuring your abilities – the person who was the best scholar would always get right down the back left-hand corner and it would be graded all the way right through the classroom . . . Sport was a big thing in that way, too, we played cricket and football. It was all very regimented.'

It wasn't only at school, that sense of structure, order and discipline. Geoff's wife Polly, who grew up in America, witnessed Geoff's relationship with his father. 'Geoff's dad was a sergeant-major in the Second World War and he ran his family that way. He was a tough character. It was very black and white with Wal, there was no grey area in the middle, was there?'

Geoff has a black-and-white photo of Wal Stirling in suit, tie and Trilby hat. He has a firm and angular face that squints directly into the lens. Geoff's memories of his relationship with his father are still strong.

'He wanted to live his life through me, too, like he wanted me to join the Boy Scouts. I remember I was crying. I didn't want to go but he was so determined that it would somehow improve me or do something for me, so there was a showdown. The arguments we had growing up, it was almost like I needed to prove to him that I was worthy.'

Wal Stirling with Geoff, aged two, in Melbourne in 1944.

As we grow older we see through time and experience the meaning of something our parents did, or wanted us to do. 'You'll find out one day when the penny drops for you, Cabbagehead,' as my own father would put it to me.

Geoff Stirling isn't blind to his father's faults, but he is also open to what he calls the 'gifts' he was given. 'My father was a great storyteller. Whenever we went in a car anywhere, he would be continually referring to motor cars or buildings and the stories attached to this and that. It's interesting how that plays out for me – I don't get lost in a forest; I can walk through a forest with the same eye for detail that he showed us. There are many aspects of him that I can value now; it's a little bit easier to see those sorts of things.'

In the last years of his father's life, as Wal Stirling suffered the onset of dementia, Geoff began to embrace with greater understanding the man whose threats had terrified him as a boy. 'It was the first time we could both look into each other's eyes. Not be glancing away. There was clarity in his eyes. These are the sort of things that I pick up; the conditioning is very much the thing that I was battling because in essence I'm not very much different from him.'

And as Geoff tilts his head to one side, he shows a strong resemblance to his father. He acknowledges that his negative experiences as a child would later shape the way he parented his own children.

The children of the 1950s and early sixties were expected to accept authority; boys and girls were meant to sit quietly in the classroom and learn lessons that would equip them for their future roles in life. At least, that was the idea. They were told that Australia was a wealthy and prosperous nation compared to the rest of the world. We were the 'lucky country', a term coined in 1964 by Donald Horne in an ironic reference – he believed Australia's wealth came not so much from the cleverness of its citizens but from its bountiful natural resources. But it was taken up by almost everybody else as meaning the outstanding state of Australia among nations. A place where a family's hard work held attractive rewards.

The basic regime for primary schools was almost the same for twenty years, as federal and state governments instituted a series of benevolent measures. Generations of school children were treated to the delights of free medical examinations, chest X-rays in search of tuberculosis, and one of the more unusual rituals of primary school, the provision of free milk to drink. Even up until the early seventies, while attending Humpybong Infants in Queensland, I received free health checks. In 1973, at the age of nine, some other boys and I were asked to march into a little office one at a time and parade before a nurse in our underpants.

Our hearts were listened to, our tongues looked at, and we were weighed and measured, I believe, and then we were told to step forward while the nurse pulled open the top of our underpants and peeped down at what sprouted between our legs. 'Turn your head' was the command and then there was a final order, 'Now cough.'

I did as I was told and stared straight ahead at the wall for what seemed like an age. What had she found when I had coughed? What was wrong? My underpants snapped back against my tummy and the nurse looked up at me and said, 'You should play the piano.' Then she told me to go and get dressed. To this day I have no idea what she meant or what it was about – what she saw that gave rise to such advice.

Every once in a while, square grey vans would appear on the corners of streets and outside places of note, like the butcher's shop. People would line up to have an X-ray taken. I remember them in the evening. The street lights added a yellowish glow and people seemed to have gone home from work and dressed themselves up a bit. I can remember being held in my mother's arms while she waited in line with my sisters and a friend of one of my sisters, a loud girl with bright red hair, dressed in a white dress with yellow sunflowers on it, yelling out as she walked up the stairs of the grey van. 'I wore me good dress for the photy!' she said as she disappeared inside.

The free morning milk was in some ways as mysterious as the Masons. From 1953 to the early seventies, free milk was provided to primary school students to strengthen our diet, a scheme originated by politicians and civic leaders who had vivid memories of the Great Depression and the heavy rationing of the Second World War. The milk was carried in by specially selected milk monitors, a prized position among students. Small glass milk bottles, and later small cartons, and a free drinking straw were handed out by the monitors in time for what was termed in Queensland 'little lunch', or morning recess.

Here the mysteries of the morning milk deepened. It was a throw of the dice as to whether the milk was cold or, horror of horrors, warm. If it was cold then it was quite enjoyable, but if it was warm then you were for it. You couldn't really dispose of it as teachers would stand guard alongside the favoured monitors and make sure the milk was drunk.

Our milk came from the prettily named Caboolture Dairies, a co-op of Queensland dairy farmers just north of Redcliffe, which was where Humpybong Infants stood.

The greatest mystery of all was opening the bottle. The caps were either gold or blue foils and the desired method was to press down with the heel of your palm in a circular motion to release the cap, then insert the straw. This just never happened. I favoured the plunging thumb. This way you found out if the milk was cold or not and you could also plunge next to a mate or some other poor unsuspecting milk sipper and cover them with an explosion of milk.

'No thumbs, no thumbs, twist with your hands!' I can remember a teacher called Mr Clancy yelling.

You were supposed to drink in an orderly fashion and this was the most mystifying thing of all. One could never have imagined that kids could find so many ways to drink a bottle of milk. One girl drank a bottle with her feet, and then, to prove a point, drank another with her shoes off. Some sucked the milk up with the straw and then blew it at others, and one boy called Bradley Phie tried to drink it with his eyes as a dare from Gordon Exeter.

Gordon Exeter had all the little-lunch milk-drinking skills, in fact he really was the Bradman of the mini milk bottle, and it was he who tried to show me how to make milk come out of my nose. I came close once but never quite got there and managed to do a pretty good job of being sick. I was sent to the office and confessed my crime of 'trying to make milk come out of my nose'.

The headmaster looked at me and snarled, 'You made milk come out of your nostrils!'

'My nose,' I said, and I couldn't quite understand what the big deal was. But there was apparently a big deal and I was caned by a moustached and seriously grumpy headmaster for not appreciating 'What it is that WE, and the DAIRY FARMERS and the GOV-ERN-MENT give you!' The Queen looked down from her frame with a half-smile; I supposed she drank her milk. But it was probably never warm. 'What SHE gives you!' yelled Mr Stevens with a gesture to Her Majesty.

I was almost under the impression that he had actually milked the cows himself he was so aggrieved, but I was content with the fact that after he gave me six of the best I sicked up some milk on his office carpet. He nearly went for me again, but I let out a warning burp and was sent on my way with the sound of his high-pitched shriek in my ears.

This must have been the same year as the piano-in-the-underpants incident, or maybe a year before. The 1970s in Queensland. My father always said we were twenty years behind the rest of Australia, but light years ahead.

2

Hillbilly Cats

The fifties and early sixties brought with them a phenomenon that was going to turn childhood into something new altogether. As the economy grew and the privations of the past began to slowly dissolve into history – and there is nothing that makes people forget the past as quickly as a booming economy – families had to face the fact that teenagers had become prime targets for economic growth. If ideas of order, respect and obedience were crates of free school milk then suddenly it seemed to go very sour indeed.

The hint of what was to come started with breathless newsreel voice-over men sounding alarm bells in that strange and almost hard-to-believe English–Australian correct-pronunciation accent. Every syllable was pronounced and spoken in a tone that seemed as if they had just sucked on a helium balloon at a child's party, rolling their r's in dire warning of the menace of the teen breed of bodgies and widgies.

These were teenagers who would gather and listen to music and dance, and as a reaction against the set order of society, they would express their individual tastes by all dressing the same. It all looks pretty tame now but back then the voice-over of the newsreels fed the viewers' interest. 'A bodgie is a male with long hair and unusual clothes. A widgie is a female with short hair and unusual clothes. Unlike usual society the male is the more colourfully, even exotically, dressed. Mostly they are teenagers, usually they come back to normal after twenty-two. If they don't then sound the sirens.'

For an older generation represented by the newsreel narrator looking at this small group of young Australians, these bodgies and widgies raised a touch of fear and alarm. Others saw them as kids having fun. They were different, they didn't look like us, but it was all right, they were just mucking around. They would come back to their senses by the time they grew up, which was twenty-two.

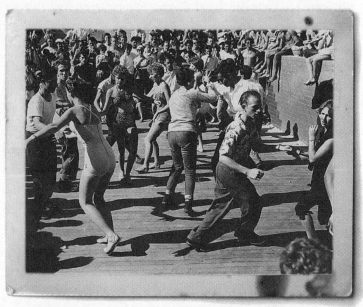

Bodgies and widgies at the Snake Pit at Scarborough Beach, Perth, in 1958.

Les Dixon became a bodgie in 1956. 'People saw us as some sort of a threat – we were going to be the downfall of society and mothers would warn their daughters not to mix with those guys, they'll ruin you. And we probably would have – you know we were the peacocks around Perth.' And he roars with laughter. 'The other young guys would be in their grey suits and herringbone waistcoats and they didn't get a look-in with the girls when we walked in.'

There were fights and even a police Bodgie Squad, a special group of detectives formed to keep an eye on the bodgie menace. Coloured clothing could spread like wildfire if it wasn't stopped.

Sometimes, though, Les and his bodgie mates were the ones who needed a bit of looking after. 'One time at East Fremantle when we were at the movies, a bloke in a jumper comes up to us and says to come down the laneway at half-time. So we did, but when we got there he and his mates were gone and all their brothers who were wharfies turned up – boy, did we cop a hiding. I ended up with a tooth through my lip, a brand-new tie that I'd bought that day was done up in such a little knot I had to cut it off with a razor blade.'

Les Dixon's eyes twinkle and he smiles a bit at the fun of it all and also because he knew what was coming next. The bodgies and widgies were a flash in the pan compared to what was about to happen. 'I was listening to the radio and Lionel Lewis, who was a disc jockey, said something about the latest thing from America, a hillbilly cat called Elvis Presley. When he started up "Heartbreak Hotel" I thought, my God, this is it, this is what I've been waiting for – it totally blew me away.'

This 'latest thing from America' wasn't just a fad; it was a new direction in culture and expression. It was music and a way of life based solely around youth.

*Les Dixon, aged seventeen, performing an acoustic set at the Ascot Inn,
Perth, in 1958.*

'It struck all right. It was a rebellious thing for teenagers because straight away old people hated it. They thought it was the end of the world. Suddenly we had our own identity, our own music, our own clothes – from that moment on it changed my whole life.'

The teenage rock'n'roll rebellion took off, and Les was there at the heart of it. 'I started a band called the Saints and we recorded a song called "Stingy Mingy Mama" – we actually recorded it in Perth. It cost us virtually nothing to make in those days.'

It's not a bad song. It has a big backbeat and it drives along, and Les does a fair job with his throaty vocals, not bad for a lad of seventeen or so. And the lyrics were his own work, too. 'You're a stingy mingy mamaaaaaaa / You don't wanna my lovinnnnnnnnnnn aah / Stingy Mingy Mammmmmma / Wowowo oh yeah.'

There's a photo of Les and the Saints in someone's backyard, his hair combed in a rocker's wave. Only two of them have instruments, a drummer and Les with an acoustic guitar, but they more than make up for it in their enthusiastic pose. Les with legs spread à la that hillbilly cat Elvis Presley, the guitar slung on his hip and his hips tilted at a suitably rocker angle.

Les sits in his kitchen as he remembers, with a red Fender guitar on the wall. Stuck on the grille of his security door is a translucent coloured hanging of Elvis in his prime with a guitar and his legs apart, hips tilted. Les sits, his respectable head of suspiciously dark hair still swept in a rocker's wave, and he rumbles with laughter. 'We used to have school dances and they'd bring the girls from the school next door. We're up there playing the old stuff, Glenn Miller, "Moonlight Serenade", and the young fellas down the front would be calling out, just so we could hear, "Play some rock'n'roll, Les, play some rock'n'roll!"'

Les and his band performing in 1956.

Les and his Saints generously obliged. And that's when 'Stingy Mingy Mama' came roaring out from Les Dixon's throat, full bore. And the headmaster got into the act with an answering howl.

'Well, the place exploded and the headmaster's yelling, "Turn the power off, turn the power off!" And boy,' Les chortles, 'did I get into trouble for that one.'

But something tells you in the way he laughs that it was more than worth it. There was something about the new music that made lots of things worth it – even defying the Sisters of Mercy.

Rose Kruger would sneak away from her orphanage in Subiaco as a seventeen-year-old to enjoy the delights of rock'n'roll dances. 'We were told by the nuns that rock'n'roll music was the devil's plaything and not to get involved. When I worked and lived at the orphanage I bought my first transistor and I used to play all Elvis'

Rose Kruger (left) *with her friend Anne in 1957.*

music. It got my blood boiling – the beat – and you could dance, and I think as a rejection of the nuns I took it up.'

Rose went along to a well-known Perth institution called the Snake Pit, a milk bar with a sunken dance floor where rock'n'roll was played and the teenagers would jive away. Les Dixon would do much the same thing, and although their paths didn't cross on the floor of the Snake Pit, life took the most interesting of turns.

This was the beginning of the commercialisation of childhood. And teenagers were the first target. The new medium of television was quick to exploit it. Televised shows like *Six O'Clock Rock* with Johnny O'Keefe and *Bandstand*, which were shown nationally, and locally produced programs like Perth's *Teen Beat*, on which Les

Dixon and his band appeared, would help to satisfy the cravings of the lucrative 'teen market'. Australian society had a new subculture and it stamped its foot and demanded to be heard.

'We were the first teenagers to have a disposable income as such,' says Les Dixon. 'Even though we weren't earning a lot of money, a lot of it did go on clothes and records, you know, that sort of thing.'

They may not have earned much, but the booming population had a booming number of teenagers who were looking to have a booming good time. Department stores began to design teenage-specific shopping areas, and new magazines and radio shows were dedicated to feeding the seemingly insatiable appetite of young Australians.

By the early sixties middle-class Australian youth had developed a culture and identity that couldn't be ignored, but out on the fringes of society there was a group of children whose presence and status remained unrecognised – occasionally seen but seldom heard. The thread of the new music would trail out into these fringes.

Donna Meehan was born in the mid-fifties in the New South Wales town of Coonamble, not far from the Castlereagh River. Her grandparents lived on a property and were given permission to set up a camp that consisted of two very small tin shacks. Donna was born in a hospital, then taken back to the camp, which by then had grown to about twenty residents.

'We didn't have a bath every night because there was no running water, so you'd go down to the river and have a swim. Life was very simple,' says Donna. 'I remember the screeching of about fifty or a hundred galahs. We used to eat bush budgies. Used to eat witchetty grubs, kangaroo stew, and if we were fortunate the uncles would bring back a lamb and you cooked it on an open fire.' She laughs a little as she remembers the aromas. 'Oh the smell of that made you so hungry and it just seemed to take forever before it was ready to eat.'

So the children would play. Play with broken bottle glass, pretending it was imaginary furniture. They would draw pictures in the red dirt and make dolls out of wooden pegs, or they played with the dogs. All the cousins living in the camp would climb trees and Donna had a special tree. 'I used to climb it and sit out there on a limb and just watch the men. Or at Christmas time we would decorate it with some tinsel and the birds would come. So I loved to watch the birds and the white man, Santa Claus, would come and bring us lollies or a doll and a book.'

And the uncles would sometimes return from work with lollies for the kids. Donna laughs again and says with a smile, 'That broken glass we played with – I don't know how we didn't cut our fingers.'

Around the campfire at night they played the music of Elvis and his band and other songs from the new rock'n'roll. 'The uncles would try to pick out the latest songs and their favourite was "Joey's Song" by Bill Haley and The Comets – it's just an instrumental. And whenever I hear it, I'm just transported back to the camp.'

It is a simple, happy tune, almost annoying in its finger-plucking glee, but as she sits in her comfortable home and remembers, Donna Meehan's voice wavers and her composure begins to fall away. And with good reason.

On the night before 22 April 1960, Donna's mum told her repeatedly that she and her brothers were going on a train ride. 'We were so excited because only rich kids got to ride the train and Mum had gone into town earlier and had come back with new clothes.'

They were in fact second-hand clothes but were as good as new to the children. There is a photo of Donna wearing her new dress, but she doesn't need to see it to remember what she wore. 'My new dress – it had, I can still see the colour – it had fruit all over it, pears, apples, oranges, cherries. The background was green and the top half was red and I had a red cardigan. I had new shoes, shiny black shoes.'

On the morning of 22 April, Donna's mother dressed her children and brushed their hair. 'She kept brushing our hair, which she never used to do,' says Donna with a half-smile, and then it disappears. 'She kept saying, "Always remember your manners,"

Donna Meehan, aged five, 1960.

and she kept on brushing our hair. An old lady who had the taxi in town was a friend of Mum's so she took us to the train. And I sat in the back thinking, Why isn't my mum singing or talking, because she always sang. Always hummed, always talked. I just sat there clicking my new shoes together.'

When the family arrived at the station there were kids everywhere, running up and down the platform, yelling, playing. They waited forever for the train to come. Then a whistle sounded and they could see grey smoke in the distance. Their excitement grew as a great, powerful train pulled up in front of them.

Donna was five, her eldest brother Barry nine, Widdy was seven, Robby was four, Kevin was two, and the twins were a few months old. They stood and stared in their new second-hand clothes and their brushed hair at the huge locomotive. Then their mother said, 'Get on the train now, all you kids, get on the train.'

They hopped inside and ran up and down. They looked at the seats. They explored the toilet, they hadn't seen one before. And like children do they opened and shut the old wooden-slat windows. Open and shut, open and shut.

Then they were told to take their seats and a white lady came and sat next to Donna. She didn't know why the lady sat there, it was her mum's seat. So she looked around a little. Then looked down at her black shoes and out the window.

Her brothers stared, their eyes big with fear. Out the window they saw their mother and aunties standing still as the great train moved slowly away from them. They stood and each of them waved a white hanky. Donna saw tears falling from her mother's eyes faster than she could wipe them away. Then she disappeared.

Donna didn't see her birth mother for the next twenty years.

As an Indigenous Australian, Donna had no citizenship entitlements. Successive governments had embarked upon programs of

Donna playing on the swing her adoptive father made for her in 1960.

'assimilation' of the Aboriginal peoples into the white Australian culture and the removal of children from their families was part of the welfare that the authorities felt they were bringing to these children.

At best it was a well-intentioned scheme. At the time the predominant view was that immersion in the white Anglo-Australian way of life was the only possible way to advancement. At worst it was seen as a racist agenda to destroy a culture and family system.

It is doubtful that a five-year-old girl, dressed in new clothes, alone on a train filled with crying children, could make any sense of what was happening. For Donna Meehan it was the first time she had ever felt real fear.

The train arrived in Sydney and the white lady told Donna to stay in her seat. Her brothers got off and were put onto another train. Donna's train left the station and headed for Newcastle. When she arrived there, she stayed in her seat, and the white lady went to fetch her some water. A young boy sat next to her. They sat together for a while, not saying anything. Donna looked out the window watching the people walking by, looking at the shoes. She had never seen so many people in shoes and then something struck her: everyone was white. 'And I thought, where were all the blackfellas – that's what my uncles would call themselves, blackfellas. And I realised they talked another language. Not that we didn't speak English, we spoke broken Aboriginal English, we had a different accent. And I realised they were all whitefellas.

'Then the white lady came back and brought with her not a glass of water but a tall, dark-haired white man and a shorter white woman. The white lady from the train bent down and said to me, "Donna, this is your new mum and dad, go with them and they will get you something to eat." And I followed them.'

Donna Meehan had become a member of what would come to be known as the Stolen Generations. Indigenous children removed from their parents. 'My mum lost seven children overnight, seven children,' says Donna, and she shakes her head slowly.

It's a horrible irony that at the time of this removal, the 1960s, the family was seen as the core element of society. To be married and a parent was regarded not only as a personal achievement but also a fulfilment of a social obligation. But for some Australians it went a lot deeper.

'You've always got this want in you for a mum and a dad, because you've never called anyone a mum or dad,' says Rose Kruger, and she pauses for a moment. 'Having your own children lightens it a little, but you always remember that you don't have what you've given someone else – a parent.'

She shrugs her shoulders. 'I married this guy who was a bit of a drinker and we had three children, one after the other, three beautiful kids. But life got worse. He got more into the drink and more abusive. I ended up in hospital quite often with broken bones. Stuck with him for twenty-five years.

'I tried to leave him in the earlier stages but I was told that if I did I would have to get a job somewhere to support myself.' Rose pauses again, then continues quietly, 'My answer to that was, my mother dumped me, I'm not dumping my children.'

Heroes come in many shapes. In Australia we tend to celebrate the odd soldier and many a sporting champion, but as my father would have said when he was impressed with somebody, 'I'll tell you this much for nothing, there's not a medal big enough to pin on that chest.' He could have been talking about Rose Kruger. Rose's courage and commitment were borne of her childhood. There is a moment from her words that I remember clearly, about when she would sneak to the Snake Pit and there, I hope that she danced and jived and felt free, that she felt that open-ended joy of youth.

Years later, after both their marriages had ended, Rose Kruger and Les Dixon came together to celebrate more than just the music of their youth. They came together to celebrate each other. Although, at first she thought Les was 'a poofter': his words, not hers. 'I was just a bit ahead of my time because I had my hair done at the Playboy International – it had tints in it and things,' says Les Dixon rather proudly.

They first met in the mid seventies, and are still together today.

Almost all of us have a tendency to look back to the past with a golden veil of sentimentality, to a gentler period, a simpler time. This is usually aided and abetted by somebody wanting to sell you something. The sixties are often painted as a golden age because the population then was encouraged to perceive how fortunate they were. Information films are a prime example.

In a government-sponsored colour film from the time, you can see a Land Rover driving slowly up a street through a new housing estate. White Australia, well, that was the only idea of Australia that existed for most people at the time, was a place where you could raise healthy, well-behaved children in quiet suburbia. Ninety per cent of women were stay-at-home mothers and on average they bore 3.5 children. There was full employment for their husbands. It was a bountiful picture, the streets were clean and it was safe enough to leave your children at the entry to the supermarket when you went shopping.

But like so much of life the reality was very different. For many families it wasn't order and plenty, and 3.5 children around a happy breakfast table. Karen Lawrence's mother had her first child when

Karen Lawrence with her seven brothers and sisters.

she was sixteen and by the time she was twenty-nine she'd had eight. 'And my father was . . .' there's a pause as Karen gathers her words, and she continues in a halting way, 'was fairly alcoholic and had a really bad temper and they tried to stay together but it was a bit of a nightmare.'

Trying to put things in perspective, she says simply, 'They had no money. They were poor. Every year we would go to my grandparents for Christmas, my mother's parents, and they would give us underwear.' There is a photo of Karen and her siblings arranged in a group showing off their Christmas gifts. Most family albums have happy-snaps of children with their new Christmas toys. Not many, though, would show them posed in new singlets and undies. Karen half laughs. 'That's how poor we were, all lined up in our underwear. It's sort of funny and sad at the same time.'

Karen with her siblings, dressed in their Christmas presents.

There were many good times playing with her sisters and brothers, but she says in a considered tone, 'I can honestly say I don't remember much love, you know, holding and hugging, but I think a lot of families were like that.' She tries to be as fair as possible with another qualifying, 'I think.'

She is quite certain that in her childhood there was no way children would have been allowed to talk to adults as they do today. Children had to obey rules, otherwise there were consequences, and when Karen's father was alive, she says there would be violent consequences. 'I remember once, it was pretty weird actually, and it makes me quite sad.' She pauses, looks away and is obviously distressed. It is sadness for her father as much as for herself. Then she does something quite childlike that makes years vanish. Like a little child, she holds up her right index finger to her mouth and rubs it a little on her lips as if she is trying to soothe away what she has said or as if it somehow can stop the pain.

'My father was not good at being kind if you had done something wrong, and I remember one time when he held me upside down and hit me with a bread knife. And I found that very disturbing. In those days there was the belief that when you smack kids it makes them better. It makes them tougher. I don't agree with that.'

Karen Lawrence never had the chance to say what she thought to her father. He came home one night, drunk, and walked around the small house they lived in singing 'Old MacDonald Had a Farm' at the top of his voice. 'We all thought, Oh well at least he's happy, you know he's not going to give my mum a whack around the face. Umm, and then he made a sort of funny noise.'

She goes still for a moment then takes a small breath and continues, 'And he made a funny noise and said, "Oh Jan, I've got a headache" – that's my mum, Janice.' Her mother started yelling out to Karen's older sister, 'Go, go down to Connie', a friend who lived nearby. 'Tell her to get an ambulance!'

'Then he went out on a stretcher and we were all sort of peering out the door as he went past. Two days later Mum came back and told us our father was dead. Just like that. And we all thought, What does that mean? Because at that age, what does that mean? And I still, I must say, I still can't understand why someone would do that to her children. But in those days, that's what one did. I was seven when my father died. In 1964, you didn't take children to funerals, children were "seen and not heard".'

Of course, this had a huge impact on Karen. 'I was quite scared of dying for a long time after that. You know, just disappearing.'

Many things in life are hard to make sense of, especially during childhood. Some things are never explained, at best they are accepted.

Donna Meehan's new parents, who had taken her from the train in Newcastle that day, were a childless couple who had emigrated from Germany.

On her first night with them, Donna was afraid of her new father because he was a tall man; in the camp she had been looked after mostly by women – her mother and aunties.

Even though the Popovs had a one-bedroom house it seemed like a palace to a little girl who had shared a bed with four other children. That night she slept on a sofa and she woke to a quiet house with no children, no cousins.

At first the 'New Australians' Elizabeth and Tim Popov were foster parents to Donna, but after a period they applied for and were granted adoption rights. Donna's brothers and sisters were not as fortunate, moving from foster home to foster home.

When she attended church with her new mum, Donna discovered that Elizabeth was a singer. 'She would go out the front and sing with a piano accordion. And I thought, wow, my other mother had a piano accordion. So I loved that. It reminded me of the camp.'

The differences between her home and her new life seemed to be vast – her adoptive parents were white and from another culture. They spoke German to each other every night, a new language the little girl had to grow used to. She not only had to manage the racism directed at her, but also towards her adoptive parents, being Germans after the Second World War. It seemed to Donna that it was her and her parents versus the rest of Australia.

'We were just three people in a quiet house, a serious house. Europeans didn't laugh, there was no humour, which is what we had in the camp. In this new house right beside a railway track,

Donna Meehan, aged ten, with her adoptive parents, Elizabeth and Tim Popov.

I remember watching the steam trains go past, thinking if I just followed that train it would take me back to the camp.'

These thoughts haunted Donna for a long time. 'I remember coming home from school in Newcastle, when I was just starting to settle into my new home with my new parents. I was really excited because I had had a good day at school. And I froze when I got to the back door because there was this song on the radio.'

It was 'Joey's Song' by Bill Haley and The Comets. She thought of the campfires and her uncles and grandfather. Where were they now?

At school she put up with the taunts of other students. Abo, Bori, Coon. Dirty, Dumb. 'You hear that a hundred times, two hundred times and it becomes a self-fulfilling prophecy,' she says quietly. She was also teased about being adopted. 'Your parents didn't want you, they would say. They called me fat, ugly, dumb.' Her adoptive parents ran a small business, so she was called rich and spoilt – she couldn't win on any front.

Later, as she grew into a teenager, her parents ran a service station. There is a photo of Tim Popov standing proudly in his Caltex uniform, with his arms crossed behind his back and his legs apart. Donna worked there, too – in her red Caltex mini dress she would walk out to the bowsers to serve the motorists. 'I was serving hundreds of people every day and they looked down on me. It was their facial reactions.' She closes her eyes momentarily at the memory and continues. 'I just knew it before people would even ask the question. They'd edge around it and say, "Oh, excuse me, if you don't mind me asking, what nationality are you?"'

Donna, aged seventeen, at the family's service station, 1971.

Donna Meehan feels she was in denial about her Aboriginality. 'Everywhere we went I was the only Aborigine – at church, at school. I certainly didn't feel I belonged, I was sitting on a fence, watching society.'

Photographs show her in clothes of that period, and many scenes look so familiar to me. They could belong in my parents' family photo albums. The holiday snaps, municipal playgrounds, school photographs. Yet one thing does stand out: yes, she is Aboriginal.

She tried to understand her place. 'I went to the pictures when I was about fifteen and saw *To Sir, With Love*. There was this gorgeous black man, Sidney Poitier, a schoolteacher who had a lot to say. I saw this blackfella and something stirred within me.' She went back every Saturday for thirteen weeks to watch it again and again. 'My spirit was whispering to me, "He survived and you will, too."'

Donna didn't know of many Aboriginal role models at that time, although a helpful maths teacher tried to encourage her to play tennis like Evonne Goolagong. That was as far as it went.

In one respect Donna was fortunate: her adoptive parents loved her and supported her culture as much as they could. 'They were good, kind and loving and told everyone, "Yes, we've adopted Donna, but we couldn't love our own flesh and blood any more."'

When Donna heard 'Joey's Song' on the radio that day, rather than try to erase the memory, her adoptive mother hunted down a copy of the record for her. So it would be Donna's song as much as Joey's.

And when she was about eight, playing in her bedroom, her German mum, in Donna's words, suddenly 'went ballistic'. '"Donna! Quick, come out and look! There is a beautiful Aboriginal man on television." Jimmy Little was singing "Royal Telephone" and he looked and sang just like one of my uncles.'

These were gifts, efforts of understanding and offerings, that planted seeds in Donna's mind that meant she would one day be able to understand and hold her identity. One day.

3

Family Nights

Many things were as hard to understand in the past as they are now. This particular one shouldn't be, it's just an exercise in biology when all is said and done, but when young people start thinking about sex, all bets are off. And as for engaging in it, well, it would be easy if it was just a biological imperative, but it's not. We're human beings and the fact that we've wrapped ourselves in various layers of cultural, religious and societal blankets that we like to call civilisation just makes the issue of sex a bit more complex – and at times incredibly entertaining.

'I was a virgin when we got married – no worries about that,' says Bob Moore, averting his eyes and tapping the table. 'But when we were courting we'd go to the movies then we'd come home and sit in the lounge and, ah, listen to the radio.' He continues tapping the table. 'And we'd, ah, play records.' With a final tap he admits, 'Oh, we'd get up to whatever nonsense we could get up to.'

Bob looks across to Loretta, who nods and smiles a little. Then he goes into full-description mode, laying out the plans of Loretta's childhood home on the table with his hands, like country people do when they're describing what they're going to do with a paddock or a bit of machinery. 'And Loretta's mother would be in bed in the room next door. The door would be open and the light would be off, but she'd be awake.'

Loretta smiles a bit more and shakes her head slightly. 'But one night she had the bedside light on and I could see she'd positioned the wardrobe door with the mirror so she could see what we were up to on the couch.'

Bob laughs, taps the table again and says, 'Pretty clever.'

Les Dixon remembered playing an age-old game that was curtailed by parental intervention. 'When I was about six my mum did catch me with the girl from over the back. We were playing the usual I'll-show-you-mine-if-you-show-me-yours.'

Loretta and Bob, both aged nineteen, in 1966.

Les' mum pulled him away by the ear. 'I got my little bum smacked all the way down the footpath back into the house for playing that one.'

Well, there are always going to be consequences and, later on, Les faced them. There was little or no sex education at that time and Les Dixon and Rose Kruger and other people their age had almost no idea of the precautions they could take to avoid pregnancy. They both had to enter into early marriages before they had even reached the legal age of twenty-one.

'If you got the girl pregnant you did the right thing. The right thing was marrying the girl, so the baby had a father, and things like that,' says Les.

A different time.

Not so long ago I found myself having a coffee in a place called the Retro Café. It's decked out in flotsam and jetsam from the fifties, sixties and seventies and serves fare with names like 'Humphrey Bogart Breakfast', 'Doris Day Sunny-Side-Up Eggs', and 'Marlon Brando Raisin Toast'.

It's modest, but it's fun. Both my children love it. They don't know who half the people are but they sit and flip through the magazines from the fifties and sixties, some of which are still around today – *The Australian Women's Weekly, New Idea*. Some I never even knew existed.

My son, at sixteen, read out a headline. 'Teenage Sex Exposed!' he said in a mock announcer's voice. I took it from him and had a look.

'Excuse me,' he said.

'Come on, it's work, Read something else,' I said to him.

It was a magazine called *Everybody's*, dated 2 March 1966.

They did indeed have a major exposé, well, as major as it could be. As I flipped through to the pertinent page I saw advertisements for underwear that made you slimmer, skin-blemish cures and a few now-dead actors who were young and handsome, but mostly the pages were filled with young women in bikinis of the period. They smiled and posed on the beach, and I saw that one was as young as sixteen. She was Katy Ford, *Everybody's* Girl of the Week. The others were contestants in *Everybody's* Miss Bikini Gold Coast contest.

Then came the double-page spread. It made stark reading compared with the smiling, bouffant-haired, false-eye-lashed Miss Bikini models. The article quoted statistics such as police in New South Wales believed that about 90,000 illegal abortions were being performed in Australia every year. Out of 3,937 cases of gonorrhoea notified in New South Wales in 1964, two males and eighteen females were under the age of fourteen; 880 boys and 250 girls were between the ages of fifteen and twenty.

Perhaps it was because I was reading this in a magazine of the period – a magazine that didn't seem to care about the double standards when compared with its other subject matter – that it came as a more visceral shock. The magazine came from the era that this pleasant café celebrated as the good old days of innocence and happy times. The article was written, it was claimed, by an English doctor, unnamed, who lived in Tasmania.

A few of the article's comments caught my eye. 'Rules are unwritten, but can soon be discovered by observation. The first set is what society says and the second set is what individuals in society do. What makes the teenager so different today from the 1940s or the 1840s? The teenager today has a mobile bedroom – a car. They are like spiders sitting in their web waiting for a juicy fly to come along. Here she is – come for a ride, Jane, in my mobile bedroom, look, the other girls do! . . . Can youth turn to anyone for advice? No, sex is not a subject the adult world allows to be discussed sensibly.'

The good old days, from a different time. Records dangled from the café ceiling, strung up with lengths of fishing line. They swung gently in the breeze.

The adult world can't discuss sex sensibly. The teenage market that spawned magazines like this one was growing, and with their ever-increasing economic power came the idea that the young should now not just be seen, but also heard. The age of the social revolution was dawning, but like so many Australian stories, there were scales of how far individual lives were affected by it.

It wasn't until the sixties that sex education began, if you can call 'Family Film Nights' and 'Family Talk Nights' held by various Christian organisations educational. There is footage of blank-faced teenagers staring from the shadows at caveman-like cross-sections of bits and pieces of the human anatomy as if they are contemplating the sheer complexity of what they are being told, and the even blanker faces of adults staring with the resigned knowledge that there wasn't really anything to contemplate at all.

Still, sex was being talked about. It didn't really get that much better. In the seventies, when I was in high school, my father took me to a father–son night in a hall down the road from our house. Inside sat almost all of the local sons watching an American film about flowers and elks and salmon swimming upstream in the spring. Outside we could hear the fathers playing two-up, smoking and telling blue jokes.

On the way home Dad asked, 'You right about all that then, are you, eh?'

I had images in my mind of great, antlered elks head-butting each other and quivering, straining salmon swimming against the flow and flinching as grizzly bears tried to keep them from their destiny. I hoped I didn't have to answer any questions. So I just nodded.

'Good, right then.' That was the father and son talk.

Later on, in the noughties, the 2000s, I gave my son a book entitled, *Where Did I Come From?* This purchase was prompted by him asking a question I had bravely deflected a week or so earlier.

While we were watching a game of football, Footscray versus Hawthorn, I think it was, a television advertisement came on – and this was a Sunday afternoon – showing a man and a woman dressed up in evening clothes dancing around the city on a cloud of happiness. Then, as they finally embraced, a deep voice intoned, 'If you have erectile dysfunction we can get you on your feet again.'

Neither of us said anything and I hoped it would remain that way. Unfortunately my son couldn't contain himself. 'What's that mean, erecticile, erectile dysfunction?'

I thought for a moment then said, 'You want a glass of lemonade?' He forgot about everything else – except the fizzy drink and the footy.

After giving him the book, I remember two things about my son's reaction. He looked at the book and then at me and said, 'Can't I wait till I'm older to read it?' He was eleven and a half. And then our conversation on our way to breakfast about a week later. 'That book,' he started.

'You read it?' I asked him.

He nodded his head.

'You right about all that then, are you?'

He nodded his head.

'Good. Right then.'

The more things change, the more – well, you know how it goes.

That was certainly the case for the bulk of Australian society and especially Karen Lawrence. When the sixties met the seventies,

Australia finally began to catch up with the sexual revolution that had swept through the rest of the Western world, and into its swirling waters dived Karen.

She had moved to the South Australian town of Woomera with her mother and stepfather, where he worked as a painter. Woomera was the base for Australia's space race, evidence of our nation's place among the world of technological and scientific prowess. So in a town that sought to reach the heavens, Karen Lawrence tuned into the world around her with growing fascination.

'I would just be glued to the television, thinking, my God, look at what those people are wearing and look at what they are doing! I started to realise there was a bigger world, and that I was pretty and I was getting a lot of attention. That's when I got my first mini skirt.'

There's a photo of Karen in her front yard posing in a short dress, while in the background a neighbour goes to open the door of an old EH Holden in a driveway. It's a photograph that says something about the blooming of youth in the suburbs and it also says something about that mini skirt.

Revolution without education has its consequences. Remember our friend, the unnamed Tasmanian doctor? The adult world was unable to talk about sex sensibly. Karen Lawrence met a boy, and she speaks about that time in shorthand. 'He had a car. He had a job. I used to nick off with him to the bush.' She smiles a little sadly. 'There was no birth control that I knew of, not really. The Pill wasn't talked about. I didn't know what a condom was . . . and that's when I got pregnant.'

She and the boy 'did the right thing', more out of ignorance of any other options, according to Karen, than anything else. Arrangements were made for them to be married – she had been a bridesmaid for three of her sisters so she borrowed their clothes.

Karen Lawrence, aged sixteen.

She drove to the wedding in a Valiant Regal and her stepfather gave her away. It was the right thing to do. 'So I played house – played Mum and Dad,' she says.

Karen gave birth to her first child in 1973, when teenage pregnancies accounted for nearly eight per cent of the babies born in Australia.

Everyone always has their own ideas about how to be a parent and, for Karen, a girl as well as a mother, there were many voices offering advice. 'Have you thought about this? Have you thought about that?' she says, then she stops herself, takes a deep breath and blows out her cheeks at the memory of it all. 'And then you think you are totally useless as a parent because you hadn't thought about that!'

She half laughs, then describes how she went about the business of being a mother. 'In some ways I was so ignorant, it all just happened. I fed the baby. I changed the baby. I got up and fed the baby. I got up and changed the baby. I did a sort of robotic thing because I didn't want to listen to people. I was sick of people telling me what to do.' And she nods her head. So there.

In a different situation, Bob and Loretta Moore found common ground with Karen Lawrence. 'Parenting,' says Bob, 'it's not easy.' Between 1970 and 1977 Bob and Loretta had three children. 'There's no course that prepares you for it – no reading any books, not a thing, so we played it by ear.'

The seventies in Australia saw upheaval in many areas of the social network, aided in part by the three high-flying years of the Whitlam Labor government. Whatever the economic credentials of this government, the social reforms it introduced and the revolutionary waves it rode affected all families.

Karen Lawrence had another child with her husband before they divorced in 1976. The couple took advantage of the new no-fault divorce laws introduced by the Whitlam government and, thanks to another change made by this government, Karen was now legally an adult.

In 1973 the voting age – the age you were considered to be an adult – was lowered from twenty-one to eighteen years. Karen could see that society was offering a new direction for women who wanted to pursue a life other than the traditional role of 'playing house'. The women's movement was a part of the changing society: campaigns for equal pay, equal opportunity, and giving women more control over their bodies. Women now had a burgeoning sense of freedom.

There was no shortage of people who opposed this new direction. 'A mother's primary responsibility is the full-time care of her own very young children and almost every married woman is driven to this, to want this by her own innermost instincts. There is no substitute for the unifying factor of the mother in the home.' So spoke Bob Santamaria of the National Civic Council on his weekly five-minute piece of social and political television commentary *Point of View*.

Well, it was his point of view in 1974. A committed Catholic and political warrior, Santamaria founded the Democratic Labor Party and was no fan of the new reforms. He wasn't the first and certainly won't be the last middle-aged man to lecture women on their role, but perhaps he knew somewhere in his sharp mind that the ground was shifting and women like Karen Lawrence would grab every opportunity with both hands.

'At nineteen I realised there was more in the world that I needed rather than just being a parent, and I was bored out of my brains with my partner – so I left him when I was twenty.'

Divorce for Karen was, in her own words, 'Great, because it meant [my husband] was out of my life.' But there were considerations other than herself. 'The children obviously didn't have their dad – and he wasn't a bad person.'

In those days people didn't understand co-parenting, a concept that would eventually be accepted as the divorce rate grew. There was, Karen says, a lot of nastiness. 'I felt during this time there were a lot more people who were nasty to each other. I was nasty to [my ex-husband] and he was nasty to me, and that affects your kids – it affected my kids.'

People began to question traditional methods of raising children and explore alternatives during the seventies. Geoff Stirling was determined that his children would have a different childhood from his own experiences in Yarraville, Melbourne. He raised them in a commune in Nimbin in northern New South Wales. 'I consciously rejected the way I was brought up. I was not a happy child. I found my teenage years, especially, extraordinarily difficult. So I didn't want that for my children.'

The Stirlings settled on fifty hectares of rainforest land, which they shared with ten other families. This was, as Geoff's wife Polly

Geoff Stirling with his first child, Melina, in 1974.

Stirling describes, their 'intentional family'. The Stirlings had two daughters, Melina and Myfanwy, and a son, Paedor.

When reflecting on their childhood, Geoff sounds almost professorial. 'The key is experimenting – their education has been the community. Both of us took the view that we would just find out what they were interested in, expose them to as much as possible and let them find their way.'

Polly Stirling has a simpler description. 'They were like free-range chooks, they were just out the door in the morning and we didn't have to worry about them.'

There, in family super-eight footage, is the lush north coast hinterland of New South Wales. Timber-frame houses nestled together with the rainforest creeping around. There is a long-haired, long-bearded Geoff Stirling, shirtless, wearing billowing purple cotton trousers, peering into the camera.

It is the perfect image of every cliché of commune living. But of course, appearances can be deceiving, especially in the eye of one who is ready to judge. If you stop and take a moment to think of your circumstances, then everyone's parents had weird hairstyles and wore odd clothes. I know mine did. If it wasn't Stubbies work shorts, it was safari suits, and compared to the massive helmets that used to pass as hairstyles on the adults of my youth, Geoff's long mane seems quite sensible.

The film plays a bit more and suddenly there is Geoff and one of his daughters climbing into a billycart, and a pretty good-looking billycart at that, then haring down a hill together. A father spending time with his kids, not just trying to give them a life, as Geoff's father had done for him, but also being with them.

All children do things that kids seem to do in films like this, play dinner parties together, ride a toy pushbike along a tricky bit of wood, wander around with the odd chook, pet or toy, this way and that. Simply living, being a kid.

'You couldn't tell me and my sisters apart,' says Paedor Stirling. 'We all had the same haircut, shoulder-length blond hair. We were half-naked most of the time.'

Life in this childhood community was a mixture of adventure and discipline. There was a café called the Tea Gardens not far up the road, a place where Paedor would work in exchange for spiders, a concoction known to many Australian kids made up of Coca-Cola and ice-cream. 'You get the ice-cream and when you poured on the Coke it would fizz up,' he says with delight.

But wanting to find their own way, the three children sought an alternative and more adventurous route to the Tea Gardens, and then they'd feel like they'd really earned their spiders. 'So we set off with a compass and a machete, no shoes, just a pair of shorts, and went off through the forest. We came across quite a few animals,

From left: *Myfanwy, Paedor and Melina Stirling, 1982.*

The Stirling family working in the Robb Road community garden in 1981.

probably some that were dangerous. Got chased away by a couple of snakes – but this eventually became our new path. It was the start of a lot of adventures; we would have an idea and just set off.'

There wasn't a cliché in sight for Paedor. 'The community wasn't a bunch of hippies running around naked, copulating – that is so far from the truth. My parents never smoked marijuana, and were quite strict, especially my father.'

Geoff admits that the discipline from his own childhood shaped him to become the type of father he is. 'In essence, I'm not very different from my father.'

Strict parenting, according to Paedor, wasn't common in the area where he lived. Although he had the freedom to explore, his parents had strong ethics and ideas about how they wanted their children to grow up. 'We couldn't talk back, there was no chance of swearing and we didn't have a television until we were teenagers. They wanted us to be outside, exploring the world and not subjected to other people's ideologies.'

One of Geoff Stirling's greatest childhood fears was the threat of being hit by his father. Paedor remembers a different method of discipline. After joyriding in an old Datsun given to him by a neighbour, he and his mates ended up upside down in an upside-down wreck. 'We dragged the car back with a tractor, left it in its spot, then put a tree branch over the window to cover the shattered glass.'

Of course they didn't tell their parents and two days later Geoff came up and said to his son, 'Paedor, have you been out in the car? What's happened to the car?'

The boy tried to deny all, but his father then said to him that he could understand the windscreen being broken with the branch. 'But,' he said, 'that doesn't explain the broken axle.'

Paedor then explained the accident and the deception. Instead of handing out a severe punishment, his father took a different approach. 'Dad said, "You've done something bad – we hope you've learned from your mistake. It was a great car and now you don't have it. You can sell it for parts, but that's it."

'And he actually told us stories from his childhood, about the experiences he had rolling cars. After he shared these stories I felt a stronger connection to him. And we ended up having a good experience out of it all.'

One thing that Wal Stirling had given his son Geoff was the gift of storytelling, and in his own way Geoff had taken his father's teachings and used them to pass on not only family folklore, but also a sense of his own moral discipline and beliefs. A different time, a different method.

Even in the more conventional families the child–parent dynamic was changing. A plethora of parenting books, led by Dr Benjamin Spock's seminal essay on raising children as individuals, *Baby and Child Care*, were indicating a shift in parenting philosophy.

In defiance of the old adage, children were encouraged to be both seen and heard, and by the beginning of the 1980s corporal punishment had almost disappeared from Australian schools. There was a widespread recognition that, like everyone else, children had rights and that their physical and emotional wellbeing were to be protected.

4

A Kid's Job

From the 1980s onwards, Australian couples were deciding to have fewer children, 1.7 in fact – who comes up with figures like this? Anyway, despite this declining birth rate the population continued to grow, due in part to a new wave in immigration. From 1980 to 2000 almost two million people came to this nation, often leaving desperate circumstances in their homeland and eager to give their children a better life.

Helen Huynh's family began leaving Vietnam immediately after the war ended in 1975. 'The country was in chaos and people were scared for their lives. My family were business people before the war and this made it really hard for us after 1975. Our property got confiscated, there was more fighting, and news of people being sent to re-education. We were just sick of death, we were sick of having no future at all, so we left.

'Thousands of years of wars but not once did the Vietnamese people turn to the sea on the scale that was seen after 1975. Culturally, Vietnamese people are terrified of water. But for

Helen Huynh, aged two, in Dalat, Vietnam, in 1988.

my family, the sea was our last bid for freedom – whatever that led to.'

Helen speaks about the early years of her family's Australian life with pride and respect. 'My uncle left on a boat at the age of nineteen – younger than I am now. An entire generation threw their future out to sea, saying, "A better future for our children."' She says these words clearly and simply but the cost of this journey is crystallised as she tells her family's story. 'Basically this generation laid out its body as a bridge for us to walk over.' She says it with no rancour or burden, just a statement that indicates she holds a deep sense of gratitude to the members of her family who came before her.

There is also an understanding that she has a responsibility to make her uncle's trip mean something. 'My generation has a sense of obligation to justify all the sacrifice that they made to give us everything we have. There is this feeling that you make it in life through your education, and if you have to work hard at it then you work hard at it.'

That doesn't mean she has no regrets in her young life, no matter how trivial they may seem. Her face opens with a wide, self-effacing smile as she continues. 'After school, when I'm doing the dishes, the kids next door,' and she points away with another smile, 'the kids next door, they're on the trampoline.'

She could see them bouncing up and down, just their heads, then their bodies and flailing arms; she could hear them trying to do somersaults and that twisting, bum-thumping, side-to-side bounce that is a staple of the backyard trampoline.

'I thought, I've never had a trampoline, I was studying so hard, even from a young age.' Then she laughs a little. 'I would always think, Mum, why piano lessons? Or Mum, I've already studied for eight hours, it's enough! And you come home with your 99.98 per

Helen with her mother in 1988.

cent HSC mark and your parents go, "Where's the other 0.2?"'
Helen breaks into a beautiful smile and laughs again. She then
admits, 'There's an incredible amount of pressure to do well.'

But the pride her family takes in her achievements is evident,
and it's a celebration of the life in this chosen country of Australia.
Helen has a heart-rending early home video, where she has been
positioned in the corner of the living room between the sideboard
and the television. She wouldn't be nine, and she sings 'Waltzing
Matilda' for her parents, fudging a few times. The song about a
thieving swagman running from a squatter on his thoroughbred
hasn't sounded sweeter.

A great part of Helen's family chores also lay in the responsibility
of being a first-generation Australian. 'The uniqueness of the
responsibilities you have growing up in Australia because your
parents did come from another country – you have to play the
cultural mediator, you play the linguistic mediator.' Which is an

Helen Huynh (second on the left) *with her grandma, grandpa and cousin in Vietnam, 2007.*

intelligent way of saying you have to do a whole heap of running around and thinking for your olds.

'Say there's a traffic infringement in our household. I'm the one who writes the letter, and I'll tell my mum to sign and she'll sign. She knows I'll read the fifty-page insurance policy, the gas and electricity bill,' and here she cracks up laughing, 'and you verify things over the phone for your mum in her voice.'

Then she says with a softer smile, 'Don't all kids have to do those things? It's a kid's job, right?'

She may be a first-generation Australian but Helen Huynh is also an articulate spokesperson for young Australians who are growing up in a world where information and its transactions have become quicker, more advanced and more wide ranging. The age of the computer and the internet.

In the last two decades the advancement of computers and their impact upon the way children grow up has been obvious. The two have become inseparable. Children are born into a world that provides instant information and entertainment. They are computer natives.

For Helen, today's children are bequeathed with the responsibility of broader society. But she sees a shift in what childhood actually means. 'The notion of "childhood simplicity", as in parochial existence, obliviousness to worldly matters, well, that needs to be discarded because we do live in a very different world due to technology – technology does define our childhood.'

And she demonstrates how that world has changed for her generation. 'We, at the press of a button, can communicate to someone on the other side of Australia, the other side of the world. We're connected by mobile phones, through the internet, so if it's someone's birthday I type in "Happy birthday" and press "send".' She smiles and says, 'That's communication for me – I don't know any better.'

All of us at some time in our lives will say that. We didn't know any better, so we will live according to the circumstances in which we find ourselves and really that is all we can do. It is constantly surprising, however, to see just how quickly and how much people can change.

My first brush with computers was as a kid in the late seventies. It was a game called Pong – you plugged a brick-like console into the television and proceeded to play 'tennis' with two sliding rectangles as racquets, bunting a floating little square across a black screen. When one of the rectangles bunted the square, the game would give a hypnotic *pong* sound.

'By Christ, that's an amazing piece of machinery,' said my father. 'But don't play too much, get off and get out to the beach.'

'As modern as tomorrow,' was my Aunty Rita's opinion.

We Ponged like mad for an afternoon then gave up the rectangles and square, and hit the beach. But times change.

Helen continues, 'If you've been brought up with a particular notion of what childhood is in terms of simplicity – as in: "Childhood is playing in the backyard and getting your hands and feet dirty" – if you define childhood in that narrow way then obviously everything my generation represents is an abomination of childhood. Because we are inside on our computers. What people need to understand, though, is that we are still learning and discovering and communicating with each other. We're just doing it on a different scale, at a different pace, in a different way.'

Helen believes, however, that there is also a dark side to technology. 'The amount of media that my generation is exposed to, the kind of imagery we are exposed to on an average day, is disempowering because of the expectation it places upon us. It defines the way we think we should behave.'

The internet offers an ocean of information and its content is seemingly as uncontrollable as the tides of the ocean. 'You've got little kids taking pictures of themselves, sexual images of themselves, and throwing it out for dissemination across the internet, so I can see the adult world thinking, Oh no, what's happening to these kids? They are out of control. Where do they get these ideas?'

In the space of a single generation, traditionally accepted social mores have been challenged and overturned. The majority of Australian kids soon had both parents working, preschoolers were looked after in daycare centres and childminding became a major industry.

The collapse of the ABC Learning Centres childcare group after the global financial crisis of 2008–2009 led not only to investigations of corporate compliance and activity but it distressed thousands of Australian families who relied upon the corporation's childcare to continue their family's routine.

Bob and Loretta Moore are now grandparents of Georgina, the daughter of their own daughter Jo and her husband Ben. Georgina is being raised in ways that Bob and Loretta could never have imagined. For a start, like many other couples, Ben and Jo Madsen have careers they pursue, but instead of daycare, Georgina has a full-time nanny.

'The world's greatest nanny, that's Debbie,' says Ben. 'She usually arrives at about eight in the morning and gives Georgie breakfast, then we head off to work.'

Jo continues, 'I get Georgie up and get her dressed in the morning – which Debbie says is a first for any of the families she's worked for. Usually the kids are in bed when she arrives.'

Jo and Ben Madsen with their daughter Georgina.

The cost of a full-time nanny is, in Ben's words, 'horrendous', but it is worth the price of paying what amounts to the yearly mortgage repayments on an average Australian house because, he says, 'Debbie is helping Georgina grow and develop those innate skills that will help her be a healthy, happy person.'

There are some aspects of Georgina's childhood Bob and Loretta don't take a shine to. 'It's a nightmare where they live,' says Bob. 'Six floors up in the middle of Sydney. You need a card to get in the door. You can't even get in the outside door.'

He thinks for a moment and says that even though he would have liked Georgina to grow up in a country town like he and his own children did. 'You've got to roll with the blows and, really, what's she missing out on? Georgie hasn't even started school yet and already she can do a lot more than I could do when I'd had a full year at school. I can remember for the first six months all I did was draw on the slate with a piece of lead or whatever. Georgie can do more at three years old.'

Ben and Jo say they don't buy Georgie a lot of things, but rather they want to give her experiences. Monday morning, she has a music class. Tuesday morning, she has Mandarin along with a group of other preschoolers. Wednesday is play day when she travels through parks with Debbie, and Thursday is Mandarin day again. Then, in Georgie's words, 'Fursday afternoon we go to ballet!' She likes to dress in her tutu and stomp and dance in front of her television with images of ballet performances from around the world.

That isn't all that Georgina watches on her television. Loretta says that Jo and Ben didn't let Georgie watch programmed television until she was about two, but instead the couple uploaded images from a computer onto the set, pictures. Photographs from the albums of both Ben and Jo's families. So when she watches she sees the faces, the history of her past.

'Photos or grandparents, uncles, aunts – so Georgie got to know her relatives as well,' says Loretta. 'There must be thousands of photos of all the family members from everywhere. She's gotten to easily recognise them after watching them come up all the time. And nobody told her to watch, to look at it, it's just there, all of us, just happens in passing.'

From learning to drive a left-hand-drive jeep while out shooting with your father to learning Mandarin, from stoking two-metre-high fires to boil a billy to music classes and ballet, the family's journey has been quite remarkable.

At three years of age Georgie is living a childhood seemingly light years from her grandparents' and even that of her parents. But while she is better educated, more articulate and more confident than they might have been as children, she's grounded in her family's strong history through the generations.

Not all Australian childhoods have experienced such a connection, but even so, wonderful things can still happen.

Donna Meehan had struggled with the loss of her Aboriginal family for more than twenty years and then, one morning, her birth mother arrived on her doorstep. 'I opened the door and there was this pretty, young Aboriginal girl and I knew in an instant it was my sister Kim, born after I was taken away. She said, "There is someone here to meet you." She stepped back and then my mum came around the corner.'

Donna and Kim had made contact through letters but they had both needed time to adjust to what the meeting would mean. Donna had no idea her birth mother was coming that day, and there she stood. 'She came inside and we had a cuppa and I just had to ask her the question – I just said, "Why'd you give us away?"'

'And her eyes filled with tears as she said, "I don't know why they took you. They just took you."'

After a while Donna played 'Joey's Song' for her birth mother. 'My birth mum said they used to play that song after the children were taken away and just wail and wail and wail.'

In the middle of all this, Donna rang her adoptive mum, her German mum, with some trepidation, thinking that she might even 'get roused on' by her. But generosity of heart is one of the most compelling of all human traits, and a mother's love wishes only happiness for her child.

'When I told my German mum I had a visitor, she asked me who it was. I said, "It's my birth mother."' Donna's face is still for a moment and then she says slowly and with a great deal of pride, 'And she was so happy. She said, "Oh, I would love to meet her." So I arranged to visit. When we got there my German mum had made a cake. My two mothers met. Just a beautiful love story.'

She smiles. 'And they sang together, my German mum and my Aboriginal mum. A soprano and an alto, they sat at the organ and sang and sang and sang.'

The sadness of Donna's childhood was finally acknowledged by the Australian government in February 2008 with the Prime Minister's apology to the Stolen Generations on the floor of the House of Representatives in Parliament House, Canberra. Beamed around the nation on large screens in civic spaces or in school classrooms, it was a moment that Donna Meehan felt deeply.

'When Kevin Rudd said the words, "I apologise to the mothers," I thought, that's for you, Mum.'

Two years later, the Australian government acknowledged one more example of the indifference and neglect perpetrated upon children after the Second World War. On the same floor of Parliament the neglect and abuse of people like Rose Kruger and all the other children who had come to Australia for a 'holiday', the so-called Forgotten Generation, were remembered with an apology.

'Today and from this day forward it is my hope,' said Kevin Rudd alongside the then opposition leader Malcolm Turnbull, 'that you will be called the remembered generation.'

There may be some who find these acknowledgements politically fortunate, perhaps even tokenistic, but as Ron Palmer, a man who has lived in this country for more than eighty years and fought under its flag, put it, 'An apology costs you nothing, and if you don't mean it then it's worth less than that. But if you mean what you say, then, brother, there's not the richest man's treasure that's worth more.'

Looking at the adult faces of the Stolen and Forgotten generations as they listened to the apologies, I'd have to agree with Ron Palmer. One hopes the apologies were meant sincerely, for seeing the changes that time and experience have made upon those faces, upon those lives, is a humbling thing.

One of the greatest crimes humans can commit is to steal a person's childhood. There are so many ways in which it can be taken away; sometimes it can be done quietly, sometimes violently, sometimes it can be done without any knowledge that the theft is even occurring.

There is nothing so open as a child's face and perhaps it's only through the lives of their own children that a person can really appreciate the briefness of life and yet the continuity of its spirit.

5

Two Photos, Two Childhoods

There is a moment when you can contemplate two childhoods. That moment caught in time, a child's first class photo.

As I remember it, the day of my first school photo I was running late. I was always running late. I played war with a red-haired, buck-toothed kid from down the road and came off second best. Got caught in mud-ball crossfire. Then I played tiggy with some of the Red Cross Home kids. They were tough. My torn shirt was testament to that. So as I remember it, that's why I was late for my school photo. My first school photo. Humpybong Infants. 1C. 1969.

It was thirty-odd years before my son's first class photo. A lot had happened. Back then, Australia was involved in an overseas war, in Vietnam, which divided our society. Now Australian troops are in action in Afghanistan and again we find our society divided, although on a much smaller scale.

Humankind has not only walked on the moon but also played golf there, governments have come and gone, computers and the information revolution, cloning, AIDS and the internet, the birth of my son and his first school photo.

Holding both photos in my hands, I notice my son's class all wear their school uniform. At Humpybong in my day we dressed freestyle. Yet there is so much more obvious diversity in the faces of my son's class photo.

Humpybong's closest call on an ethnic school kid was Pascal Ferrier. He came from Melbourne. In my son's class there are Anglos, Chinese, Turkish and Vietnamese: a rainbow of cultures. It's so obvious a difference.

But there is still the same innocence in the faces, still the girls firmly push their hands into their laps for modesty's sake, still there are the crazed face-pullers. In my son's class it was a boy called Alan, who achieved a very rare feat for a class photo: he's cross-eyed. God knows how he got away with it. God knows what his parents said when they saw it. Although I can well imagine.

William McInnes (second row, fourth from the right), *in 1969.*

I was my class' face-puller. My basin-cut head was squeezed into my best attempt at a 'Killer' Karl Kox snarl. My face was dirty, my shirt ripped and my tongue protruded and my dad . . . well, he looked at the photo and he grabbed me and wanted to know why he'd paid good money for a photo of a human prune. I wonder if Alan had better luck.

I look at the faces in both photos and suddenly realise I know the names of most of my son's class and yet those of my classmates escape me. Let me think, has time made me forget so much? Let me think.

There's Lynn Wakefield next to me, I remember she had a wart on her thumb. There's big Jeff White up the back – he's a plumber now. Trevor Barsby, he won a couple of Sheffield Shields for Queensland with his thumping bat. Karen Greenway ended up a librarian and Jenny Barter, I last saw her in a supermarket with a basket full of meaty treats for her dog. She's a bank manager these days. That's it. Five names from a class of thirty-eight. Who are they? Where are they? What happened to them?

That's when I recognised Steven Draper. Dibbs, we used to call him. Snowy blond hair and freckles and a grin as big as a Cavendish banana. I stare at Dibbs in the photo. The last time I saw him was in 1983. I was riding along the Bruce Highway between Rockhampton and Mackay. In the driving rain I saw some poor sod ahead trying to hitch a ride. For some reason I slowed down. As I drew near and cut the engine, I saw it was Dibbs. Dibbs Draper. We looked at each other for quite a while. He was going north to Airlie Beach to try to get a job on a yacht. He wore thongs, shorts and a torn windcheater. He was right, he said. Didn't need a lift. He'd wait. He smiled and looked down the highway through the rain.

'Life's been funny,' he said.

I heard later from a friend that he'd been told Dibbs had died. Somewhere. Somehow. I hoped he had heard wrong.

With the photos in my hands and thinking of Dibbs and the faces whose names I can't remember, I suddenly feel the fear all parents feel. What will happen to my child? Where will he go? Will he be safe?

I have an urge to hold my son and tell him how much I love him. How I will try to help because life can be unkind. Life can be funny.

I look at his class photo again, at that rainbow of young, innocent faces and suddenly I see something else. I see how that collection of cultures and races stand together and sing our national anthem at school assembly. I see that as they sing, they are Chinese and Anglo and Turkish and Vietnamese, Greek and Indigenous Australians.

Australians. I see them march to class hand in hand. I hear them laughing together, just as I laughed with my classmates.

This was the class that I helped mind on an excursion, to an IMAX cinema to see a film about giant kelp, of all things. I sat at the end of a row to aid any little ones who had to dart off to the toilet in the dark.

I looked away from the 3D seaweed on the screen to a sight of little people with their funny 3D glasses, all sitting in their seats with their little arms outstretched and their little fingers, their starfish hands, wiggling in the hope of touching the fish that swam around the weed on the big screen. They all were open-mouthed and smiling.

Whatever the next thirty years and beyond may bring us, as my son stands in his school photo, I feel such a pride in him and his classmates. In the strength and resilience of their youth and of the diversity of our country.

Australia is many things and there are many childhoods, but even though every generation changes it is the sum of its predecessors, and we just have to remind ourselves of that. Every step is a continuation, not an ending. We have to remember, in a way, to just come back by the time it's dark.

Postscript

Dibbs Draper didn't die. I found this out only this year, 2010. A friend of his sister's told me as I bought a coffee from a café not far from where I grew up. Everyone had heard the rumours of Dibbs' death and nobody was quite sure how they had started but Dibbs, she assured me, is still around. 'Two little kids and as much of a ratbag as ever.'

The
Australian
Soul

6

My Front Doorbell

My front doorbell rings. Well, it doesn't ring, it shrieks. We've been meaning to disconnect it for years but never have. I don't quite know why that is, but we must have had better things to do. One thing I do know is that when the bell shrieks it's a sure bet that whoever it is standing out on our verandah isn't known to me or my family. Well, they wouldn't be a close friend or neighbour. For once anyone has pressed the bell and heard that sound there is no hurry to ring it again.

Usually I open the door to find an unfamiliar face. Maybe a student trying to flog an electricity plan or television-cable connection option. Once I opened the door to find an Indian student who wanted to tell me all about the wonders of Foxtel, but couldn't help himself from laughing at the noise.

'Can I, please,' he uttered between giggles, 'ring it again?'

Another time I discovered a Jehovah's Witness who seemed to be in a state of shock and numbly offered me a clenched copy of *The Watchtower*. As I prised it from her hand she turned silently

---

Page 89: *Sister Vianney Hatton in 1971.*

away and carried on. Then there was a mumbling man who shook nearly as much as the Witness. I had seen him before, wasted and out of it down around the local railway station. This time he shook from a mixture of the substances he recreated with and the effects the noise of the bell had upon him. He was like a punch-drunk fighter sniffing at the noise of the bell for the final round.

He almost shaped up. 'Gets you going,' he said, and he went on to mumble and jabber his tale of stencilling our house number on the driveway. Apparently the week before I had ordered such a service and it had been carried out. I knew I hadn't but said nothing. He was trying to make a bit of money, I thought, so I nodded.

'Ten dollars,' he mumbled and after I had fished out some change from various pockets, he advised me that he didn't actually have the correct numbers for our house so had chosen a couple of other digits that looked vaguely similar to our address.

So outside our house is a street number that should be at the other end of the block.

Then there was the time Lois had been standing out there. Lois is a local. She likes to shout at people and bellow at voices that don't exist down the phone outside the local library. One of the few public phones left. She usually prefaces her assault with 'Excuse me!' and then fires off salvos of indignant rants about almost anything one could imagine.

She has been a presence in the area for as long as we have lived here and she has her good days and her bad, depending on when she takes her medication. On good days she has a veil of sad melancholy on her face, as if she is listening to some unbearably beautiful yet sad piece of music.

This was not one of the good days. There was no beautiful music.

'Yes, Lois?' I ask.

She lets me have it with both barrels. 'Excuse me! That bloody bastard doorbell is a ridiculous bastard! And what, can you tell me, has Channel Seven done to my television set? What have you done to it? They bugging it?'

There are charity collectors of all ethnicities wearing homemade ID badges for groups with vague names and noble intentions. Couriers who simply stand and stare and wait for you to sign an indecipherable signature on a palm pilot.

Sometimes the faces are familiar, like the Egg Man. Every second Thursday in the late afternoon the bell rings and there stands the Egg Man, a diminutive old Greek man who sells eggs laid by his chooks. He stands, smiling slightly, with his white hair and goatee beard, and says simply, 'Hello.' And offers his dozen eggs.

It is as if the shrieking bell has heralded our front door to open upon a whole range of the different faces of Australia. Sometimes the faces seem to be caught in another time and some seem to be portraits of the future, but they are all, to me, Australian.

The other day, a Thursday, the front doorbell rang and I go to open the door expecting the Egg Man and his freshly laid dozen. Through the dappled thumb-smudge patterns of the coloured glass I see a familiar looking shape. No, it's not the Egg Man. It's Ron Palmer.

His lanky frame is propped up against a verandah post and he is wearing an outrageous pair of wraparound sunglasses. Even though they cover half his face I can tell that he is smiling.

'How do, brother?' and he offers me his hand.

'Nice glasses,' I tell Ron.

'Aw, bloody eyes are going, doctor's orders, what can you do?'

He has always looked old, Ron, even the first time I met him almost twenty years ago, and he has always been the same lanky, laughing man. I was quite startled once to see a photo of him as an eighteen-year-old, who, like many other young Australians, had joined up in the fight against the Japanese. He was in the Second World War uniform of the RAAF.

It was so startling because around the photo, propped up on the wall of his home, were more recognisable shots of Ron, surrounded by children and grandchildren and one with Santa Claus in a park. His big lopsided grin beaming out. To see him look so familiar and yet so distant was quite something. And now here he was at my front door, looking, it must be said, a little worse for wear. He laughed out loud when I asked him how he was.

'Bits and pieces falling off left, right and centre – but nothing a bit of Tarzan's Grip and a rubber band won't fix. Now are you right for the Carols in the Park?'

For the past several years Ron has appeared now and then, asking me to front up at various community events he, or whichever community group he has been working with, is organising. It would actually be easier to list the community groups and organisations he hasn't been associated with, such is the list of his commitments.

Ron Palmer with his grandchildren Harry (left) *and Monty* (right).

People who like to rag him call him Mr Footscray, but for the last eighty-odd years that is how he has defined himself.

From the Labor Party and St Vincent de Paul, the local mission for the homeless, countless arts festivals, the local brass band and historical society, and the matter he wanted to discuss – the Yarraville Carols in the Park.

'Now, son, you'll be there, won't you? You don't front and I'll keep on ringing this clanger of yours until you do.' He smiles and he rings the bell again. The dog barks and somebody yells and Ron Palmer laughs. 'Love a bit of action, brother!'

He is eighty-four years old. I look at him. Eighty-four. When I saw him as an eighteen-year-old in the uniform of a fighting man I had to laugh.

Eighteen-year-old Ron Palmer.

'Very dashing,' I said.

'Oh, mate, we were all young and beautiful once.'

I told him he still looked pretty good.

'Oh hello, I was in the airforce, brother, not the navy!'

He said 'brother' in the way old Labor men do, with no real ideological bent, but more as if it were a suitable substitute for 'mate'.

I asked him, as I looked at the eighteen-year-old Ron, what he had felt when the Second World War ended.

'Bloody relief, you clown, what else?'

No, I told him, I'd like to know what he had wished for, what he had hoped for Australia.

'Oh, there you have it,' he said, and he laughed. 'Well, I didn't have a clue, really. Thought we'd pretty much go on as usual. Be about eight or nine million of pretty happy people.' And then he laughed even more. 'Well, there you go, was I ever wrong? Don't expect a good tip from me for the Cup.' Ron Palmer pointed his eighty-year-old-plus finger at the image of his eighteen-year-old self. 'That young fella didn't know what was coming, but I love a bit of action, brother, so he won't be disappointed!'

Outside my front door Ron Palmer goes to ring the doorbell again, but I assure him that I will front at the Carols in the Park the week before Christmas. He gives a nod and a wave and tells me I'm a good man.

I tell him I don't know about that.

And he yells back from his car, 'Well, you're something!' and waves again.

It was a different world, a different Australia back then when he was eighteen, but somehow I can't imagine Ron Palmer would have been much different. I think of what Australia, and we, have become, and to coin a Palmerism, well, we're something.

7

Postwar Prophets

At the beginning of its federation, Australia had been a nation of contrasts. On one hand it was seen as a social utopia. It had a forty-hour working week, universal suffrage, a high court of appeal, a form of arbitration commission to settle industrial disputes and a flourishing democracy that heralded the world's first labour government.

So rare was this that a bemused Russian revolutionary and political agitator by the name of Vladimir Ilyich Lenin ruminated on the odd nature of a democracy that could change control from capitalist to labour ideology without the use of force and revolution. 'What sort of peculiar capitalist country is this, in which the workers' representatives predominate in the Upper House and, till recently, predominated in the Lower as well, and yet the capitalist system is in no danger?'

Yet at the same time, this Australia was also a nation deeply suspicious of any people of a different 'race' and instituted the White Australia Policy to protect the 'Australian way of life'. It was an economic as much as a racial policy. Alfred Deakin, prime minister from 1903 to 1910, and proponent of the White Australia described it as: 'the maintenance of social conditions of life under which men and women can live decently. It means equal laws and opportunity for all, it means protection against the underpaid labour of other lands; it means social justice and fair wages. The White Australia policy goes down to the roots of our national existence, the roots from which the British social system has sprung.' This policy is now largely considered racist and prevented many people from migrating to Australia.

The other defining strain within Australia was a raging sectarianism. Religious faith was a separation point for Australians. To put the situation into a rough and ready sporting metaphor, there were minor grade faiths you could belong to, but the A grade seniors were the Protestant faiths and the Catholics.

You might have been forgiven for thinking that a world war that was fought for democratic freedoms against fascist, racist and theological tyranny may have loosened the religious divide in Australia. After all, the Second World War was ended in the Pacific when the Allies destroyed two major Japanese cities with two single bombs. Apocalypse and the ability to shower it upon citizens came not from the heavens and brought by an angel, but from an advanced military industrial society and a gleaming silver aircraft.

It was the nuclear age and the Church in Australia may have sniffed the portents of a humanist endeavour to create a new society and opportunity not through faith of the altar, but from scientific, industrial and societal endeavour.

At the end of the Second World War, Ron Palmer was one of the million or so Australians who had served in the country's defence forces, and when he returned home there was never any doubt where he was going to settle. His family had been part of the Melbourne suburb of Footscray before it had even existed – his father's side settled in the area in 1851, eight years before the district was created. Ron had every reason to believe that life would go on much the same as before the war took him away from his beloved 'Scray.

Prewar Australia was a fairly closed, homogenous affair, with a narrowness of view. Australians thought of themselves primarily as a British people. This was demonstrated most compellingly by the late wartime prime minister John Curtin, who considered Australia a great bastion of Britain. And this from the man who asserted Australian independence and self-determination over the use of Australian troops by recalling infantry divisions from the Middle East theatre to the Pacific – in the face of stiff opposition and condemnation from then British prime minister Winston Churchill.

'Oh, we were Aussie as,' says Ron Palmer, 'but you know the Poms were . . . Well, Pommy land was the Mother Country. It was an imperial age, brother, and we were part of the empire. Happy to be there, too.'

That Australia of the imperial age had defined itself in pretty narrow terms. It liked to think of itself as white, egalitarian and safe. By and large it was, and everybody identified themselves through particular tribes. There were sport and geographic tribes: Sandgropers and Croweaters, Vics and Blues, Apple Islanders and Banana Benders. Or, rather, Western Australians and South Australians, Victorians and New South Welshmen, Tasmanians and Queenslanders.

But the 'sameness' of Australia meant a basic and deep-seated division. Religion.

When Ron Palmer came home to Footscray, a civic thanksgiving was held to honour returning servicemen. 'It was a council do and we all mucked in together — all of us. We could have been anybody as far as any of us cared. Catholic, C of E, Baptist, Methodist, Jewish. There was even a Bullen's Circus at the Catholic church hall at St Augustine's down there at Yarraville.'

'At the Catholic church hall?' I ask as if I have uncovered some vital historical marker.

Ron Palmer looks at me. 'Yeah . . . it was a big hall.'

When I ask Ron if there was any other religious aspect to the reception he looks at me again and laughs. 'Oh, brother, you're a trier. Well, we said the Lord's Prayer and sang the national anthem, but as I said, it was a council do. We couldn't care less, seen too much other stuff to think otherwise. We were all just pleased to be home. I would have had a beer with a lamp post I was that glad to be home.' And then Ron has a think. 'In fact, I had a cuppa with a couple of Baptists.'

There's a pause and I say to Ron, 'So you knew what religion the other blokes were?'

Ron nods. 'Yeah, well, that was a part of the package back then. You all knew what brand you were and mixed in those sorts of circles.'

It strikes me that I had always assumed Ron was a Catholic, but had never asked him. 'And what circles did you mix in, Ron? The Catholics?'

There's a pause and Ron Palmer's eyes twinkle behind his outrageous sunnies. 'Brother, I'm an Australian, I mix in lots of circles.'

I leave Ron with his laughter and see that even though it was a council reception or 'do', in Ron's words, people still identified fellow citizens through their faiths. In the late forties and early fifties, Australians were about as religious as they had been fifty or one hundred years before.

In 1947, sixty-seven per cent of Australians labelled themselves as Protestant while twenty-one per cent were Catholics. Three years later, in 1950, about forty-four per cent of Australians said that they attended church at least once a month. Organised or orthodox Christianity had a great influence on most people's lives. And not just through the trip to church for the Sunday service or mass. The Church or your religious faith was a key determiner of your social and political life.

Ron Palmer believed that the emergence of the world from the Second World War into the Cold War also had an effect on the faith of Australians. 'It all went sideways a bit after World War Two because of the problems we were having with the Russians. It was all right while we had the bomb but then the buggers let off one in the late forties and it was on for young and old. Nobody knew what was going to happen, so going off to church was a part of holding on to your routine.'

For most people, one of the most striking characteristics of this era was the combination of their anxiety about the threat of nuclear destruction and the unprecedented prosperity.

For many people who attended church and Sunday school as children, they found that it would define the rest of their lives. Linda Visman and Graeme Dunstan were two young Australians who had a religious upbringing. She was a Catholic and he was a Baptist.

When Linda Visman looks back to her early church experience she sees that much of her family's life was related in some way to the local church, its activities and the people who attended alongside her family. She felt an ownership and pride in her faith. 'Some of the hymns I loved were those that asserted our Catholicism, especially

Linda, aged ten, wearing her Confirmation dress.

"Faith of our Fathers". I was much chagrined when I learned later that other denominations claimed these hymns too!'

So even a commonality between the faiths was bypassed in favour of competition. It would have been interesting to find out if the hymns sounded different in the different houses of faith.

'Well, it depends if anybody got stuck into the communion wine or not, I s'pose,' says Ron Palmer, with a wink.

Graeme Dunstan grew up in the Melbourne suburb of Essendon, although his mother was from Stawell in rural Victoria. The family's middle-class aspirations were dashed by the death of Graeme's grandfather in France in the First World War. The family had always been very loyal to the Baptist Church, and the Church returned

Graeme Dunstan in 1949, with his mother, Bessie, and his sister, Wendy.

the loyalty in kind. It was church welfare that got people through the hard times.

Graeme was a good Baptist boy and went obligingly to Sunday school. 'My mother was determined that I would be a Christian,' he says with a smile. 'And I went to Sunday school every week – as early as I can remember. So Sunday school, Bible stories, I had it all.'

He quite enjoyed those Bible stories and found the Jesus story inspiring. And there were other inducements. 'There were picnics and I was in the boys' club called the Pathfinders. You know it was all part of family life back then.'

Linda Visman remembers that the Catholic Church extended its presence in people's lives to more than just the practice of the mass. 'The Latin mass was an ongoing institution and we attended every Sunday. We also went with our parents on Holy Days, like Ascension Thursday and All Saints Day, as if they were a Sunday.'

Hers was a fairly typical Catholic family, steeped in the Church's ancient traditions and guided by its precepts. 'We believed all we were told: that the Pope spoke with the authority of God; that the bishop was his representative; that the priest acted for Christ in the sacraments and was a respected teacher who would lead us to heaven.'

The church was also involved in its parishioners' everyday lives. 'The church had sodalities – clubs, I suppose – and they were for different groups in the parish. Men joined the Holy Name Society; women the Sacred Heart Society; girls the Children of Mary; and boys would become altar boys serving the priest during mass.

'The sodalities had their own Sunday each month, so on the Children of Mary's Sunday, we would attend as a group, all wearing our blue cloaks, white veils and Children of Mary Sodality medal, and carrying our missal, the Catholic prayer book.'

Sometimes Linda's parents decided not to go to the main church and instead walked three or so kilometres from their home to Oak Flats. There, a Sunday mass would be held in the community hall.

'I loved the early morning walk, especially when we went on Christmas mornings. Then there was the added joy of knowing that on our return, as well as being able to eat, there'd be presents under the tree for us to unwrap.'

It didn't matter that the presents were almost always homemade, courtesy of Linda's dad and his workshop in the shed. 'The wooden scooters he made for me and my little sister were as prized as any bought ones.'

In the early post-Second-World-War years, the divide between Australians due to their religions was marked and known by those of every faith and openly encouraged by the churches themselves.

Maureen McLoughlin has a steady gaze and a spirited nature. She loves a chat and is clear in her opinions. She grew up in a

Maureen McLoughlin, aged nineteen months, with her family.

staunch Labor household, which meant, 'We were Irish Catholics. My dad was a wharfie, although he said to us kids to say he was a stevedore foreman because people looked down on wharfies.'

As she grew up there were a few rules in her home that were known by all. 'We voted Labor, always. My dad said at least with Labor we get crumbs, but we get nothing from the Liberals, they're for the rich.'

And there were other rules handed down by the Church. 'You weren't allowed to go to non-Catholic religious services.' And she stresses with that level gaze, 'There were three times I was asked to be a bridesmaid and they were all in non-Catholic religious services and you weren't allowed to go in.' She gives a slight shrug of her shoulders. 'If you came from a strict Catholic family you didn't do it, you'd go to the church and stand outside and wait till they came out.'

It got too much for Maureen when a very good friend of hers – non-Catholic – was getting married. When she asked her priest for permission to attend, he told her it would probably be all right. But once she was at the wedding she was disappointed on two counts. For a start, 'This friend's uncle was a dreadful bigot – an Orangeman.' Orangeman was the term given to some Irish Protestants, who also immigrated in large numbers to Australia along with the more commonly known Catholic Irish. Secondly, 'At the reception people

Maureen, aged eighteen, with her brother John.

were rubbing it in, making jokes about the Catholics disobeying the Pope to come along. It was all very derogatory.'

It wouldn't be the last time that bitterness and old feuds from other countries would be reinforced in Australia, and it seems a little sad that Maureen was mocked when she wanted so much to go to the wedding. She might have asked herself whether it was all worth it, especially when she found the Presbyterian service lacking the high theatre and ritual of the Catholic mass.

She remembers quite a lot of argy-bargy between the faiths and living under the adage of giving as well as you got. 'Bishop Kelly told Catholics not to go to Kodak because that company discriminated and wouldn't employ Catholics. They lost a lot of business.'

There were whispers about the Post Office and even Qantas. 'They were definitely businesses whose policy was not to employ Catholics, but then,' she adds, 'there were others, like Mark Foy's, who would only employ Catholics.'

Mark Foy's was a department store in Sydney that stretched around a whole city block and was well known for a few reasons. It was the one big department store that would stock the uniforms of the major Catholic schools, as opposed to David Jones, which specialised in Anglican school uniforms. The store gave birth to a famous Australian saying, popularised by a politician by the name of Paul Keating, when describing a person of pomposity or overwhelming confidence, 'They've got more front than Mark Foy's.'

Mark Foy's was the first Australian shop to have an escalator, and perhaps this was another point of difference between the faiths: the use of stairs in shops. Protestants would work their legs for the bargain upstairs while the Catholics got a free ride.

There were some Australians, though, who would take a trip through other faiths to find what they were looking for. In his adolescence, Graeme Dunstan discovered an interesting point of

difference between the Protestant faiths. 'When I became a teenager
I discovered that Baptists didn't dance,' he says with a straight face.
'But Presbyterians did!' and he laughs. 'So the way you got to meet
girls, of course, was to go to a Presbyterian church dance.'

A Presbyterian who knew a little about music was Margaret Bennett.
She grew up in the Sydney suburb of Auburn and her parents came
from different faiths: her father was an Anglican, her mother a
Presbyterian. 'Oh well, the Anglican didn't take,' she says.

Having been a teacher in the country, Margaret moved to Sefton,
in southwestern Sydney, as a young mother where she and her
husband bought a kit house, the first on its street in an area that was
just developing. When she moved there her mother told her Sefton
had a Presbyterian church and that Margaret should attend. 'I told
Mum that I'd go with her, but on one condition – she mustn't tell

The wedding of Margaret and Gordon Bennett, 1947.

them I play the organ.' Margaret had been in enough churches to know that after the pastor, the hardest worker in a congregation is the organist, who becomes a general factotum to the parish.

The church, like the area, was in its early stages and was nothing more than a tin shed with a dirt floor. Margaret said it had 'the oldest organ you'd ever seen'. The minister had the endearing habit of running out and shaking everyone's hand as he saw them coming up the street. When he visited Margaret's mother at Bondi Junction and saw the piano in the corner, he asked who played. Margaret's fate was sealed. Her mother said to her, 'I couldn't tell a lie, I told him you played.'

From that moment Margaret became the organist and a pillar of the church, and with her teaching skills she also started taking the Sunday school classes. 'I was the chief "chucker-outer" and I would give the children a practised teacher glare – a filthy look – if they mucked up in church.'

The Presbyterian church in Sefton and the congregation of 1952.

That church became a huge part of her life. She helped run the socials and cake stalls and even mowed the lawn. 'I could go round the world on the money we raised for that church,' says Margaret, but she never questioned the worth of the work she was doing. It was building a community.

It's fun to think of her being able to spot an undercover Baptist like Graeme Dunstan on the prowl for a foxtrot with a young Presbyterian parishioner, then issue him with a 'filthy look' and engage in her role as chief chucker-outer. But the Sefton church socials, like its hand-shaking minister, were a pretty generous affair.

The socials and youth groups weren't just an avenue for meeting members of the opposite sex and building the church itself, they could also help with finding a vocation. And sometimes the two would go hand in hand.

John Cottier came from a not particularly religious family. Like many Australians, his parents would go to church perhaps once a year. Indeed the closest they came to practising religion was living in the same street as the vicar. So John's parents were surprised when he told them he was going into the ordained ministry for the Church of England. 'I was a little bit harum-scarum, I suppose. I wasn't wild but I was a reasonably lively young man. I just went out at night, had girlfriends and met with the blokes, you know, went to billiard nights and played hockey.'

It was the church youth group that eventually drew him in. 'We had a very lively church, St Andrew's in Aberfeldie near Essendon in Victoria.' He says it was the centre of people's lives. 'This was all pre-television, you see, and we had a meeting on Sunday evening and another during the week, so when we had the service of about two hundred people a good proportion would have come from the youth group. Then after the service we'd stay behind and mingle.'

He considers that it was all fairly tame compared to what kids of a similar age get up to today, but he says, 'We were up to high jinks and the lot.'

John spent so much time on the social aspects of St Andrew's that he found himself working as a Sunday school teacher and helped the local vicar with pastoral duties. The vicar challenged him to take his work with St Andrew's further by considering joining the ministry.

'This became a standing joke in the youth group. They couldn't believe this would happen and neither could I!'

John's parents thought along the same lines: they doubted he had the necessary determination. But before too long he was off studying at theological college.

'It grew on me,' he says. 'One visiting preacher used to say it's like falling in love – some people have a sudden experience, some people go out with a person for a long time, try a lot of different things, some people marry their next-door sweetheart.' He considers that analogy in terms of his own choices. 'I suppose I was the one who tried different things and over a long time it came to me.'

Vianney Hatton found a calling through the Catholic Church. Vianney grew up in Bondi in Sydney but was schooled in the Hunter Valley, where two of her aunts were living. They were both nuns. At that time in Australia it wasn't unknown for siblings and nieces and nephews to enter religious orders, indeed it was actively encouraged.

'In our family, sisters were very prominent and were looked up to and revered; the Church and religion were very much part of my life,' says Vianney. 'We always said grace before meals and

Vianney Hatton in 1955 at the old Trocadero on George Street, Sydney.

Vianney on her graduation day in 1956, with her parents,
Eileen and Jack Hatton.

there were always morning prayers, and night prayers before we
went to bed.'

With the encouragement of her parents, especially her father,
Vianney was the first of her family to undertake tertiary education,
earning a diploma in physiotherapy. She then did something that
gets in the way of so many parents' presumptions about a career
for their child – she fell in love. 'My father felt, of course, that I'd
had this education and it was not going to be used in any way, so
he was not too happy about that.'

Vianney's father wouldn't be the first who didn't approve of the
bloke his daughter brought home, but then he didn't have much
room to move because Vianney's love had been present in her life
for a long time.

'I was in love with our Lord Jesus and I wanted to be with
him,' Vianney says today with the same certainty she had back
then as a young graduate. So she followed her aunts into service as
a nun. The order she joined was the Blessed Sacrament Sisters in

Vianney Hatton, Sister of the Blessed Sacrament, 1959.

Melbourne, a strict, enclosed and deeply contemplative order that adored the Eucharist for an hour every day and night. If the young kneeling women felt themselves dozing off during the adoration, they would stand up and keep going. This was serving religion through withdrawing from the world, and the attractive young Vianney had no reason to believe that the order would not stay like this for the rest of her life.

Such a choice by this articulate, intelligent woman seems hard to accept today. The nuns' time was spent in prayer, silent toil, arranging candles, washing vestments, polishing the chapel – all the housekeeping that comes with unceasing religious devotion and ritual. Vianney Hatton was dedicating her life to Christ.

The nuns earned a living baking and selling altar breads, and it was hard manual work. Their culture was hierarchical: strict rules were in place and if you wanted something you had to ask the mother superior, literally on bended knee. The only time the outside world made contact was when family and friends were allowed to visit under the supervision of the older nuns.

Perhaps it was just as well that outsiders only visited occasionally because the Sisters of the Blessed Sacrament may have had a hard time keeping up with the changes taking place in Australia and the rest of the world.

As Ron Palmer put it, 'Things started racing along when the Russians became the Soviet Union then pinched half of bloody Europe, and the Chinese went Red in the late forties with Mao and his five-year plans – they were cracking hardy. To top that off Bob Menzies got elected and then everything went bloody south.

'Suddenly there were communists everywhere and Menzies was smart enough to make the most of it. Well, I suppose he believed what he said to be honest, but some people were just scared silly and would believe anything.'

Many Australian Christians were obsessed with the 'Red Menace'. In the space of a few short years the Soviet Union had gained atomic power, mainland China became a communist force, and the USA had the atomic bomb. The world seemed poised on the brink of a major conflict almost every year, and the Cold War was just beginning.

First there was the crisis in Germany with the Berlin Blockade, and then, in the early 1950s, what began as a United Nations police action to bring order to a Korean nation split by civil war turned into the first significant conflict of the Cold War.

It wasn't a theological war, even though Christianity was an important part of the capitalist system. Christian faith was seen as a point of difference between the freedom-loving people of the West and the apparently godless communist masses. The whole chart of life and society was beginning to change but old concerns mixed in with this changing landscape to create a potent mix of fear and suspicion.

The Korean War, fought for three years from 1950, brought the dangers of the communist threat closer to home: it was not just happening in far-off Europe. Added to this was an old bogeyman of the Australian people, the possible threat of Asian expansion. It wasn't enough that there were commies out there, but they were Asian as well – a case of the Red Menace being tinged with Yellow Peril. Red Menace, Yellow Peril. It sounds like a bad paint colour, but it made for a pretty hectic time.

'Brother,' crackles Ron Palmer, 'people think we were all living the life of Riley – what was it Howard said? Relaxed and comfortable! It was going off left, right and centre. You had the Cold War, the Labor split, the DLP, the referendum on communism and the Bulldogs even won a bloody flag! It was going off!'

When the leonine Robert Menzies, a Presbyterian, became prime minister, he replaced the Catholic Ben Chifley of the Australian Labor Party. Menzies was genuinely concerned about communism spreading around the world. 'The threat of the communist menace is a very grave problem,' he said for the newsreels in his learned barrister's voice. Many agreed.

Val Noone came from a working-class Irish Catholic family, and the extent to which the fear of communism had permeated society, especially the Catholic Church, was made evident to him when his young sister died in 1952. 'One of the nuns said to my mother, "Well, maybe it's just as well she's passed on because she won't have to be here when the communists take over and everything goes wrong and they start persecuting us."'

Val Noone, aged eleven, with his brothers in 1951.

Menzies was a supreme politician. Having suffered first-hand from the damage caused by political division, the head of the Liberal–Country Party government saw a chance to exploit the presumed closeness of the leftist Labor Party and the Australian communists. Not that Ben Chifley was a friend to the Communist Party of Australia. While prime minister he had sent in troops to break up a coalminers' strike called by communist-oriented union officials. The tensions within the Labor Party were there to be exploited.

The Communist Party had been banned once before, after the signing of the pact between Nazi Germany and Soviet Russia in 1939, and now Menzies sought to reintroduce the Communist Dissolution Bill in 1950. With the country at war in Korea, where more than 17,000 Australian troops would serve, it's hardly surprising that the Australian Labor Party let the bill pass, but then events took an unforeseen course.

'I tell you, when anybody wants to bag us Aussies and tell us we're a bunch of drongos, we've got no time for anybody and we're intolerant and all that palaver – just tell him to look at the commie referendum,' says Ron Palmer.

A raft of organisations wanting to overturn the bill that was seeking the dissolution of the Communist Party lodged an appeal in the High Court of Australia. They wanted the High Court to declare the bill unconstitutional.

The High Court ruled in favour of such a decision, with only one dissenting judgement. The highest court in secular Australia had declared the legislation against the godless creed of communism was not in the interests of freedom of speech and the democratic principles of the Australian people. Menzies then sought a referendum to amend the constitution in respect to communists and communism.

'It went bung when poor old Chif fell off the perch and we ended up with that fella Evatt,' grumbles Ron Palmer. On the night of 13 June 1951, a tearful Robert Menzies announced the death of Ben Chifley from a heart attack and called to end the Parliamentary Ball. Although ardent political opponents, the two men had enjoyed a relationship of deep mutual respect.

'Maybe if Chifley had hung around a bit the split would never have happened; I mean, he was a Catholic, Chifley, old-style Labor, and Evatt wasn't anything much except a pretty strange bloke. He was a gifted advocate but he had poor political skills,' according to Ron.

Of course, there was another side to Evatt. He successfully led the fight for democratic rights against Menzies' attempt to ban the Communist Party. And he went on to become the first Chair of the United Nations.

As the leader of the opposition Herbert Vere Evatt campaigned furiously for the 'No' vote in the referendum, defending what he saw as inalienable democratic freedoms, but at the same time reigniting the view that the Labor Party was sympathetic to communists.

Even though the fear of the 'Red Menace' was widespread, the Australian people voted down the Menzies government's amendments to the Constitution. 'It wasn't that they didn't like Menzies, they did. He'd just hammered us that year in the federal election,' explains Ron Palmer. 'It's that they didn't want the government to become too powerful. It was a wonderful thing when you look at it – even though folks were scared witless, some of them put their democracy ahead of those fears.'

But now the country was set for religious and political turmoil. Australians, especially many Melbourne Catholics, became engaged in a campaign against the threat of communism. Most Catholics were like Maureen McLoughlin's wharfie, sorry, stevedore father – rusted-on Labor supporters – and many working-class people, if not most, didn't like Menzies and wouldn't vote for him. But after the defeat of Evatt's Labor Party by the Menzies-led coalition, a bitter split developed in the left. It was over politics, but some used religion in their propaganda and methods of organisation.

Evatt had blamed his defeat by Menzies on a group of concerned Labor members known as 'Groupers', who were predominantly devout Catholics and ardent anti-communists. They were led by B.A. (Bob) Santamaria, a journalist and editor who was the driving

Maureen McLoughlin's father (left), *with her Uncle Willie in 1929.*

force for what was to become a political movement and philosophy propelled by a religious faith. The bitterness and recriminations of the Catholic divide within the Labor Party was to keep it out of office for twenty-three years and distort the political nature of Australian society.

Three times in federal elections over that period the Labor Party would gain a higher proportion of the vote, but because of the preferential electoral system and the new theological political party, Santamaria's Democratic Labor Party, Australia would have a conservative federal government for more than two decades. His organisation, the National Civic Council, was a grassroots political movement that could also pass as a think tank. It evolved in the late 1950s from the Catholic Social Studies Movement, which Santamaria founded.

Whether or not the Labor split would have occurred, or may have been less severe, if Chifley had lived longer is open to debate. 'I don't know if Chif's living longer would have stopped Santamaria and the Groupers, but Evatt becoming Labor leader certainly helped fan the flames,' Ron Palmer recalls. 'Chifley, Curtin and Scullin were the three previous Labor leaders and all were Catholic, and then you had Arthur Calwell, who then probably would have got the nod for the leadership in time and you know . . . maybe Santamaria would have held off for a bit, but he was up for a fight. It was bitter all right, religious fights always are, but you've got to remember that nobody died over it, we [the Labor Party] just got a lot of sore arses sitting on the opposition benches!'

Although Bob Santamaria never stood as an elected member of any parliament, he was always willing to put his hand up for a television or press appearance. Sir Frank Packer allowed him free air-time once a week to broadcast his agenda on a five-minute talk-show called *A Point of View*.

'Good afternoon,' Bob Santamaria would say in his cartoon-quavery voice and he'd be away on his five-minute rant. The show ran for years and I can remember watching it on Sundays at noon, with my father, a committed Labor man to his boots, nodding and uh-huhing in the background. This funny looking bald man with wet lips and measured delivery was, to a boy like me, a bad distraction from watching the midday movie.

My mother would watch my father. 'Good God, Colin, you're fascinated by that man. I don't know how you can sit and watch him, that DLP fellow threw eggs at you and called you a communist!'

'I know he did – but he was just a yahoo. I don't want to like the bastard, but for the life of me that bald-headed bugger just makes sense sometimes. But he's got no sense of humour, love. Too much religion.'

My father would nod a bit more and then invariably say, 'Too much religion is never much chop in the end. You can't think straight.'

With his own thoughts strong in his mind, Val Noone, an avuncular and thoughtful man, reflected on how he trod a traditional path to the priesthood. 'Under the heading of doing something extra for God, we were asked to go to mass one extra day a week as well as Sunday. I became an altar boy, one of the young lads who help in the performing of the mass, so I had a fair bit to do with the rituals of the Catholic Church and they interested me a lot.'

During his training as a priest Val crossed paths with B.A. Santamaria. 'He spoke at the seminary and who among my generation didn't hear him?'

Like many other Catholics, the Noones were deeply affected by the Labor Party–Catholic split. 'That division in the Labor Party led to very big rifts in many families – people had terrible times at barbecues because one had taken the Labor side and one had taken the DLP side. My father had been active in the movement, he had been a shop steward in the Vehicle Builders Union and my mother would say to him, "You can't vote for the DLP, it's a vote for Menzies!"

'And my Dad would reply, "No, it's a vote against the communists!"'

Santamaria would tell an ABC television interviewer: 'My basic opposition to communism, as to Nazism, is based upon the fact that they are totalitarian and being totalitarian, they are thereby, by their very definition, opposed to any religious principle whatsoever.'

Val Noone, Catholic priest, 1968.

Val Noone points out that Santamaria didn't always oppose totalitarianism: 'He supported Franco and Salazar in his youth, then Rhee, Ky, Thieu, Smith in Rhodesia, Pinochet and Suharto in his maturity.'

There were many in Australia who would agree with these sentiments, especially among the wave of immigrants who'd arrived after the Second World War.

8

Spreading the Word

Both the Chifley and Menzies governments favoured a 'populate or perish' policy to secure Australia's future – its economic prosperity and also as a bastion of the white race. Waves of immigrants, or 'New Australians', poured into the country to help build a nation. They joined the fast-growing industrial economy or filled the workforce of the grand infrastructure developments such as the Snowy Mountains Hydro-Electric Scheme.

Many of the first wave of immigrants came from the Mother Country, England, and from Ireland, but increasingly refugees from battle-scarred, postwar Europe started to arrive, people who had suffered persecution and hardship under both the National Socialists of the Third Reich and the occupation forces of the Soviet Union. It was little wonder Santamaria's comments resonated with many of these people, these New Australians.

Not all Australians were as welcoming as the beaming immigration ministers who greeted shiploads of people at the various arrival docks for the newsreels. First it was the weather-beaten and bespectacled

Arthur Calwell with his raspy voice and massive chin, and then the Liberal–Country Party's urbane and handsome Harold Holt. The RSL, the Returned Services League, for example, was strongly opposed to the 'mongrelisation of the Australian people'.

But come to Australia they did, and many found the long journey brought them closer to the origins of their faith. The experiences of Susan Balint's family, the Hoenigs, are among the countless tales of peril and hardship. Susan's German mother was born a Lutheran and had converted to Judaism to marry Susan's father, a Hungarian Jew. They were secular Jews and urban sophisticates rather than the more orthodox schtetl Jews from Poland and Russia.

This difference didn't matter in a time of intolerance and hatred, and when the Nazis invaded Hungary the family was split. Susan, her younger brother and her mother were able to obtain false identity papers, helped by the fact that her mother was born a Christian, and they hid in relative safety in Budapest. Susan's father wasn't as fortunate.

'In about 1942, when the Germans came into Hungary, my father lost his job because he was a Jew. So he was sent to a labour camp,' Susan says. Her father stayed at the camp for about nine months and during this time she recalls going to visit him, on Sundays. 'I remember a big haystack and sitting on that, and then . . . and then he was taken away to a concentration camp. I had no idea where he was, he was just away.'

He was transported to the Mauthausen concentration camp in Austria.

Chance and generosity helped save the family: their caretaker in Budapest never gave them up to the Nazis. 'We lived in our old apartment, not the ghetto, and the caretaker could have given us away but he said, "Don't say anything, don't say that you are Jewish." Yes, the caretaker and his wife and their sixteen-year-old daughter could have easily given us away, many people did, but they didn't.'

Susan's brother wasn't circumcised, which added to their gentile masquerade. Amazingly, at the end of the war, their father returned to Budapest and the family were reunited. 'Well, my father came home from Mauthausen concentration camp . . . he was away and suddenly he was back! It was,' she remembers, 'a difficult period.'

An attempt to emigrate to the United States of America failed and after some to-ing and fro-ing the family arrived in Sydney. Susan's father soon found work in Melbourne, as an industrial chemist with Hortico, a major supplier for Australia's primary industries.

The family drove down from Sydney. 'We passed through this vast, vast land of just plains and sunshine. And it seemed to go on and on.'

Her parents had little knowledge of Australia and didn't know whether it would be all right to be Jews here, fearing that persecution may follow them, so they didn't openly identify themselves as Jewish. But they did keep basic rituals, like the Seder dinner. 'We desperately wanted to fit in, desperately. I often spoke with my hands and that was a no-no. You had to be very British and not use your hands,' Susan recalls.

Some attempts to meld into Australian society went a little sideways. Even with their experience of driving through the unending plains, somehow the Hoenigs assumed that in Australia horses were the preferred mode of transport.

'"You have to go to riding school," my parents said, "all Australians can ride." So on a Sunday my brother and I put on jodhpurs and went out to a riding school. And I learned to climb onto a horse and canter.'

And when a group of women invited Susan's mother to the school Mothers' Club for afternoon tea they asked her to bring a

Susan Balint (centre, wearing sunglasses) *with her family in 1973.*

plate. 'My poor mother took them literally, and showed up with a plate, just a plate without a scrap of food on it.'

As the family became more settled and secure, Susan started to go to Sunday school. 'I felt I knew quite a bit about the Christian religion and I wanted to keep the amount of belief that I had. Remember, I was told during the war, "Don't say you are Jewish!" so in some way I felt I belonged by going to Sunday school.'

Susan even played the Ghost of Christmas Past and visited Ebenezer Scrooge in a stage version of Charles Dickens' *A Christmas Carol*. 'I wandered about in a blanket with leaves stuck on me or something,' she explains. If that sight was hard to fathom, Susan says her attendance at Sunday school really confused her parents. 'For so many years they denied their Judaism. Then they come to this free land and they didn't really know, was it safe to be Jewish or wasn't it safe to be Jewish?'

After attending a state primary school she started at the selective Mac.Robertson Girls' High School. Here she met other Jewish girls and their families and soon the Hoenigs began to embrace both their old and new cultures. 'I rediscovered my Jewishness. In Grade 12 I had religious instruction and I found it very interesting. I met other girls who were in the same position as me. They'd come from Europe and had denied their Judaism, or they had grown up in Australia and were learning more about their faith. I felt this empathy, a closeness, a similar interest.'

Some of Susan's friends came from homes that were more observant and as she became increasingly comfortable in her 'Jewishness', her parents, particularly her mother, also rediscovered this part of their life. 'My brother was turning thirteen and that's when you have your bar mitzvah. And my mother said to my father, "Well, he's going to be thirteen, he should have a bar mitzvah!" but my father said, "No. No. I've suffered enough, I don't want him to be Jewish." So my brother never had a bar mitzvah.' The Jewish community was small and there was still fear and trepidation surrounding life as a Jew.

Susan Hoenig met a boy named Michael Balint at a school dancing class. Also the son of Jewish refugees, his family were friendly with the Hoenigs and they faced similar issues. 'His family didn't tell him and his younger brother that they were Jewish. It was only when we started going to uni in 1957 that he joined the Jewish Students' Club.'

Susan can remember little or no discrimination towards the Jewish faith. 'When I did Law there was certainly discrimination, against the Catholics, though, more so than the Jews. I was just a young woman. I had a good time, joined the Jewish Club, but I didn't feel any discrimination at all.'

As she grew closer to Michael she became more and more involved in the Jewish community. 'It's funny, in a place far from my roots, I've discovered my roots.' But she feels as Australian as she does Jewish.

A diversity was beginning to appear in the make-up of Australian society.

Even though Bob Santamaria's anti-communist words were welcomed by some of the Australian populace, Val Noone saw him as a talented TV presenter but, 'He was more of a debater than a thinker.'

Santamaria said that Melbourne's Archbishop Mannix was his mentor. However Val Noone considered the archbishop, who was then in his eighties, to be more of a tool of Santamaria's. Certainly the strength of the DLP and Santamaria's forces was at its greatest in Victoria, for Santamaria had the support of the senior officers of the Catholic Church in that state. In Sydney Cardinal Norman Gilroy was more content not to openly attack the Labor Party, and indeed preferred the traditional relationship between Australian Catholics and the ALP.

'Santamaria rattled a lot of people's pans and tins, but really he was just a one-trick pony,' was Ron Palmer's view.

Even though the DLP was a nationwide organisation and boasted a senator from Queensland, Vince Gair, the former Labor premier, my father always considered the Groupers and the whole split as being a Melbourne push. He had his own thoughts on why the movement was so strong in the southern capital. 'Too much religion, too much time on their hands – they should have gone to the beach a bit more.'

And in a way, even though the 'Red Menace' and the cry of 'reds under the beds' would echo through the decades, my father had a point. After the early turmoil of Cold War flare-ups and the wool crisis and credit squeeze of the fifties, the early sixties exploded with an economy that grew exponentially each year. There were more and more enticements to lure Australians away from indulging in too much religion – and it wasn't just the beach.

The churches were facing a battle for the Australian soul with a much tougher and more appealing opponent than communism. The economic boom brought with it a growing middle class, a ravenous consumerism and a plethora of materialistic distractions that tempted a generation away from the congregations.

Adolescents were given a new name, 'teenagers', and a new music and culture were tailored to them and only them. The rock'n'roll of the fifties and sixties was fairly tame in hindsight and was controlled by major entertainment corporations from America and, to a lesser extent, the United Kingdom. But it had the heady pulling power of sex and image and indulgence.

Bruce Ballantine-Jones was a thrill-seeking teenager; by his own admission he was a pretty loud and boisterous kid who liked being the centre of attention. His parents were nominal Anglicans and he received little or no support from home from a religious perspective. 'Never, ever went to Sunday school,' he remembers.

When his parents separated, Bruce ended up living with his father in Kings Cross. 'I was attending the National Art School at East Sydney Tech, which was just up the road, and I was enjoying it,' he adds wryly. He then lets fly with a litany of his teenage escapades. 'The problem was, I was enjoying it too much. I wasn't working very hard at my studies. I started to drink quite a bit, I was only fifteen, and I smoked – of course, all the cool guys smoked back then.'

Bruce Ballantine-Jones, aged fifteen, in 1957.

In the late fifties there were lots of 'cool guys' performing to thousands of Australia's teenagers. The apostles of rock'n'roll stomped around the various arenas of the nation. Bill Haley and The Comets, Little Richard, Eddie Cochran, Gene Vincent, Bo Diddley, Jerry Lee Lewis and even Buddy Holly.

The churches grew alarmed at the dramatic drop in attendance, especially among the young, so the Protestant churches banded together to bring another charismatic, handsome young man from America's South to perform in stadiums. Only he didn't play to a backbeat and guitar, it was more a case of the old adage of fighting fire with fire. The American evangelist Billy Graham created a sensation as he barnstormed into Australian halls, stadiums and sporting arenas with his brand of revivalist missionary showmanship.

'I didn't come to Australia to teach you anything new,' said Graham to the newsreels, bobbing on the spot with enthusiasm and conviction. His wavy hair, bright eyes and heavy-browed good looks beamed out across cinema screens and television sets. 'Or to say anything new – rather we've come to remind you of some old truths.'

And many were in the mind to listen. Hundreds of thousands of Australians went to Billy Graham's Southern Cross Crusade.

Two teenagers at the time had very different reactions. Bruce Ballantine-Jones and Graeme Dunstan saw the Crusade in the nation's two biggest cities. Ballantine-Jones says he was a lonely and lost young man. After his father kicked him out when he wouldn't get a job he went to live with his mother and stepfather and 'bludged off them for a while' but then they kicked him out, too.

He went to the rally. 'Out of curiosity my little brother and I went to see him down at the showground.' There, at the Sydney Showground, in place of a grand parade and ring events, Billy Graham stood at a lectern facing a stadium of would-be pilgrims. On the scoreboard, instead of the points for and against, a message blazed in capital letters: JESUS SAID, 'I AM THE WAY, THE TRUTH AND THE LIGHT.'

At the height of the Cold War the evangelist called the time in which they were living, 'a confused age, an age of despair'. This touched a chord with Bruce. 'I remember hearing his message about the coming judgement of God, for those who rejected Christ, and that you had to be ready because that judgement could come at any time.'

Billy Graham, tie loosened, hair slightly ruffled, but still with certainty and clarity, asked those at the showground to, 'Enter the narrow gate. The Bible says, "Jesus says there is a gate – it's a narrow gate, but thank God there's a gate."'

And Bruce Ballantine-Jones accepted that invitation. 'A voice inside me said: "Bruce, if that day came today, you're not ready," and that put the wind up me,' he says, smiling. 'So when he gave the invitation to come forward and accept Jesus as your Lord and saviour, something said to me, "Bruce this is your moment."'

And he did. It was a revelatory experience. As he stepped forward, he said, and accepted Jesus Christ, an enormous sense of release came over him.

But in Melbourne, at the Myer Music Bowl, for Graeme Dunstan, brought up by his mother with the hope of him being a good Baptist boy, the fervour and belief of Billy Graham was simply a sales pitch. He was tempted, but didn't buy. Was it the message or was it the mode of the message, the delivery and style and not the content, that touched and moved people?

'We went and sat on the hill and got this great sell on Christianity. It was powerful. And, you know, the big, "Come forward now, make your decision for Christ!"' He smiles and rocks back and forth at the memory, hearing the Southern drawl calling to him.

'I was teetering on the edge; I thought, Will I do it? And I decided . . . not to. And that was the high point of my Christianity. That point of doubt. After that I ceased to believe. Didn't feel motivated by the Church at all.'

It might have started on those searches for a dance with a girl at the Presbyterian social but an evening at the Myer Music Bowl tipped him into a journey of experimenting and dabbling in other faiths. 'It was the American sell.' He almost shrugs his shoulders. 'The big sell, it was a little over the top. So that's how it was for me. They weren't it.' There is a frankness in his expression that might be taken, for a moment, as sadness, but the eyes tell you that there was a great deal more searching in store for him. As

A Christian youth group in Kings Cross. Bruce Ballantine-Jones is standing far left.

far as being a good Baptist boy, that was it for Graeme Dunstan. Once he left home to join the army he never set foot in a Baptist church again.

Bruce Ballantine-Jones was happy with what he had found at the Southern Cross Crusade and pledged his life to the Lord, a life that would lead down a few paths, including a stint in the advertising industry, but ultimately to Bruce becoming an evangelical Anglican minister.

In the wake of the Crusade, youth groups were suddenly as hip as they ever could be. Bruce came into contact with this social network and he, of course, wasn't the only young Protestant up for adventure. He joined a little youth group that met in Kings Cross every Sunday afternoon. Armed with an accordion, some scripture and a lot of enthusiasm they cut loose in the Cross. 'We'd sing a few hymns and one of the young folks would give a message and so forth. After a while I had a go.'

And have a go he did, the little boy who liked being the centre of attention if he could. He made speeches and attempted to convert people in Fitzroy Gardens in the Cross. And he got one. Only one. One convert who became a missionary in Sardinia for thirty years. And joined a growing number of Protestants spreading the word.

9

Opening Up

From its beginning, Christianity was in the business of converting people to its beliefs and scriptures. As Evangelical Christianity was thriving after the Southern Cross Crusade, a bump in their attendances allowed churches to look beyond the wilds of Kings Cross and call for missionaries among its members, a trend that had been simmering for the past decade.

The Anglican Church had been active in the then Australian territory of Papua New Guinea since the nineteenth century, and Judy Hall was one young Anglican who answered the call of service. She came from a working-class family in Queensland and was an active member of church youth groups, including the Comrades of St George. She was sure of her faith from a young age.

'I was about fifteen and I went to see the parish priest, begging him to help me because I knew God meant me to be a teacher. He told me to put a sign on my desk that said, "I can do things through Christ".'

Judy Hall (second from right) *at a church youth group in 1961.*

She became a teacher when she heard that the Church was calling for missionaries. 'I was a fairly pushy broad for those days, I suppose,' she laughs, 'so I actually went when I was twenty. I was the youngest missionary ever to go and they only accepted me because I wasn't going to stay away forever.'

Judy arrived in Papua New Guinea in 1962, as did John Cottier, who was by then an Anglican priest and had completed a year's training to become a missionary. 'It was the biggest missionary year, so I was just one of a mob,' he says. But he bumped into another one of the mob and soon they became two. Judy Hall and John Cottier had gone to Papua New Guinea to change its people, but found that their missionary work made a huge and dramatic change to their own lives.

'We shared our first kiss under the cross at the cathedral,' says Judy Cottier, and soon they were married.

The photographs of their time in New Guinea have that wonderful crispness, a Kodachrome, Technicolor feel to them. The Cottiers' smiling faces and deeply suburban Australian look are surrounded by the highlands and bare-chested, grass-skirted and loin-clothed Papuans. There are images of John in a blazing white cassock performing a religious service before a single wooden cross in the grasslands. More startling is a photo of Judy kneeling before a stainless-steel box with a young baby in it – the Cottiers' first child.

'There was one patrol we did soon after our son was born – we put him in a tin trunk and walked three or four days from a remote mission to an even more remote place, which was a first-contact patrol,' John remembers. 'The trunk had a lid on it which

John and Judy's children, John Jr and Trisha, play with family friends in Papua New Guinea, in 1971.

A Papua New Guinean policeman holding the Cottiers' baby son, John Jr, in 1966.

wasn't closed, you'll be pleased to know, and it was strung on a pole and . . . And we found,' he says with a sly smile, 'our baby was a very good ice-breaker.'

There's another photograph of a highlander with a rifle slung over his shoulder. Perched on top of the other shoulder is the Cottiers' young son, his nappy slightly skewiff.

John becomes animated as he recalls the baptism ceremony in which his son and a hundred highlanders were baptised in the name of the new faith. 'The bishop came and baptised them. We didn't actually put them under the water but they stood knee-deep and we scooped up the water and poured it over 'em – plenty of it,' he smiles waving his arms, 'plenty of it.'

The highlanders wore grass skirts and when they emerged from the water there were new garments waiting for them. 'Their skirts were pretty tatty and when they came out, they could take them off and either put on a new grass skirt or a white calico cloth – so they shed the old and put on the new.'

It's a pretty clumsy, if accurate, metaphor, and it's probably not the first time he's told the story. After a pause he adds, 'And the dancing was magic.'

I realise what these photographs remind me of: it's the sharp colour and the wildness of the scenes that does it. Old breakfast-cereal collectors' cards from a Nabisco packet – they must have been from the early 1960s. My mother, for whatever reason, put them in a telephone-number file, which meant you'd pick one up every time you were looking for a telephone number. On these cards were scenes from a series called 'Our Wild Territory New Guinea' and white people, presumably administrating Australians, would appear among exotic-looking Papuans.

I always found these cards archaically funny – Australia as a would-be imperial master. But the memory gave me pause for

John Cottier conducting a service in Papua New Guinea, 1967.

thought. These cards would have been distributed at the time the Cottiers were doing their missionary work there, and the images in their photographs look even wilder and more exotic than the breakfast-cereal cards.

There was a difference, though. The white administrators on these cards are all grim-faced professionals – it is, after all, a 'Wild Territory' they are inhabiting. The Cottiers look happy. They are smiling and glad to be there. In fact, the smiles on the Cottiers' faces in the shots from their youth group days are no different from the ones from New Guinea. They were happy to be doing what they were doing; they believed in what they were doing.

'We would send out word that the priest was there and the next morning the people of the area would assemble and I would talk to them, religious stuff.' John makes it sound low key. He is a man with an easy manner but has an evident pride and enjoyment in their work in New Guinea.

'I don't feel the slightest bit apologetic,' Judy says of the missionary work. 'Until you've had the experience of telling an animist people who live in fear that God is good and loving, you have no idea. We take it for granted – we believe, whether we're religious or not, that creation is basically good. They thought evil spirits ruled the world. We emphasised a good creator, that God was someone you could talk to.'

To Judy, the Papuan Highlanders believed in black magic and curses, and Christianity, she says, liberated them from that.

Papua New Guinea was not Australian Christianity's first attempt to convert Indigenous communities. Many Aboriginal people have been rounded up by government officials and moved into church missions since the late nineteenth century.

Beryl Carmichael was born on the banks of the Darling River in Menindee, not far from Broken Hill in New South Wales. While living at the Menindee mission, which was run by the Aboriginal Protection Board, she learned the traditional beliefs from her father, who was one of the last of her people to go through initiation. During the early years of her life, elders would teach the children. Their religion was inseparable from their culture and matters of daily life. The older women would show the young ones how to make string bags and practical tasks were interwoven with spirituality.

When Presbyterian and Methodist missionaries arrived they lived in the community with Beryl Carmichael and her people, introducing them to Christianity. Beryl was even baptised twice.

Sitting on the banks of the Darling River, she laughs at the memory. 'I was about eight or nine and I went up to the missionary and told her that I wanted the Lord to come into my heart. It was the first time I left poor old Mum and when I knocked on the door the missionary said, "Yes girlie, what do you want?" She must have

Beryl Carmichael.

thought I wanted flour or sugar or something, eh! So I told her I wanted to give my heart to the Lord. She said I was too young and I had to argue with her for a while!'

The missionary then took Beryl into the church and read her scripture and lessons from the Bible and confirmed that young Beryl did, in fact, wish to become a Christian. 'I came out that door and I reckon I was on cloud nine – the Lord just lifted me right off the ground, I just ran all the way home.'

Despite her elation Beryl knew she still had to face her mother's reaction to the news. 'Well, I got home and then I just stood, stood around the corner, and I thought, Oh gee, I've got to tell Mum now.' She laughs but says that the concern wasn't warranted. 'My mum was really happy for me, actually.'

Beryl's mother was familiar with the missionaries' work because the Australian Inland Mission had taught Christianity to the Menindee mission's three hundred residents.

'We were very receptive to the work of the missionaries because they spoke about a creator up there and we – the Menindee people – already knew there was a creator up there. Through our stories we were reinforcing the law to our children and it's the same as the Ten Commandments in the Bible. When you come to think about it, they walk hand in hand.'

The old mission is gone now, not even a wall remains, but the beliefs instilled by the teaching of Christianity are still strong, and Beryl believes the generosity of many of the missionaries proved highly effective. 'The first missionaries would share with us and that was our way, but the Catholics, they were the first to start the divisions on the mission.'

She explains how the Catholic missionary would tempt people to go to mass. 'The Catholic priest came out in his car and he just opened the boot, and he had lots of clothes and stuff for people in there, and he said, "We got all these nice things for you if you come round to our church . . ." And he was recruiting for his church, just getting the numbers for his church, not teaching.'

In the years to come Beryl would become a different sort of missionary in her own right, but always carried with her the idea of two faiths walking together.

Her generosity of spirit was mirrored in the lives of the Cottiers in Papua New Guinea. Over the couple's twelve-year stay, saving souls and converting an animist people to the teachings of Christianity, they found that the very nature of the country they worked in would change them profoundly.

The Cottier family grew during their stay: three children were born. From their lounge room Judy Cottier remembers, 'I had my third child, and . . .' she pauses, 'and he died at about seven days old.' John becomes very still and folds his arms. He looks away but listens intently.

Their son was born a haemophiliac and if he had been in Sydney an injection could have saved him. But the Cottiers weren't, of course, in Sydney and events conspired against them.

'The hospital was quite remote, we'd had a big storm so the rivers were up and we couldn't get out. The doctors were on patrol and they couldn't get back – everything that could go wrong went wrong, and that was that.'

Judy brought their son David home and as she says his name her voice softens and she smiles. David's brother John Junior and sister Trisha had made grass mats at school, and used them to gently wrap their brother. Here Judy holds her hands up and gesticulates to emphasise her point. 'One of the good things about death is that it's ever present and you understand it and you cope with it. So we dug the grave next to the chapel and we picked the flowers to go with it.'

If there were any thoughts of why this had happened, why God had let this happen, they weren't thought by Judy Cottier. 'Through all that time I just felt absolutely held in the arms of God.'

Perhaps if this family tragedy had happened away from New Guinea, perhaps here in Australia, where the hospitals are not remotely situated and doctors are not away on patrol and cut off by swollen rivers and storms, then perhaps it would have been harder to bear, but the Cottiers' faces still show the pain of David's loss acutely. And despite this pain, they show acceptance. It is a remarkable demonstration of their faith and belief.

It is also evidence of two people learning and growing from the land they were trying to change. And perhaps a poignant example of Beryl Carmichael's idea of faiths and beliefs walking hand in hand.

These days the idea that the sixties was a revolutionary decade has become such a given fact, such a cliché, such a marketing tool, that it's hard to understand the impact that all the changes had on the lives of people during that time. After all, icons of revolution and dissent such as Che Guevara were used not so long ago to advertise an ice-cream that the whole family could enjoy.

But a decade of upheavals and changes it was, especially for Australian Catholics. The experiences of Val Noone, Vianney Hatton and Linda Visman were evidence of that. Vianney Hatton took her final vows as a Blessed Sacrament Sister, Val Noone was about to become a Catholic priest and Linda Visman began a career as a teacher and a life as a wife and mother.

'It was a very heady time to be active in Church life, the sixty to sixty-four period, when I was in my final years of study,' says Val Noone.

On 11 October 1962, Pope John XXIII opened the Second Vatican Council or, as it was to become more popularly known, Vatican II. With its aim of modernising and letting fresh air into the Church, Vatican II had a huge impact on Catholic life.

Val Noone explains, 'The mass became a much more communal event, the altar was turned around and the priest faced the people. The language spoken became English – this was a change the Protestants had brought in three hundred years earlier, but for Catholics it was a big shift both in practice and in the mentality of people, and that was a good thing to be part of.'

Certainly the changes gave the Catholic Church a more visible sense of renewed energy and engagement in the community; one of the points of difference between Catholic and other Christian faiths had been its use of language.

'If you wanted to have a crack at a Catholic,' says Ron Palmer, 'you'd bang on about all the Latin mumbo-jumbo, you know, they could have been speaking Martian for all anybody knew. But when that went out the door all the petty bigots lost a free hit, so to speak. Folks began to see there wasn't that much difference between any of us.'

For Vianney Hatton the changes were fundamental to the very reason of her order: the Eucharist was now seen as food for the hungry, not as a static object of adoration. 'Many, many big changes there,' she remembers, 'especially for the sisters – a change in their habit, their clothing and their customs.'

The nuns began to move outside, doing works away from the building in which they lived. 'We took a while to adjust, we really did. We had to learn how to walk and talk and how to relate.' Vianney pauses, smiles and says almost shyly, 'It was a very different world out there from when I entered.'

Reacquainting themselves with the world was a prolonged process. The order had a farm on Victoria's Mornington Peninsula, and a big house in the Melbourne suburb of Armadale where they had lived until Vatican II. 'We needed to be at the farm to water the grounds and so on, and I can remember helicopters flying overhead and sirens and so much activity.' The world, when they entered it again, was so noisy, so busy. It was only much later that Vianney learned about the disappearance of Prime Minister Harold Holt in the area and connected all the activity around the farm with the dramatic but unsuccessful search efforts to find the missing leader.

In the early twentieth century, the Blessed Sacrament Sisters had been taught that dancing was a mortal sin, but as customs relaxed a bit further, somehow Vianney and her friend and fellow sister Maureen got hold of a Tijuana Brass record. 'It's one of the earliest music memories from the time of our "emancipation".

Maureen and I would listen to "Spanish Flea" and dance around our basement room.'

Herb Alpert and the Tijuana Brass were a firm favourite of my dad's. The idea that two young Catholic sisters celebrated this emergence from the strict code of their order by dancing in a basement to the sounds of my father's preferred good-times barbecue music is quite startling.

Vianney also took up the guitar again and learned to play some of the songs on the radio of the day. 'Ruby Tuesday' by the Rolling Stones was a particular favourite. 'I can't think that we gave much thought to the meaning of the songs – we had to grow up ourselves again, but we did absorb and claim some of the songs of the protest movement, like "Where Have All the Flowers Gone" and "We Shall Overcome".'

It was indeed a different world.

During the sixties more Australians than ever before finished high school and went to university. They were exposed to ideas and ways of thought that not only challenged the authority of the Church but also of wider Australian society.

More women had access to higher education and with increasing wealth across the country they were able to enter the workforce in greater numbers. Modern Australia was beginning to provide more options and choices with its technological and social advances.

It wasn't just more leisure time or a few rock'n'rollers thumbing their noses at authority, as was the case in the late fifties – a challenge that the Protestant churches answered with Billy Graham and his Southern Cross Crusade. It was now beyond Billy and his crowded stadiums. Society was challenging an established order and offering women products that could turn their perceived role as nurturing childbearers and homemakers on its head.

The contraceptive pill promised to transform women's lives, giving them freedom to control their reproductive cycles, liberating them from the designated role of wife and mother. But it forced many women, especially Catholic women, into an ethical and moral dilemma.

Linda Visman was one such young woman. 'I acted against the Catholic Church because when I was first married I went out teaching and I didn't want to have children straight away, so I did take the Pill. This was frowned on by the Church, well, it still is,

Linda Visman at her wedding in January 1969.

and I can't remember if I stopped taking it because I wanted to have children or whether I was feeling too guilty about it.'

For whatever reason there was a dividend for Linda Visman. 'So I ended up with five sons,' and she laughs. 'Five beautiful sons.'

Along with the moral dilemmas over the Pill, Australia was a nation at war, a war that forced many people, including Val Noone, to consider where they stood in terms of their faith.

In 1962 the Menzies government decided to send troops to join the American military in opposing the North Vietnamese communist forces in their civil war with the South. And in 1965 he increased Australia's commitment to the war by sending a battalion.

Val Noone explains that 'The Americans and Australians intervened to prevent self-determination in Vietnam because, as US intelligence reported, eighty per cent of the Vietnamese people wanted Ho Chi Minh as their leader and, for reasons of empire, the Americans did not.'

Vietnam was a country haunted by the ghosts of former attempts to subdue the local upheavals. The French had tried to reclaim the nation but failed and then in 1964, after the Gulf of Tonkin incident, in which it was reported that communist forces had fired upon an American warship, the US began a major bombing campaign and sent in hundreds of thousands of troops. This incident was discredited by the release of the Pentagon Papers in the early 1970s, showing that the American claims were false.

It was an inauspicious start to a controversial war that cost a great many lives for a result that was as obvious in the early sixties as it was at the war's end in 1975. Victory for the communist-led independence forces.

Graeme Dunstan had spent three years as a staff cadet at the Royal Military College, Duntroon, before resigning and completing his engineering studies at the University of New South Wales. He'd gone to the academy in an effort to emulate his heroic grandfather, 'As a way of winning my mother's love.'

Graeme's questioning, outspoken dissent and his own search for spiritual meaning caused him grief at Duntroon. 'At Duntroon, you could be C of E, RC or OPD and I tried them all. There were chaplains for the Roman Catholics, the Church of England, and Other Protestant Denominations. But no Buddhists, no Hindus.' He spent time with each chaplain but couldn't find what he was looking for. After a while, Graeme would go on church parade, be marched to the chapel, but refuse to go inside. Instead he would walk back to the barracks. This refusal led to the Duntroon commander personally writing to him, ordering him to attend. Graeme says that for his freedom of conscience and for his principles he faced a court marshal, but he resigned from Duntroon instead.

At Duntroon he had attended lectures about South East Asia and its politics and he'd read some military history. 'I was shocked – honestly, the Holt government's commitment to war and conscription came to me as outrage. I was the first of my clan to go to university and so I was more questioning. Rebellious, you might say, and since I'd been studying all about South East Asia it came to me that we'd been set up.'

As in America, the war at first proved popular in Australia. It was seen as the next in the long line of conflicts stretching from the First and Second world wars to the Korean War and the Malayan Emergency, in which Australians could prove themselves in battle. The Vietnam conflict was also seen as another instalment in the 'Free World's' battle against communists, and this very characteristic of the war found fertile and determined supporters among the more conservative Catholic population. Bob Santamaria and his followers were enthusiastic and vocal in their support, so much so that these religious warriors would go to great lengths to control the agenda.

But opposition to the war was growing. During 1968, the Gorton government was considering holding an early election but after comments that Gorton was favouring a change from forward defence, of which the Vietnam adventure was a prime example, to a more scaled-down, contained idea of defending Australia within the nation's own borders, Bob Santamaria and the National Civic Council stepped in. They were opposed to any withdrawal from South East Asia and threatened Gorton by withholding DLP preferences to the government in crucial seats, raising the possibility of eroding the Gorton majority. No early election was called.

The conduct of the war was not progressing well after the initial expectations of success. Inevitably the battles were more prolonged and soon the public's unprecedented access to images of the ravages of the war on the Vietnamese people on the TV news each night, along with the increasing wantonness of the destruction, were dividing public opinion.

A form of conscription, in which young men of military age were chosen by lottery, was one of the most emotive and divisive of issues. In the First World War the Catholic Archbishop of Melbourne, Daniel Mannix, was a leading voice in the opposition to the conscription campaign of Prime Minister Billy Hughes. But now Catholics were split on the issue: even though there was real doubt over the Vietnam War among more progressive Catholics, the fear of communism still raged within the Church.

Val Noone, a Catholic priest by this time, was in no way a supporter of communism, but as the war progressed it seemed harder to justify the growing civilian deaths. He was forced to make a choice that would change the course of his life.

Initially Val thought the protesters were missing the point – they should be raising money for the starving in Africa. And it wasn't the role of a priest to take on these issues; his job was to perform rituals and engage in pastoral work.

'During the early years of the war, I was working as a chaplain to Catholic youth groups,' he explains, 'and some of these students began to ask me about questions of conscience of the day.'

The students wanted to hear Val's opinions of the Vietnam War, but with his training as a parish worker, his role was to put both sides of the argument forward but take no position himself. The students warmed to the subject and as Val was an accessible and open man he looked upon the students' repeated hammering of the questions, 'What would you do if you were called up? Would you go and serve in Vietnam?' as questions he should answer.

He remembers how terrible it was to see young men sent off to war. This was made all too real for him when he attended the twenty-first birthday party of a man who was home on leave, just long enough to celebrate before he had to return to the war.

The atmosphere of the party was 'really weird' – the celebration barely masking the horrible fact that the boy had to return to the war. 'He'd be shooting at people and they would be shooting at him. Everyone,' Val recalls, 'was acting like he'd just been across town and back.

'I thought, I owe it to these kids to say what I think, what I believe, and so I said if I was called up I wouldn't go, I don't believe it's a just war.' It was a case of the shepherd being led by the flock.

'Now that was a very big moment. In my memory these young people pushed me to get clearer where I was up to and to make a commitment.' And make a commitment he did, for in 1968

Val Noone speaking against Australia's involvement in the Vietnam War, 1972.

Val became a vocal opponent of the Vietnam War and the next year spoke at a support meeting for a conscientious objector at the Melbourne Town Hall. He brushes it off now, but at the same time recognises the important direction in which his stance was taking him.

'Oh, I was only one of about twenty or thirty people speaking, but that small thing put me in a very public position. To take a strong view on Vietnam, it was better for me to be out of the pulpit and do it from a lay perspective.' And with the surety of a man who took his role as a priest and his faith as a Catholic as a calling, he adds, 'That's one of the things that changed my life.'

Val Noone is a sensitive and compassionate man who is acutely aware of the role of the priest in the Church and his own position and direction in life. As a result he left the priesthood. He never looked back. 'In the end, what led me to resign from being a

Catholic priest was my decision to get married. The Church can encompass a lot of things but what it can't allow is for a priest to marry. By 1973 I had met my wife and I decided I wasn't going back to parish work and I wasn't going back to the priesthood and that's what I did.'

His decision has never meant for a moment that Val Noone is not an active and enthusiastic Catholic Christian. 'The teachings of Jesus are as relevant today as ever; just because you leave the priesthood it doesn't mean you leave the Christian faith. And all false gods need to be investigated.' In the decades since this is exactly how Val has lived his life.

The great antiwar moratoriums that drew hundreds of thousands to march in the streets in protest were a graphic demonstration of the activism and the winds of change blowing through Australia. The year 1972 saw the election of the Whitlam Labor government after more than twenty years of conservative rule, and the new government soon implemented a wave of social reforms, and the end of Australia's involvement in the Vietnam War.

'What does it mean to live in peace – this became one of the questions of the counterculture,' says Graeme Dunstan. Then he has another thought: 'And drugs, of course. Cannabis was our sacrament – no question.'

Another pause.

'It was sacred to us.'

Another pause.

'And LSD.'

He had completed an engineering degree and had started an arts degree majoring in sociology. While at university, Graeme, the Duntroon drop-out, became a visible and active organiser of the

Mary and Val Noone signing the marriage register, with Father Con Reis at St Columba's Catholic Church, Elwood, Victoria, in 1974.

student resistance to the war and conscription, even to the extent of having broken crowd barriers to race through a Secret Service cordon and clutch the bumper bar of the limousine carrying the American president Lyndon B. Johnson. Johnson was visiting to shore up Australia's support in the Vietnam conflict, and also as a show of solidarity for Harold Holt, whose government was going to an election.

The New South Wales conservative premier Robin (Robert) Askin had famously shouted to the driver as Dunstan and two other protesters slid under the presidential limo, 'Run over the bastards!'

To which the American president was reported to have replied, 'I like your style, Bob.'

Dunstan survived Lyndon and Bob and the wheels of the limo to continue his spiritual search. 'We wanted to know what meditation was, what these Indian gurus were talking about, what would we believe?'

In 1973 he became a leading light in Nimbin's Aquarius Festival and although he said, 'Trying to organise hippies is like herding cats – it can't be done!' Graeme Dunstan managed to invite a diverse collection of religious groups such as Hare Krishnas, Children of God and followers of the Maharishi. 'I was encouraging spiritual groups to come and share their lifestyle and the Hare Krishnas were the biggest group. They came with their tents and they were doing a great service by chanting through the festival twenty-four hours a day.' He laughs and his eyes sparkle. 'Well, that was all right for them but it bugged everyone else camping there! They got a little tired after a while.'

This reminds me of the first time I encountered Hare Krishnas, which was also in 1973 and, of all places, at the Brisbane Agricultural Show. I left the show late at night after the fireworks, clutching my showbags in one nine-year-old hand and holding onto my mother with the other. We stood, my family and I, with a group of other people watching some Hare Krishnas banging cymbals and singing their chants.

In the street light they shimmered in their flowing robes, and the noise and colour of the sideshow alley area just inside the gates added a macabre touch to the evening. They didn't seem to really be looking at anything and somebody asked somebody else, 'What did they want? What are they doing?'

A few people gave them money. My mother said, 'They're just people looking for something, like the rest of us.' I remember dropping a Redskin lolly into the bowl as we walked past.

I think I understand how those other campers at the festival might have felt. Twenty-four hours!

Graeme Dunstan's Aquarius Festival was part-spiritual search and part-hedonistic adventure. 'People were blown away, it was sensory overload. Anything seemed possible, everything seemed possible. You'd walk down a path, past a couple making love,' he holds up his hands by way of explanation, 'they were walking naked and got carried away and nobody cared.'

Anything may have seemed possible to Graeme Dunstan, but Vianney Hatton's journey of emergence from a strict religious order by way of dancing in a basement to Herb Alpert's 'Spanish Flea' led ultimately to the University of California, Berkeley, near San Francisco – the very epicentre of flower power and counterculture. This would possibly have tested even Graeme Dunstan's idea of imagination and adventure.

As a consequence of the changes to her order after Vatican II, Vianney found herself studying theology at Berkeley. 'I was very, very lucky because in 1974 I had the opportunity to study overseas,' she says. She continues with a nod of her head and a smile that splits her face, 'And that was just fabulous.'

Vianney Hatton (centre, front row) *at the University of California, Berkeley, 1975.*

What was so fabulous about it? As well as widening her knowledge of her faith and her world, she deepened her knowledge of human experience by falling in love.

The photos of her time at Berkeley show her almost unrecognisable to those of the Blessed Sacrament Sister, save for one thing, her smile. Vianney Hatton's open face and her smile greet the camera in two particular photos and the eyes of a fellow student stare only at her. 'I did have the experience of falling in love, which was wonderful,' she says with a shrug of her shoulders. 'I guess I was in my late thirties, really, and the temptation was there, and the questions were there, and the longing was there and the pain was there, but looking at the other person I knew that he was meant to be a priest. He was meant to be a priest, he was meant to be a priest.' She repeats the last phrase quietly and carries on.

Linda Visman with her five sons, in 1999.

'And that was as much a part of him as . . . oh . . .' her voice trails away and she shakes her head slowly. 'It would have been wrong, it would have been wrong. Even though I loved him.'

After another brief moment she smiles her wide smile. 'They say that doors open and you find your way. Well, in my case, that door closed.'

In the case of Linda Visman the door didn't just close, it slammed shut. On both love and her faith. While pursuing her career as a teacher in rural New South Wales and as the mother of five children, she had gradually moved away from the Catholic Church, but after a bout of depression, she found God again and joined a Bible group in the central west town of Narromine. It was supposedly non-denominational but was populated mostly by Baptists and was fundamentalist in nature.

'I became quite involved in that and after about a month I met someone there and it just seemed that we looked at each other and we had an instant attraction. All of a sudden I realised that there was more to it than friendship – that we were in love with each other.' She says this simply and without dramatic effect.

For a woman raised in a strict Catholic household she knew that what she was doing was not a part of the Church's canon in any way, shape or form. 'We continued to go to the Bible group and we fought against it, we believed it was wrong, we believed it was something that should not happen. Both of us had children, both of us were married and even though we were both unhappy in our marriages we tried to work it out. A good Catholic girl does not divorce her husband.'

It's not unusual that even though Linda Visman had moved away from Catholicism, the strains of belief and commitment ran deep. As a young girl at her First Communion the only thing that she could remember was how the thin wafer of the Host stuck to the roof of her mouth. 'My mouth was dry, I suppose from nerves. I kept poking at it with my tongue, trying to loosen it. I did wonder if I was doing something awful to Christ's Body and when the Host did finally come loose, I made very sure not to touch it with my teeth. I didn't want to be accused of chewing His Body!'

It's a funny story but also one that shows the almost supernatural fear that could grip the human imagination with the ideas of ritual and notions of right and wrong.

Linda received letters and visits offering support to bring her back to God because, as the letters put it, it was her friend Bev who was possessed by the devil. In the end it meant no more Bible study for Bev and Linda.

She remembers writing in her diary at the time page after page, 'Where is God? Is there a God? Why has all this happened? We both tried so hard over months to overcome this, we did the best we could.

'We called on God to help us, we called on others to help us, but . . . if there was a God he turned his back and if there is a God of love he doesn't sound very loving to me.'

She makes me think of my mother's remarks about the Hare Krishnas outside the Brisbane Show. 'They're just people looking for something, like the rest of us.'

When does anybody know if they have found what they are looking for? Linda Visman didn't stop trying.

She and Bev lived and taught at an Aboriginal community about 300 kilometres from Alice Springs. The two lived together for almost twenty years, and then Linda went to her home town to visit her dad, the man who had made those wooden scooters for her and her little sister, ready to unwrap after Christmas mass. Those had been the days when everything seemed so certain and ordered. While visiting her father Linda met and fell in love with a man who, as a teenager, had been at school with her.

Linda Visman believes in 'something bigger' but her experience at the end of her Bible group led her to a discovery, that, like Vianney Hatton, a door had closed. 'A door did close, not just close, it slammed. And that was the door to organised religion. And, eventually, faith itself.'

Organised religion was losing its grip on the Australian soul. Church attendance declined from forty-four per cent in 1961 to only twenty-five per cent in 1980. Sundays were no longer sacred, with shops and pubs open for trade and football and cricket and even race meetings drawing avid worshippers to the stadiums.

The memories of Billy Graham's Crusade and his call to accept Christ echoed somewhere but were drowned out in cries of 'Ball', 'In the back' and 'Howzat!' around the nation.

In the 1980s one of Australia's most popular public figures ever, Bob Hawke, was prime minister for nearly a decade, and although he came from a religious family – his father Clem was a Protestant minister – Hawke described himself as an agnostic. Once, such an utterance from the leader of the nation would have been unthinkable, but now it was seen as part of the attraction of this charismatic politician.

Asian immigrants were arriving in greater numbers, bringing with them Buddhism and Eastern traditions that challenged the dominance of Christianity. There was also a confidence in practising their faith and indeed some Australians found a home in such religions, even if they had been restlessly searching all their lives.

Graeme Dunstan's countercultural questioning led him to delve into many religious and spiritual traditions: shamanism, hatha yoga and Taoism. In Nimbin, during the counterculture community-building years of the late seventies, he was introduced to Buddhism by monks who had been ordained in Thailand.

After much experimenting he settled, with his trademark liveliness, on Buddhism.

He sits in a hall with a mandala behind him, where he attended the first Vipassana (disciplined meditation) course held there and recalls the pain of the course which taught him to sit so silently on that hard wooden floor.

'I was counting down the minutes, I can remember the raging of my mind when I couldn't talk to anyone, these amazing thoughts and fantasies, and I can remember the absolute sense of bliss and contentment coming out of it – this confirmed me as a Buddhist meditator.'

Buddhism is his spiritual refuge now. 'I could never remain a Christian because I could never accept the unfounded faith that once saved by Jesus (and accepting that Jesus was the son of God) everything would be all right.'

For Graeme, Buddhism offers a spiritual practice without a supernatural belief or deity. 'What Buddhism provides, is that it is about practice. It's what I found in Buddhism – moral conduct – which I hadn't found in Christianity.'

He also found a connection between his Dharma practice and his commitment to political activism. 'Gone forth into homelessness' as the Buddha advised, Graeme is now a grey nomad. 'I am journeying for justice, protesting for peace and speaking out for sustaining the Earth.'

Bruce Ballantine-Jones had not lost his faith in Christianity, but he had been an ad man before becoming an Anglican minister, so he was well versed in the recognition of a declining brand. 'The problem was that in the Anglican Church as it was, things had hardly changed for hundreds of years. But because society was changing it was a very competitive market out there.'

Gradually, from the seventies onwards, a stream of Anglicanism evolved that was a much more informal kind of church. It was a classic example of a product make-over. Bruce smiles good-naturedly but is not at all apologetic. 'We changed our service format, we got rid of robes and dog collars and old liturgies, which I personally enjoy but weren't working as a means of attracting and holding people. And we introduced modern music – we got a band. I suppose you could say the Church became more customer oriented.'

The idea that the Church was forsaking some of its own rituals to fill the pews is one that didn't go unnoticed. A growth in the fundamental and Pentecostal churches followed, along the lines of American churches.

And it didn't matter where these services were held, for any building can be a house of God. Next door to the home I grew up in was a bingo hall. One year on Tuesday evenings for about six weeks, a man with slicked-down hair and thick glasses showed slides of his travels around the Middle East. It was advertised as a great adventure in the wilds of the world and sounded vaguely educational so my mother was happy to let me go. The man told stories of an Arab city that had huge fruit trees growing along its streets and how citizens would be able to pick the abundant fruit. It seemed like such a good idea.

The only problem was they weren't Christian. He showed a photo of a man who wore a moulded stainless-steel bowl over his head. He did this because he suffered from headaches. The next slide was of the same man without his bowl and it appeared as if the top of his head had been scraped out. The presenter told us that if the man had been a Christian such brutal treatment wouldn't have been necessary. 'He could have taken some Aspro or even a Bex.'

Pamphlets were handed out at the end of the lecture inviting people back for entertainment the following week. On the reverse side was a picture of a group of people wearing suits and smart dresses burning in hell. I asked the man with the slicked-down hair what hell was like. He put his hand on my shoulder and smiled. 'Well, it's a little like having a pneumatic drill run through your kneecap.'

I went home and told my mother what the man had said. She looked at the pamphlet and shook her head. 'These people don't know what hell is. They don't know what heaven is. They scare you into trying to believe. No matter what happens to you, you must never be scared into believing.'

She threw the paper in the fire and it quickly caught alight. The burning people in smart suits and dresses disappeared in the rolling flames.

My parents were both deeply suspicious of what my mother called 'Home Brand religions', named after the generic jars of food that were popping up on supermarket shelves at the time. 'Always go with a brand name – they have to tell you what the ingredients are and you know where it's made,' she said.

To my father these new religious services were 'Yank hand-me-down happy hand-clappers'.

Whatever they were, the repackaging of Christianity to Australians was underway. Two major arms of the Protestant faiths merged: the Methodist and the Presbyterian churches became the Uniting Church, a move designed to strengthen an already strong congregational base. That was the plan, but the organisers forgot to tell the Sefton Presbyterian Church, because it stayed the Sefton Presbyterian Church. Even after Margaret Bennett moved away she would occasionally drive by to see the church where she used to play the organ and run the Sunday school. But with time comes change, and the building was deconsecrated. 'I felt a bit sad when it closed down,' she says.

Abu Ahmed, on the other hand, saw the vacant church as an opportunity to practise his faith. Abu fled a war-torn Lebanon, where sectarian violence was a matter of everyday life, and arrived in Australia in 1977 with his family. They lived at first in Lakemba and Lidcombe, then moved into a unit in Villawood.

His is a story of a well-trodden path, an immigrant who saw his original home fall into civil war and hatred, seeking safety and opportunity by travelling to the other side of the world and finding a new home in Australia. He was one of the growing numbers of Muslims making Australia their home. At the end of the twentieth century Australia was not only a multi-racial nation, it was also multi-faith.

Abu Ahmed eventually moved to his own home in Sefton, and seeking a place of worship, he and other Muslims in his area and from the surrounding suburbs bought Margaret Bennett's old church. When neighbours realised it was to become a mosque many complained to the local council, which in turn tried to prevent the plans going ahead.

The building under planning laws was zoned a church, not a mosque, and the matter was settled in court with the council winning along the lines of this argument. It was never simply a planning issue, though. Racial and religious tensions grew as they had many times in Australia's past. The words 'GO AWAY' were graffitied on fences and some neighbours initiated a campaign to disrupt services.

A senior community member, Rashid Raashed, told a journalist, 'The council thinks it is only Christians who live here. I mean we are all Australians, that is the beauty of [Australia's] multicultural theme. So if these people are allowed to live in this country with the right of citizenship, they should be accommodated to have a place of public worship. Which we, of course, bought and we're using it.'

This was a moment when the tiered nature of Australian society came into focus, and an example of when the institutions of secular Australia – the court and justice systems – defended the rights of citizens to assemble and worship. The New South Wales Supreme Court ruled that a mosque and a church are both places of worship and the Sefton mosque had every right to exist under council planning and zoning regulations.

The mosque has become a part of the Sefton suburban landscape and there are no more campaigns to disrupt the services. No more graffiti.

Makiz Ansari at the Gallipoli Mosque, Auburn, New South Wales.

And the old organist and Sunday school teacher still drives by occasionally. 'I'm glad it's still there, it's being used as a religious thing – even if it's another religion. I can still drive by and see in my mind's eye the old church and the things that happened in that church.' The priest who would run out to shake people's hands, the Sunday school lessons when Margaret Bennett would have to get out her 'filthy look' to quieten unruly kids, the weddings, funerals and music, and the lives that had filled the Presbyterian church.

'I would rather have the mosque than the church pulled down. If it's just a block of flats, well, no thank you. I'm glad it's still there.'

With each wave of immigration and settlement there are the echoes between modern and preceding generations' experiences. Makiz Ansari's family fled the Soviet invasion of Afghanistan and arrived in Australia via India in the mid-nineties. Like Susan Balint, who came to Australia and rediscovered her Jewish faith, Makiz has rediscovered the traditions of her Muslim faith.

The time came when she sought to explore her Islamic traditions more vigorously and seriously, especially after the September 11 terrorist attacks on the United States, which deeply shocked her and triggered within her the drive to investigate Islam. In fact, Makiz decided to investigate the whole notion of God, the purpose of life, spirituality and love for humanity in order to try to reconcile the barbarism of those terrorists attacks. 'So I went straight to the Quran myself. I read the Quran in English and the experience was deeply profound. I discovered that killing, suicide, holy war or terrorising people were against the very principles and essence of Islam, or any spiritual tradition.' Makiz believe she has moved from blind faith to faith by knowledge.

Makiz, 2009.

Throughout this journey, Makiz had contemplated wearing the *hijab* (veil). She put on the scarf as a trial, and to this day she says, 'I have not regretted the decision – it makes me feel comfortable.

'I have had some very bad scarf days, though, trying to get the hang of it,' she says, laughing the way any young woman with a fashion problem might. In fact, she reminds me of Vianney Hatton, giggling about how she would wear her habit.

Makiz grew up in Australia, this is her home where she celebrates her Islamic outlook in comfort and peace with her non-Muslim friends and colleagues. 'I am happy to call myself an Australian Muslim,' she says, 'with an Afghan heritage.'

10

Just Wait Until the Fireworks

Throughout the ebb and flow of life in Australia there are areas of tension between Muslims and Christians. Like the recent debate over a proposed Islamic school in the outer-Sydney rural town of Camden. Camden is old Australia: the family farm of John Macarthur, founder of Australia's wool industry and major character in the Rum Rebellion, still stands overlooking the lush green of the town. It's surrounded by flood plains so it has remained relatively unchanged for decades. The great sprawl of Sydney has reached as far as the old dairy town of Narellan, but Camden has stayed very much the same.

The proposed Islamic school changed that. Australia may well be multi-racial and multi-faith, but there are many Australias. Like the Sefton church–mosque debate, Camden's local council refused permission for the school to be built citing planning guidelines, and insisted there were no racial or religious considerations. But at a council meeting reported by the *Sydney Morning Herald*, a *Camden Advertiser* reader, who wished only to be identified as 'Hayley', was quoted in November 2007 as saying, 'The thought of our beautiful Camden accommodating [sic] to this religion is disgusting.'

Big hats were worn and Australian flags were waved by some at the meeting. The fact that so many of the people opposing the school were products of religious schools was never really raised.

In May 2009 a group of Camden churches and Christian ministries issued a joint submission to oppose the school's development. The local Catholic church did not add its support to the submission, perhaps indicating an acknowledgement of not only the right of independent schools to exist, but also of the plurality of faiths in Australia.

Co-signed by the local heads of the Baptist, Anglican and Uniting churches, the submission stated in part that, 'Islam is not simply a private religion. It is driven by a powerful political agenda and it's an ideology with a plan for world domination.' It sounds like a broken record: take out Islam from the statement then add Judaism, Catholicism or communists.

But I do not live there and it doesn't mean those people who opposed the school are intolerant racists. And there were many in the communty who were in favour of it. Change and traditions are often in conflict around Australia; someone's heritage is another person's development opportunity. It's interesting to add, though, that in the historic town where heritage buildings stand along the main street the Camden council gave approval for a McDonald's restaurant, which was described as having a Frank Lloyd Wright feel to it, to be built.

Yes, remember, there are many Australias.

Vianney Hatton lived and worked in the Sutherland Shire during the 2005 riots in Cronulla. She initially thought it was all a beat-up, but she listened to the local parents who had been concerned about the drug and alcohol culture associated with the beach. She saw that an underlying resentment had been building for some time.

As an old Bondi girl she loved the beach. 'I felt sad that Cronulla was getting a bad name. I felt resentful that alcohol-fuelled tempers had occasioned such violence and I felt a sense of injustice that we could not share the beauty and resources of the beach suburb with those who came from elsewhere . . . even foreign countries.'

The cohesion of a plural society is always likely to be tested at such times and perhaps religious faith cannot be shared; after all, religion is a discipline. Perhaps in the journey of the Australian soul a breadth of thought is not always possible.

Beryl Carmichael thinks otherwise. She is dedicated to keeping alive the once threatened traditional Aboriginal beliefs in addition to a Christian ethic. 'You can't separate anything – it's all connected. Like even our affinity with the birds, the animals, the reptiles, the land and the sky, everything's connected. You've got that one-ness with everything. It goes beyond country, right to your spiritual self.'

Her father, a tribal elder, would tell stories around the campfire. She says, 'I felt it was my duty and responsibility from an early age to carry it on for old Dad and pass it onto the future generations. It's important for them to understand. That spiritual self is inside them. Find it and nurture it.'

It's possible for a message of understanding and learning to be passed between two faiths. When Vianney returned to Australia from her theology studies and work in the United States in 1983 she went to work with her fellow sisters in Redfern. 'The idea was just simply to be part of the scene there with the Aboriginal people. Not necessarily to do anything, but to provide a place where those who were more actively involved might come for refreshment and prayer,' she explains.

Pretty soon Vianney worked out that her major concern was to earn money so the order could continue to feed people who came into the house. She taught religious education a few days a week at a boys' primary school and eventually returned to work as a physiotherapist – her father must have heaved a great sigh of relief and pride after all those years Vianney had spent at university. She could see around her in Redfern that a great many of the residents were not economically or socially empowered. Among them was a man called Harold. He was intellectually gifted but was also a member of the Stolen Generations. Along with that experience, the trauma of his brother's sudden and violent death had unhinged him. He attended a clinic every two weeks to receive slow-release medication for his brain-damage-induced depression. He was nicknamed Johnnie Walker because he was always pacing up and down. Barefoot and restless, he never stood still.

Harold would come to Vianney's house for tea and a sandwich. 'Plain white bread, thanks, Sis, none of that healthy stuff.' Sometimes he would have a shower and put on a change of clothes, but mostly he would just pace up and down.

One Christmas Eve, Harold visited the house, pacing up and down. He had a few places he could go to to sleep, but perhaps they were closed so he just kept pacing up and down. What was he doing? Why was he here? Whatever the reason, Vianney was growing anxious. She was due to go to midnight mass and although it wasn't the custom to give needy people money, she had to get Harold on his way and, anyway, it was Christmas. So she gave him some money and he left.

Later, as she was about to leave there was a knock at the door. Harold. He shuffled past, mumbling.

'Couldn't you get a room at the Salvos?' asked Vianney. No answer. What am I going to do with him at this hour? she thought.

Vianney (left) in 1986, with other sisters who worked in Redfern.

'What do you want, Harold?' she finally asked.

He looked at her. 'You going to midnight mass, aren't you Sis?' he said.

Vianney nodded.

'You can't walk down Wilson Street on your own at night. I've come back to walk you to mass.'

Vianney says she saw him differently after that. It wasn't simply a matter of her giving and Harold receiving, it wasn't simply a matter of charity or of the empowered and the disempowered. It was a moment of illumination and awareness, of love and respect between two people.

A state of flux exists in everyday life and for many people the uncertainties surrounding us make a more disciplined form of faith attractive. Although Bruce Ballantine-Jones and other Anglicans had dressed down the rituals of faith, their structure of beliefs exists within a rigid set of rules. 'If you package Christianity in a medieval or out-of-date way, you're going to turn off the market you're trying to attract,' he reasons.

To Bruce, in the evangelical churches the authority is the Bible, along with traditional moral beliefs. 'People want to know the answers to the real questions – how their sins can be forgiven, how they can have eternal life, how to find God. The liberal churches don't answer those questions.' He believes the liberal churches get involved in social causes. 'Everyone wants justice for Aborigines and peace for the Middle East – you don't need a church to get involved in causes.'

Judy Cottier sees things a little differently. 'Many people who want a cut-and-dried and absolutist religion find it appealing,' she says. But she regards herself as a liberal Anglican. She supports women priests and as the principal of a Perth Anglican girls' school she brought the Reverend Kay Goldsworthy from Melbourne to be school chaplain. Kay became Australia's first female bishop.

Bruce Ballantine-Jones' beliefs are quite simple. 'Christians believe what Christ said: "Nobody comes to the Father except through me." You can respect other religions and have friendships with people from other faiths without accepting that they have got it right.'

Judy is more fatalistic about faith. 'If I die and it all turns out to be wrong, it doesn't matter because it enriched my life.'

And perhaps the lives of others, too. When the Cottiers returned to Papua New Guinea to visit the people and places they had once known, they found their son David's grave had been well cared for. 'We left them forty years previously as a very fledgling Christian people. When we returned to the Simbai Valley the whole church was flourishing. There was a Simbai bishop running it and there must have been twenty or twenty-five clergy who had come out of that valley, some working there and some in other places,' says John Cottier. 'I believe the Christian message that we have is great. I don't believe that everyone who doesn't have it is lost. I think it's so great and I want to share it – it is a freeing, life-giving and enriching experience. But I didn't think they were condemned souls without Christianity.'

The Pentecostal mega-churches, with their use of music and video 'and an active style of celebration, have much in common with Bruce Ballantine-Jones' idea of presenting a more attractive packaging of the same message.

Many young Australians such as Chris Gresham-Britt find the modern churches' informal style appealing. He attends a fairly small non-denominational church, and said he was attracted to worship and meaning through music. He's good-looking in a young muso way, designer haircut falling over his intelligent, handsome face.

'When I was confronted with what the Bible actually says it really challenged my perception, and when I chose to become a Christian, I felt like a part of a minority group. It definitely wasn't cool at school, but because I was so challenged I really wanted to pursue it. I was willing to go against the flow.' In Chris' case that meant his parents. Although they didn't stand in the way of his faith his parents are more typical of the prevailing Australian attitude to organised religion.

'I don't feel the need for nurturing,' says Chris' father. 'I have social needs and I have sporting needs but I don't feel the need to ponder the existence of a god.'

His mother Meredith agrees. 'I think there are many other ways of expressing a belief structure, of expressing a spirituality, other than going to church.'

Chris Gresham–Britt.

But Chris sees a passion rising up in young Australians. 'It's not affecting everyone, but I think there are a lot of people out there, and you can see this as a musician, who are searching for meaning and a lot of young people in our culture are starting to find that with God.'

It's not only Protestant evangelists who are trying to find new markets. When more than three hundred thousand Catholic pilgrims attended World Youth Day during Pope Benedict's visit to Sydney in 2008 it was, in a way, a rallying cry from the faithful to secular Australia. The government openly welcomed the celebrating Catholics and put a dollar value of the event at between $152 million and $193 million for the local economy. The Sydney Chamber of

Commerce went even better, punting on a $230-million-dollar benefit.

Not all Australians welcomed the celebration. The president of the Atheist Foundation of Australia, David Nicholls, wrote in a press release posted on the association's website in May 2008: 'Australian support for this superstitious entourage makes it a guilty party in the religious oppression of millions of people on a scale never before witnessed by humanity.'

He went on to say in the same press release that atheists are rightfully upset that governments are spending lavishly on supporting a particular belief system, which is demonstrably no better in its historical and present political and social context than any other.

When you take the big-picture view of such an event and what it may or may not represent, it's a valid expression of opinion and belief. But if you look at the ground level of such events, what you find are people.

Rehearsing at Barangaroo, the dockland site once dubbed the Hungry Mile by waterside workers, what you find late at night is a group of people. People playing parts in the Stations of the Cross.

The temperature has dropped to next to zero and Pontius Pilate's attendants are trembling, not through remorse or doubt but through sheer cold.

'It's so cold, man, a singlet would be good.'

'Any sort of undergarment.'

'Just ignore it. Remember, it won't be so cold on the day.'

'How can you ignore it?' says an attendant in a sulky tone.

For Suzi Doherty, who is lending a hand as a stage manager for the event, there is no time to waste; everyone has to get down to the water for the scene of the execution of Christ. Jesus seems to be pretty stoic about it all, which is as it should be, but the thieves are a worry.

She radios in: 'We're taking the thieves down and putting some clothes on, but can you tell me where the Roman soldiers' clothes are?'

The soldiers' clothes don't turn up. It's 4.30 in the morning and the centurions are without their wallets, car keys or clothes. The production manager offers to put them up in a hotel for the night, but one centurion snaps, 'Dressed like this? They'll think we're on together.'

The other Roman soldier, his tunic and helmet plume waving in the breeze, closes his eyes. 'Why did I say I'd do this?'

With Jesus nodding his head and saying it's all good, the images and resonances of what she sees makes Suzi burst into laughter. 'Somehow it at all must have meant something, made some sort of crazy sense,' she said.

As if World Youth Day wasn't enough of a celebration, a Catholic drum thumper if you like, Australia of the new millennium is about to celebrate its first Catholic saint, indeed its first saint of any denomination. Mary MacKillop is edging closer to canonisation.

The political commentator Bernard Keane took a jaundiced view of the whole exercise in his piece on the Crikey website of 14 December 2009. 'The promotion of Mary MacKillop's sainthood is a very smart piece of marketing by the local Catholic Church and its international masters. It appeals to that lurking cultural cringe in the Australian mindset that the surging nationalism and swagger of recent decades has not killed off the pleasure to be gained from international recognition, no matter how dubious.'

Val Noone, not surprisingly, felt a little differently about the proposal and he speaks about Mary MacKillop with disarming warmth. 'Mary MacKillop, well I think she's good value. She stood up to the bishops. What more do you want? Her canonisation is a bit of a win for the little guys.'

Perhaps in time Mary MacKillop will become a hero of secular Australia, a woman who fought for the underprivileged and poor to be given an education and opportunity.

'What a corker,' says Ron Palmer. 'Good for her, it's like being named a Hall of Famer. Good for her.'

On my way down to the carols I walk along the Maribyrnong River. You can see the changes that time has brought. Just down from the Flemington Racecourse, where once there was a factory, a Buddhist temple is being built. There is a huge sixteen-metre high golden statue, the centrepiece of the complex. She is known as the Heavenly Queen Mazu and is revered by Buddhists for helping people.

The temple towers above the river, yet doesn't dominate, and it enchants the train commuters, bike riders and joggers of the local area.

Not far away in Footscray are Catholic, Anglican and Uniting churches. It's a bit of a melting pot, Footscray. Even though the property values have gone through the roof it's still one of the most culturally diverse areas in Australia. Somehow it seems to work, not perfectly, but it does seem to work, perhaps because it was always a transitional suburb, always changing. And Ron has seen it all.

I see him. Ron Palmer standing by the stage of Yarraville Gardens Christmas Carols and he is in his element. Surrounded by people. In fact, the park seems to be full of people. Families, friends, visitors, some people who stand alone. There's a choir that sang at Dr Geoffrey Edelsten's wedding at the Crown Casino.

'CDs are available,' says their manager.

'Couldn't get the Tongan choir, which is a shame, got another do on,' says Ron.

I nod my head. I can hear the voices of the Tongan choir in the Anglican church around the corner from my house as I walk past on a Sunday. Loud, clear, beautiful voices.

'But this mob are pretty handy,' nods Ron.

There are all sorts flowing around the stage, little kids, mostly, and some harassed-looking parents – mostly fathers – searching among the throng for sons and daughters.

There's a man who has come to play harmonica in the community concert before the carols begin. He walks up to me and says, 'You remember me, don't you? I played here three years ago.'

'Yes,' I say, 'I remember you.' I think to myself, I've been doing this thing for that long?

Then I look at Ron. He is talking to his Santa for the night. A man who has been a lifelong conservative voter and a friend and fellow organiser of the night. 'Now, Bill,' Santa says to me, 'don't throw the lollies when I come out this year because the littlies go off their heads and rush around like mad things. We don't want a stampede like last time.'

I nod my head and Ron Palmer laughs.

I have an abiding memory of Santa *ho-ho-ho-ing* in his friendly voice and then turning to me and yelling under his breath, 'Christ, it's absolute bloody bedlam – BEDLAM!'

'You just wear the suit, brother, and we'll take care of the stimulus package,' says Ron.

Santa shoots him a look and smiles. He shakes his head.

Ron turns and he laughs. 'What about his mob!'

The federal Liberal Party had just elected a new leader, Tony Abbott, from a field of three contenders, Abbott, Malcolm Turnbull and Joe Hockey.

'We'll be right,' says Santa.

'Maybe, but Bob Menzies must be rolling in his grave. All of them Catholics, all of them.'

Santa laughs. 'Oh well, times change.'

And that's true. It would be hard to imagine that Australia's longest-serving prime minister, the Presbyterian Robert Menzies, could ever have thought such a thing possible. Three Catholics standing for the Liberal leadership. And nobody in the population really cared. That is how much Australia has changed.

The journey of the Australian soul continues. Institutional Christianity no longer dominates the landscape like it did in the forties and fifties. It has to compete for influence in a crowded marketplace of multi-racial and multi-faith Australia. A marketplace that shrinks as the number of non-believers grows.

There is a line from Sarah Watt's film *My Year Without Sex* that best explains the philosophy of much of modern Australia. 'God just isn't my way of explaining things.' But still, for many, religion and faith are an important part of life, and all go to make up the Australian soul.

The Christian festival of Christmas has grown to mean many things – a mad rush of consumerist excess, a time of reflection, and a celebration of the life and teachings of Jesus Christ – a man who may be, depending on your beliefs, the Son of God, a holy prophet, or a rather eccentric man of great courage, generosity and passion. But it can also embrace a wider community spirit.

Later on, as Santa makes his entrance on stage and as the lollies are held back, Ron Palmer yells out to the waving, red-suited man, 'Just remember, brother, that suit is the right colour!' Santa turns to give his old mate Ron a special two-digit Christmas wave and Ron shrieks with laughter.

Nearby, a little boy stares up at the scene with his sister. She wears a hijab. Ron ruffles the boy's hair.

'Merry Christmas, champ.'

He does indeed love a bit of action, Ron. And I remember asking him what religion he was. What circles he mixed in. 'Brother, I'm an Australian – I mix in lots of circles!'

Here on this night, with these people, that seems to be a pretty good circle to be in. The Australian Soul.

And I hear Ron yell to nobody in particular, 'If you think this is good, just wait until the fireworks!'

The Australian Heart

11

Coffee at Balnarring

Early in the new year of almost every year I find myself at Somers. My family, two of my best friends and a best friend's daughter share a couple of weeks there. Somers is a small village on Victoria's Mornington Peninsula with a modest yacht club, some dirt streets, a general store and the odd growling koala. There's not much else except lots of families, dogs on the beach, lazy days in the sun and the occasional pod of dolphins.

When you think about summer holidays, that is all you really need. As well as the abovementioned attractions, there are certain holiday rituals that have to be observed, and some of those necessitate venturing away from Somers.

There is the Stuff Patrol. The Stuff Patrol is an op-shop crawl around the surrounding areas where vital Stuff can be found. Stuff. Yes, Stuff. Holiday Stuff, old records, wooden tennis racquets, books and old movies. The result is a fashion parade on the verandah of old clothes and cast-offs found among the shelves and hangers of various shops that stretch from Crib Point to Hastings

Page 185: *Ron and Marjorie Palmer on their wedding day in 1958.*

to Mornington and then finishing off at Balnarring, just up the road from Somers.

Sometimes you end up keeping the Stuff, but more often than not, at the end of the holiday it's returned to the shelves of the op-shops via the collection bins.

It takes a morning to travel through these shops but it's like a trip through an exhibit from the last sixty years of Australian history. There are bits and pieces of Australian lives. There are things that have been owned, worn, forgotten about and given to the op-shop. There are presents or gifts that have never been opened, a collection of festive beer steins with a real estate company's logo (masquerading as a heraldic crest) from the Hastings Anglican op-shop. In the Crib Point Uniting Church op-shop there's a gadget that promises a time-saving miracle in the shape of the priceless 'Vego-Matic'. It dices, slices, chops and shreds and, 'Best of all,' screams the writing on the packet, 'no more tears while chopping onions!!' Two exclamation marks, no less.

Records are scarcer than they used to be, I notice, as are VHS video cassettes. CDs and the odd DVD sprinkle the shelves and there, we stop and laugh at the bold declaration of a certain 1980s permed-hair soap-actor-cum-pop-singer on his claim to 'Take over the UK and then the US' with the release of his self-titled CD.

We're holding his CD in the Balnarring op-shop and passing it between us, laughing. He looks like he comes from another planet but really it's just another time and, as my friend Liam says, 'At least he had a go.'

A great expression. An Australian expression for accepting that the vagaries and twists of fate and life may in fact mean that big dreams don't amount to much. At least he had a go. He never did take the UK or the US or even Balnarring by storm, but yes, at least he had a go.

I pick up two old wooden tennis racquets to use on the public courts up at Florida Avenue in Somers. And then I see a souvenir magazine for the 1969 film *Battle of Britain*; it's the sort of program exhibitors of films used to put out when they premiered a movie. It's full of stories of how the film was made and who was in it, plus stills from the action.

Most of the actors were those ubiquitous English knights, Sir John and Sir Michael and Sir Laurence and Sir etc. They're all dead and gone and all the young actors, or emerging talents, as the program puts it, like Michael Caine, are as old as Moses. In fact he himself has become now a Sir. Sir Michael Caine.

I take my Stuff to the counter to pay and an oldish woman smiles. In welcome. The people who work in the op-shops always seem to be the same age and type. Usually women, middle-aged to elderly, and always up for a chat and a story about almost every article they sell.

'Wooden racquets! Oh I remember those!' exclaims a middle-aged woman.

I presume she's remembering them fondly. 'Yeah,' I say, 'they're great, aren't they?'

The woman looks at me.

'You really know when you've hit the ball well,' I say.

'Well, not really, they never had much power,' says the op-shop lady. 'Just old junk when you think about it. Like the difference between a new car and an old model T.'

My friends, children and the women laugh.

'Yes, you really know when you've hit the ball well!' says one of my mates.

The woman laughs a bit more. 'I used to play comp tennis and it was such a relief when the aluminium racquets came in with the bigger heads. My husband hated them. You'd like him.'

The op-shop lady then tells us how she and her husband would play competition tennis and every year they would travel to Mildura for the Easter tennis carnival there. 'He got so mad when I pulled out an aluminium racquet. He said, "You can't play with that, Jimmy Connors uses one of those!"'

She says 'Jimmy Connors' as if he was the worst thing anybody could possibly be, and maybe to some in the 1970s he was. Jimmy Connors was a brash, powerful American tennis champion who thrashed Australia's ageing star Ken Rosewall in the 1974 Wimbledon Championship. Jimmy used an aluminium racquet. And Ken Rosewall used a wooden one.

I ask the woman if she went along with her husband and changed racquets, and she laughs. 'Oh, he wasn't my husband then. We had a game, I beat him, then he got in a foul mood and said it was because of the racquet.'

I tell the woman she Jimmy-Connored him.

'Oh well, he proposed the next week and I accepted. And he borrowed my racquet! That's all he was after.'

I ask the woman how long she's been married.

'Thirty-five this year.'

One of my friends whistles. 'Thirty-five, that's a fair effort.'

'Chicken feed compared to her,' says the woman, nodding to her companion.

We look to the older woman. She holds up her hands. 'Fifty and never a cross word!'

My friends and I nod and my daughter comments that this is longer than I have been alive. I nod.

'That's a long time,' my daughter says.

One of the women has taken our Stuff and is adding it up. She looks at the *Battle of Britain* program. 'Oh, I remember this one, it went on forever. We went to see it on a date! Night away from the children. Hubby went for the planes and I went for Michael Caine!'

Sir Michael Caine.

The older lady looks down at my daughter. 'Yes, it is a long time, but sometimes it feels like it was yesterday,' she says.

We pay and walk across to the café at the Balnarring shopping centre for a coffee, milkshake and an opportunity to check my emails. The kids go in and order and as we three old friends sit down, I get my laptop out and fire it up. Liam watches his daughter muck around with mine and asks as I swear at my computer, 'How long have you been married, Will?'

I swear again.

'How long?' he asks.

I glance up and see him looking at me. 'Been married seventeen this year and together since . . .' I think, trying to do the maths in my head, '89. So I guess twenty-one. 'Twenty-one years.' I think about it a bit. 'Shit, that's a long time.'

'It is,' says Liam. 'It's longer than six years.'

He says this in relation to his own marriage. He says it openly with a bit of a laugh and no bitterness. He and his wife separated nearly eight years ago.

'Well,' says my other friend Mal, 'at least you had a go.'

We all laugh.

I swear at my computer, not at the machine this time, but at the emails I find waiting for me.

'Good news?'

'Work and . . . stuff I can deal with later.' I go to switch it off and then offer it to my mates to use.

Mal readily agrees. 'Yeah, I'll just check my account.'

I assume it's his bank account or some such thing but then I see this isn't the case when he starts crawling through RSVP, the online introduction service. He has never been married although he was in a relationship for more than ten years. He's never been short of company: he's an attractive, generous fellow who's a lot of fun to be with.

'Why are you looking at that?' There's a tone in my voice that makes him look at me.

'Why shouldn't I look at it?'

'Well . . .' I say.

'Well what?'

'Well, it's one of those sites.'

'Shit, Will, you sound like a fossil sometimes.' He goes back to the computer.

Liam laughs. 'Yeah, you'd never use an aluminium racquet.'

I give him a look.

'Or like Jimmy Connors.'

I laugh a little.

'And you'd just watch movies for aeroplanes, not Michael Caine.'

'Oh, shut up. He got shot down in that film anyway.'

I ask my RSVP friend if he goes on it a lot. 'Of course, that's how you meet women. It's like going out or to a pub or a dance or I don't know. Just to meet people. This thing can save you a lot of time and hassle.'

I look at him.

Liam says, 'Yeah, you don't have to comb your hair or wash. Very handy.'

I look at Mal on the computer.

'Oh, leave him alone,' Liam says, 'he's just having a go.' More laughter.

But I begin to see that the ways of the heart are many. Look at the women from the op-shop. Eighty-five years of marriage between them. Add me and that's more than a century up before

William McInnes and the op-shop lady.

lunch. Then look at my two friends. One split from his wife, the other checking out his account on RSVP. Australians walk down a great many paths in the pursuit of matters of the heart and romance.

There was a time, perhaps not too distant from the wedding of the older op-shop lady, when a firm rule of thumb existed in Australian society. The ultimate idea of romantic life was for a man and a woman to fall in love. They proved this by marrying, then consummating the marriage and having a family. You got married and stayed married. Happily ever after.

That's how it was for Rae and Graham Stevens. In 1947 they were married and in 2010 they were still married, living in the house they built together in the years after the Second World War.

Their romance and marriage were indicative of a smaller, more localised Australia. In the forties and fifties Australians usually married someone like themselves: seventy-eight per cent married within their religion, and they were likely to marry a friend of the family or someone from the same neighbourhood.

Rae and Graham lived in the same Melbourne suburb, East Bentleigh, and their families knew each other. They sit in the house they built together and remember the day they met.

It was at the twelfth birthday party of Rae's best friend, who also happened to be the younger sister of Graham Stevens. The girls were giggling and excited, which is the way all twelve-year-olds should be at birthday parties, and when a dark-haired, dark-eyed young fellow walked in, somebody had to ask the question.

'We were having a photo taken and I said to Graham's sister, "Who's that?" And she said it was her big brother. I didn't take any notice really, but that's the first time I ever saw him, when I was still at school!' says Rae.

But she did ask the question.

Graham can see in his 'mind's eye', a phrase he uses quite often, the moment he first saw Rae. 'She was standing on the front lawn over by the side fence having her photo taken. She was second from the left.'

'I've still got that photo,' says Rae, nodding.

'And there was something that clicked then, I was sixteen and you were twelve.'

It's a clear memory, an instant in their lives, but after a brief pause Rae can't help herself. 'You must have been seventeen, there's a five-year age difference.'

After a short intake of breath, Graham answers, 'Well, four and a half.'

It's the sort of exchange people who have lived together a lifetime, and then some, often have.

They can both picture the first time they met, 'I often wonder why I remember it, thinking back. I don't know who the others were but I can always remember it. Didn't think anything of it, but I remember it.'

Graham's other abiding memory of Rae is her riding a horse. 'A bloody ratbag, she looked like, she was a real character when she was young. Riding bareback on the horse like that, it intrigued me quite a bit. Look, I don't know what it was. One of those silly things they call instant love I suppose.' There's a slight pause and romantically Graham Stevens puts it all in perspective: 'But as I say, all women give me the irrits, bar one, and I married her.'

It wasn't until Graham returned home to East Bentleigh on leave from the battlefront of New Guinea, serving in the 4th Field Engineers of the 3rd Division of the Australian Imperial Force, that their relationship blossomed. The pair exchanged letters but it was as friends, according to Rae.

She didn't read too much into those letters at first; for her, writing them was a way of taking a patriotic interest in the welfare of the troops fighting overseas. As well as knowing Graham Stevens, Rae knew a lot of other local men in the Australian Armed Services. During the war she worked for Australian Paper Manufacturers in South Melbourne, where Southbank is now located.

'And every time the troops were going overseas or coming back there was a big march through the city, so we girls used to race up onto the bridge and wave and sing out to all the servicemen. I still go every Anzac Day with one of the girls, there's four of us left, and I said to her last Anzac Day, "We've stood on this bridge, this bloomin' bridge, most of our life." We saw them go and we

Graham Stevens in uniform, 1943.

saw them come back. So my interest in the war was just general patriotic interest.'

But patriotic interest bloomed into something more when Graham came home on leave. In fact, the bareback-riding Rae Peters thought Graham Stevens was a good sort. 'I used to go to the movies a lot with the girls from work and thought he looked a bit like Gregory Peck. Because Graham was dark, like Gregory Peck, who was a big heart-throb at the time. Gregory Peck, not Graham.'

He might have looked like Gregory Peck but their first date was a trip to see a Marx Brothers film. Unlikely as it may seem, that was romantic enough because after the mayhem of Groucho, Chico and Harpo they shared a kiss outside Rae's front gate.

When Graham returned to New Guinea and his role in the Engineers the letters grew more personal, to the point where Graham sent one suggesting Rae should perhaps think about buying a ring.

'Well,' he explains, 'we got a bit more romantic than what we were in the beginning.' And that's about it as far as Graham is concerned.

Rae decides to take over. 'He probably doesn't even remember. The letters became more romantic. They were censored, you weren't allowed to say anything about where he was or anything. But I remember one letter to him, I wrote, "Take care, look after yourself, take care – for me." I must have thought he was going to be the one.' She smiles a little.

Graham gives a studied look and shakes his head.

'I knew he wouldn't remember,' says Rae.

'I remember,' he says, 'you writing saying I owed you a hundred pound.'

This brings us to the matter of the ring. 'You said,' says Rae with a bit of an elbow, 'when we decided we had a future together, you said, "Well, you'd better pick out a ring." Barbara, his sister,' Rae says with a nod in Graham's direction, 'saw one over in the jewellers at Footscray.

'And I thought, Oh, that was nice; still got it, there it is,' says Rae happily.

'So I bought the ring,' Graham says.

'And he did, he sent the money down of course, and that was it.'

There was no real moment, according to Graham, when he knew they would marry. 'It was just a natural progression, wasn't it?'

And that was what marriage meant to Graham and Rae and a generation of Australians. 'Didn't give it much thought, it was just the natural thing to do.'

Rae Peters (left) *and Barbara Stevens, Graham's sister, in 1944.*

'Yes, well,' says Rae, 'you probably thought it was for life. I hope – it's a bit late now.'

Sixty-two years later it's a safe bet that is exactly what it means. It actually might have been longer but Rae had her mind set on being an Easter bride so there was an eleven-month wait before the walk down the aisle in 1947. They both recall their wedding day; Archdeacon Hewett performed the service at St Andrew's Church in Brighton.

Graham also remembers the first time he saw his fiancée Rae Peters waiting for him on the railway station at Royal Park when

Rae and Graham on their wedding day in 1947.

he returned from the Second World War. His recall is as clear and fine as the sunlight that shone on the platform. 'She wore a blue spotted dress, and a blue hat. Navy and white shoes. Yes, I can see her there. Left your mother, knocked me over. And we kissed. And we've been married sixty-two years. And you only get twenty for murder,' he says.

'Thirty you get, I think.'

Graham Stevens continues staring ahead and smiles.

You also get three children, and these kids, along with more than four million others born between the end of the war and the early sixties, were at the forefront of changes that would redefine the Australian heart.

Sixty-plus years married, three children, Rae a housewife and Graham never out of work. Theirs was a template or the very model of Australian Postwar Marriage 101. But there are many Australians, so it is only right to assume that not all lives and matters of the heart will comfortably fit within this model.

12

Love in a Distant Land

One million 'New Australians' came to Australia between 1945 and 1955. This influx of people from Europe helped to change the nature of Australia and triggered its metamorphosis from a parochial, generally homogenous community, as typified by the story of Rae and Graham Stevens, into a multi-racial, culturally layered society.

Tony Bárány and Marta Dravetzky met on a ship carrying migrants to their new home.

Born in Hungary, Marta and her family fled the approaching Red Army of Russia in 1945, first to Germany, where they lived for five years. 'As we crossed the Hungarian border it was the night of Good Friday. When we reached a high place we stopped and looked back. We could see the bombs, which would light up the background and we could see they were right behind us. The Russians were just two kilometres away.'

Tony Bárány grew up in a Budapest suburb. After his father died when Tony was twelve, he and his mother moved to the centre of Budapest and it was there that he fell in love with aircraft. When he finished school Tony was lucky enough to receive a placement with the Hungarian national airline and studied aviation for five years. His love of aircraft was fed copiously with the huge number of warplanes flooding the European skies during the Second World War.

His passion seemed unquenchable: he enlisted in the Hungarian Pilot Academy and moved to a training station in Germany, near Berlin. As the war neared its end, the German commander of Budapest wanted the air cadets to fight for the Nazi war machine.

'My commandant didn't want us to die for Berlin, so we said we were leaving. At that time the English, the Americans and the Russians were coming closer, closer, closer to Berlin. We picked up the way towards the Americans because we knew we were going to be prisoners of war, and we wanted to become prisoners of Americans.'

Tony's plans were undone by the zoning of Berlin by the victorious allies; the city was carved into three zones, and Tony and his comrades found themselves prisoners of the English. After eleven months in a prisoner-of-war camp Tony Bárány was released to Belgian authorities to work as a coalminer.

'And then after that I have relatives in Paris. I just pick up and go to Paris. Now don't ask me why I decided to come to Australia, because I don't know myself. It just happened like that.' He nods his head and smiles slightly. 'You know, when you are in good conditions, you do foolish things. Like going to Australia, I suppose. It must have seemed like a foolish thing to some. To travel to the other side of the world on an immigrant ship. But displaced persons had little choice, and an offer of a new life or a chance to see another part of the world was temptation enough.'

Marta was eighteen years old when she emigrated. 'I had to sign a two-year contract to work – same as for Tony – wherever the Australian government wanted us to work. It was mainly, of course, in very menial jobs in factories. I would have loved to have gone on with my studies but that was not possible.'

But there were some benefits. 'The English migrants had to pay ten pounds; they were ten-pound Pommies. But we didn't have to. We were DPs – displaced persons. The ship we came on,' says Marta, 'was a seven-and-a-half-thousand-ton ship and there were more than a thousand people on it.'

For Tony it may have been one of life's 'foolish things', but for Marta and her family it was just another move in their transitory lives as displaced persons. 'After five years in Germany, you didn't feel very much, you didn't know where you were going, what you

Tony Bárány en route to Australia, 1951.

were doing. You were living in a strange country. I learned German; I could speak German like a German but it still wasn't my home. You were in a permanent state of shock. You didn't know what you were coming to. I cannot describe that feeling.'

One thousand people creaking along on the open sea. And 'creak' is the word, for the ship they travelled on broke down shortly after they left. As they sailed through the Strait of Messina Marta saw Mount Etna spewing red lava into the sea. And in Egypt vendors were allowed to clamber aboard and sell their goods. They told the passengers they didn't need warm clothes in Australia because it never gets cold, so they wouldn't need their winter coats.

After lurching through the Suez Canal the ship broke down again in the Indian Ocean and underwent repairs in Colombo. Setting sail once more, it finally gave up the ghost and broke down completely about 500 kilometres off the Western Australian coast, and it was towed into Perth. There, the passengers were transferred to another immigration ship, and made their way to Melbourne.

It was quite a journey. You may wonder how the passengers filled their time. Well, Marta Dravetzky and Tony Bárány fell in love and, like Rae and Graham, it was a case of finding love within a familiar cultural group. 'My family group consisted of my father, my mother, my sister and another friend of mine, Marie, a young mother and her daughter. That was our close family group. But there were also other Hungarians on the ship who were friends. And in the evening we had dinner dances.'

During one of these dances Tony, who had seen Marta at the hostel before the ship embarked upon its stuttering journey, asked her to dance. Marta was a beautiful, dark-haired young woman who wasn't short of admirers, but she remembers when Tony Bárány asked her to join him on the dance floor.

'I remember because he clicked his heels like a nice Hungarian gentleman would. Like somebody who came from the Academy. He clicked his heels and of course he had to ask my father first if I could dance with him.'

The courtship progressed and when you consider the sixty-five days they spent on the ship it's no wonder, although Tony didn't always ask Marta's father for permission.

It was hard to keep things to themselves. 'You couldn't be secret – it was only one ship, one thousand people – how could we be secret? But we did meet on the ship every day,' says Tony.

Marta found a way through her job providing meals for the ship's nursery in a small kitchen. She prepared bottles of condensed milk to supplement the diet of shipboard toddlers and one of her duties was to sterilise the teats of the baby bottles. 'It was very overcrowded on this ship and I had my own little room . . . a small kitchenette next to one of the bars.'

'Big enough for the two of us,' says Tony, smiling.

'Our first kiss took place in the kitchen and the second kiss took place in a cabin next to the kitchen, while I put the teats to be sterilised on the stove.

'It was a longish kiss,' Marta continues, 'so the water boiled away and the teats all burned – everything. All we could do was throw what was left into the sea . . . It was a long kiss.' And she sighs.

'He was slim and had very red hair – and I wasn't going for red-haired men – so look,' she says in something approaching exasperation, 'these are things, I suppose, that are chemical attractions; you can be attracted to people who are not your type.'

And so love took its course and teats burned and sank into the sea.

Tony blended into the family and became firm friends with Marta's father, so much so that he felt comfortable enough to propose to her in Colombo, then ask her father for her hand.

With her family's blessing the two were married – but not until they had reached Australia and the migrant hostel at Bonegilla, near the Victoria–New South Wales border.

When they arrived the single men were being sent to Tasmania as forestry labourers. The fact that the two were engaged was of no interest to the authorities; a contract was a contract. 'Tony and my father got together,' says Marta, 'and decided the only way around it was for us to get married at Bonegilla.' A Lutheran minister was found, and he was suitable to both parties – Marta being a Protestant and Tony a Catholic.

Marta Dravetzky and Tony Bárány (middle, back) *with Marta's family on their way to Australia.*

Tony and Marta Bárány outside their home in Henty Street, Yagoona, in 1958.

And just as Rae Stevens had relied on her future sister-in-law to find a ring, so it was with Tony's in-laws-to-be. 'My father,' says Marta, 'had Napoleon gold, a gold coin, and a fob watch which he sold to a jeweller in Albury.' She pauses briefly, remembering. 'A very old fob watch, which I was sorry about, but he bought us rings and also material for a dress.'

The Hungarian community in the camp banded together to help the couple celebrate their wedding. 'Someone in the camp sewed a very nice dress for me, no veil, but a very nice dress. Somebody even got some ice-cream for our so-called reception. And somebody else baked cakes. Under the circumstances everybody tried to make it special for us.'

Tony laughs. 'The flowers!'

'Oh yes,' says Marta, 'somebody went to get flowers on his motorcycle but he didn't get back in time, only when I got out of church! So I didn't know what to do with my hands during the ceremony. But when we left the church I was thrown this very nice bouquet of white flowers.

'The good thing was that the Lutheran minister spoke German. As you know, the Adelaide Lutherans were from Germany. So the minister spoke German and was able to perform the ceremony very well.' She looks across to Tony, who gazes at her archly, knowing what is coming. Marta nods in his direction. 'I'm not sure how much he understood, but he said yes.'

A photograph of the wedding shows two displaced persons, from different ends of Hungary, thrown together by a combination of a world war, an epic sea voyage and some foolish things, as Tony would say. Surrounded by their Hungarian community on the other side of the world, they embraced a life together as a married couple in a new home.

Tony and Marta's wedding, conducted by a Lutheran minister in Bonegilla.

What about those people who made a similar journey to this nation who weren't surrounded by a community and family?

Immigrant men formed the backbone of Australia's nation-building projects, such as the Snowy Mountains Hydro-Electric Scheme. But the country needed more young, single women to marry these men. The government subsidised European women to emigrate to Australia on the condition that they would stay and work for at least two years, and in the hope they would marry and have a family. There is a priceless piece of footage of Arthur Calwell, the Chifley government's immigration minister, standing at the dockside with a face and manner that could only belong in old newsreels. He is surrounded by a collection of men, some of whom who stare at the raggedy haired, bespectacled, big-chinned man with his heavy suit and Drano voice with utter amazement. 'We want hundreds and thousands of men like yeeeouuuuu and we want many, many thousands of young women teeeeeeuuuuu.' And his big chin dips, his eyes look down and he swallows the last words in embarrassment at the suggestion that he was in any way encouraging a bit of New Australian hanky-panky.

In 1959 Beate Hirsch was one of those many, many thousands of Calwell's young women who came to Australia. She was from Germany and wanted to see and learn about the world as much as she could. She thinks it was her desire to flee from bad memories that gave her this urge to find out what the world had to offer. A thoughtful and gentle woman, she has a considered manner that lends itself to understatement. 'Not a very good time living through wars,' she says simply and it's only after a bit of prompting that she gives a clearer picture. 'Well, we lived through bombings and we were always evacuated to different places where we got bombed again and we would have to flee once more. And the church bells, I can't bear the sound of church bells. They remind me of sirens and warnings and bombs coming our way. It's an intimidating reminder of the past.'

Beate Hirsch's father died fighting in Hungary in 1944; the last time she saw him she was three years old. 'For me that was not the best thing to happen. I didn't get on with my mother – she preferred my brother. She'd only ever wanted a son.' Beate smiles softly and tilts her head to one side slightly. 'It's a family kind of thing,' she explains. 'And that sort of made me leave home very early.'

In 1959 her desire to learn about 'people's cultures and countries' led her to seek emigration to Canada, but an economic downturn in that part of the world meant unemployment was rife. She cancelled Canada and looked to Australia.

The staff at the Australian embassy in Bonn were very helpful, she says. 'They told me all these wonderful stories: how nice the weather is – lots of sunshine, palm trees and blue seas; everything was included. And I thought, why not?'

An offer she couldn't refuse. Like Marta Dravetzky before her, Beate Hirsch had to sign a contract promising to stay and work in Australia for two years. 'Once the two years were up I could go home or stay. If I ran into trouble I had nowhere to go, not even home to Germany.'

When she arrived in Melbourne there weren't any palm trees or sunshine, just cold and teeming rain, but there was a posse of cameramen and journalists. 'I wanted to go and experience a different culture; to have a partner or to get married – that was never on my agenda. When we landed in Melbourne reporters came to the ship and took photos of us. And then they let out that me and many other girls were supposed to be part of "fifty *Fräuleins*" coming out to look for husbands. That absolutely blew me out of the water because I had no idea I was included in that. I was never told this at the embassy.'

They didn't tell Beate's friend, who was also dragged from her cabin for the photo, either. The girl had a German fiancé who was a station hand at a property in North Queensland. Thankfully the Melbourne papers, unlike Beate's friend, didn't travel that far in those days, so the marriage went ahead. Beate's photo, though, would be seen and admired.

Beate Hirsch knew very little English and had no family or cultural network that she could rely on. She was also, by her own admission, quite naive and would take people at face value. As a young woman in a strange land it seemed she was fair game. At her first immigrant hostel she was forced to barricade her dormitory doors to fend off male immigrants who wanted to meet the new

FIFTY FRÄULEINS ARRIVE (WITH AN EYE FOR A MAN)

FIFTY German girls hoping for husbands reached Melbourne in the liner Castel Felice, last night.

They were the first to answer the appeal made by Australia's Minister for Immigration, Mr Downer, during a recent tour of Germany.

He urged more single girls to join the flow of German migrants in order to provide wives for migrant men already here.

Altogether 1300 German migrants were in the Castel Felice when she berthed last night.

And here are four of the girls with orange blossom hopes:

BEATE HIRSCH, 23, a typist from Munchen Gladbach — she will live in Melbourne.

ILSA KRUSPE, 24, a seamstress from Nuremburg — will stay in Melbourne.

MIGNON MERLE, 21, a ballet dancer from Berlin — will also settle in Melbourne.

A newspaper article showing Beate Hirsch as one of 'Fifty' Fräuleins'.

girls. Bellowing in broken English they broke the windows, pounded on the doors and hosed inside with fire extinguishers. Beate quickly looked for a way out of the hostel.

She found work the day after this incident, though it was more a matter of necessity than convenience. A trained secretary with accounting skills, her English wasn't good enough to gain employment in that field, so she took work as a housekeeper in a Polish-speaking household. 'I had no real freedom; I had to be on call twenty-four hours a day. My employer's male visitors were rude and impolite. I had to put up with a lot of awful things there – sexual propositions and touching.'

Soon a letter arrived from a man who had seen the picture of young Beate taken on the ship. 'He made a brief note in English: would I be interested in meeting him because he had seen my picture. I thought about it for a time then decided to try it.' She made a phone call and ended up talking to a man with a 'kind of Canadian accent' called Eric. She set up a meeting, with her girlfriend from the ship acting as a chaperone.

Eric was, according to Beate, a very sophisticated sort of chap for he knew how to talk, how to behave, how to treat a woman. 'And of course, being me, naive and trusting, I fell for him.' Months later, they embarked on an outback holiday and, there, the embassy in Bonn's promise was fulfilled. 'We had plenty of hot weather and sunshine. We swam and fished in streams near our little camp. We saw some of the Aboriginal wall paintings in the rocks.'

Surrounded by the culture of the oldest Australians, this New Australian found she had fallen in love with this land – and with

Beate Hirsch, 1959.

Eric. 'It was a wonderful time. We explored all sorts of things and of course love came into it as well. Oh, everything was fine. It was absolutely gorgeous. He proposed to me, we were going to get married in June. We even talked about how many children we were going to have.' And Beate Hirsch smiles her faint, soft, sweet smile.

There must have been something in the air, for marriage was on the mind of Ron Palmer in the 1950s, too. Well, in a manner. 'I had a lot of things on my mind. Always do!' he says with a grin.

I ask him how long he's been married. 'Now there,' he intones solemnly, 'is a very important question. I'll have to consult the brains of the organisation – but she's not home at the moment!' And he laughs.

'You mean to tell me you don't know how long you've been married, Ron?'

He thinks for a bit and comes up with, 'Well, it's more than fifty years.' He thinks for a bit more, then lets out a loud 'Aha!' and proclaims, 'It was after the Bullies had won the flag, and after the Split in 1955 and after the Olympics, so let's say the late fifties, fifty-nine, nineteen-hundred-and-fifty-nine!' Then he laughs. 'Or maybe fifty-eight. But we've been together a long time!'

'How did you and Marjorie meet, Ron?' I ask.

'Now, there you are!' and he launches into his tale. 'Met playing cricket.'

'Cricket?'

'Oh yes. Met playing cricket out there,' and he points towards the Mervyn G. Hughes Oval, which his home overlooks. A broad expanse of green that leads down to the Maribyrnong River, and Flemington Racecourse beyond. The ground, of course, wasn't called the Mervyn G. Hughes Oval back in the fifties when he played there in the Churches Comp.

'The Churches Comp?'

'Very strong competition,' he says, and nods. 'We were playing against the Hyde Street Methodists and there were these girls scoring.'

'Who did you play for?'

'The Bappos, the Baptists. I opened for the Bappos.'

'Are you a Baptist, Ron?' I ask, thinking I might've finally found out his religion.

'I just played for the Baptists, didn't mean I was a Baptist. They were after the best team so that's why I was opening the batting. Now don't interrupt, let a man finish.'

I can't help myself, I ask Ron if the Methodists were a good team. He allows himself to be sidetracked.

'Oh yeah, oh yeah, not as tough as the Salvos, but up there. The Salvos were hard as . . .' Then he gets back on track. 'But forget the Salvos.'

'Okay.'

'Now, I was going with a model at the time.'

'A model?'

'Isn't hard to do, brother. And I was sitting there and some of the boys were belly-aching about having no girls to go out with, how hard it was to meet a girl. So I got jack of this and I said, "I'll show you how it's done." I went over to these two girls who were scoring for the Methos and I said to the pretty one – well, they were both good-looking – but I talked to the girl who was pretty lively, a good-looking sort, and I said, "Hello, g'day there, I'm the opening bat for the Bappos and there's a dance, a ball down at the Maison de Luxe in St Kilda. Would you like to come down to this ball with me and have a dance?"'

'And?'

'And she said yes. I went back to the boys and said, "There you go, that's how you do it!"'

'And the rest is history?'

'It certainly is. The model was history! She just went on her way and, you know, there was Marjorie. Yes, she was the one.'

In the annals of romantic language I doubt whether a sweeter or more enticing opening to a romance has ever been uttered. 'Hello, g'day there, I'm the opening bat for the Bappos.' Eat your heart out, Romeo; Juliet may be your stars and you her moon but Ron was the opening bat for the Bappos and Marjorie was a pretty lively scorer for the Methos.

I think for a bit, then come to the realisation that if Ron, as opening bat for the Bappos, had time to approach the scorers for a chat then he must have got out quite early, perhaps relatively cheaply. So I ask Ron how many runs he got that day.

He stares at me for a few moments before launching into his answer. 'Oh right, you ask a man a question like that. Haven't a clue. Couldn't care. Got the world's most beautiful girl. True romance . . .' Ron smiles and it's obvious he can't help himself. 'But whatever I got, I'm sure it was with a bit of style!'

A bit of style. It's easy to imagine the start of this romance because Ron Palmer was so absolutely of that time. It's so easy to see him on the banks of the Maribyrnong in the 1950s with his lanky charm and knockabout nature. Completely at home.

But for people like Rae and Graham Stevens, the 1950s didn't have as much of a rosy glow as many may like to think. 'I always thought the fifties were rather grim, really did,' says Rae.

'There was stacks of work around,' says Graham, joining in, 'but the money wasn't very high.'

'There wasn't much money, and women got very low pay,' Rae adds. So for housewives like Rae there was little incentive to find work outside the family home. 'And in a lot of advertising you'd see the women standing with their little aprons on. You were supposed to be all nice and clean when your husband came home and the house spotless.'

Graham nods slightly and stares off into the distance.

If certain aspects were grim for people like Graham and Rae, then for couples like Tony and Marta Bárány, learning about their new home and how different they were from other Australian couples brought them closer together – to each other and to their original cultural community. They were New Australians, and when she uses the term Marta makes quote marks in the air with her fingers.

'So the Australians didn't know quite how to treat us New Australians – they didn't know what kind of people we were. We worked in a factory. We worked with very nice people, but we had nothing in common with them, they were mainly working-class Aussies –'

Tony interrupts, 'They were more nasty than nice.'

'Well that, too, sometimes,' Marta allows him. 'Okay, yes. So these people were of a different class – you know, we had nothing in common. The Australian middle-class people, they didn't want us.'

It's a revealing progression through the past of these Australians, for although they were displaced persons Tony Bárány had dreams of being a pilot and had attended an elite academy as a young man. Marta was the daughter of a senior bureaucrat in the Hungarian Treasury. Yet they found work in factories, trying to plan a new life in a society that, as Graham Stevens noted, had plenty of work, but it was low paying work.

Marta and Tony. Marta is dressed in a traditional Hungarian costume.

'It must have been an uphill battle to integrate into the Australian society. What did you do?'

Marta answers. 'What you did was, you forged friendships in the Hungarian community and you built the Hungarian community around you.'

Perhaps when you are in love and life is an adventure, a lack of a 'home' community doesn't really matter, but for Beate Hirsch, her 'gorgeous time' with her boyfriend Eric was coming to an end. By this time she had a job in a fashion boutique and had noticed that

Eric's visits were becoming less regular. 'In the meantime I found that I wasn't well. And,' she pauses for a brief moment, staring with her brown eyes, then takes a breath and carries on, 'I went to see a doctor and my suspicions were confirmed. I was pregnant with Eric's baby.'

When she told Eric the news he made it completely clear that he wanted nothing to do with her or the pregnancy. He suggested, in Beate's words, 'all sorts of things' including arranging an abortion, or him taking the baby and organising adoption. 'And then when nothing worked he came up with this story about how when he was sixteen he was imprisoned by the Nazis in a concentration camp at the Czechoslovakian border and that they carried out experiments on him and he was not supposed to have children or get married. He told me that my baby would be deformed or stillborn. All because of these experiments. Everything went sour. He went away and refused to see me anymore.'

It doesn't say much for Eric's sense of responsibility, but he knew he was playing with a loaded hand. Beate was young, pregnant and unmarried. Let her deal with it. He disappeared.

For single women like Beate there was almost no help from the government. So many gave up their babies for adoption or had illegal terminations – the second-highest cause of death for young women in the 1960s.

In desperation, alone, in a society she had not yet come to understand, Beate decided on a drastic solution. 'I thought I'd end it all. I was living in a small bungalow with an outdoor kitchen that had a little gas stove.'

Fortunately, or unfortunately in Beate's opinion, her landlord found her and called the ambulance. She was taken to hospital and survived, waking there to an overwhelming feeling of guilt and shame. 'It never left me. I had no way out because my two years weren't up and my mother wouldn't have accepted me home anyway.'

Beate was now eight months' pregnant and for all intents and purposes alone. Well perhaps not. 'It was a disaster in those times to have a child out of wedlock. I had nobody to go to. But I found the Australian people were absolutely marvellous. I really got a lot of sympathy, a lot of help you wouldn't have found in Germany. I would have been a real outcast there. My employer at the time kept me working as long as I could.'

Despite all the compassion and kindness, in Beate's mind there was no other option than to welcome the first man who showed any interest in trying to help her. 'I'd gone to the beach because I was sad and lonesome and a man started talking to me. We got friendly and saw each other occasionally. After a while he told me he wanted to marry me even knowing the full circumstances, but I didn't want to get married.'

Peter, this man she had met, wouldn't leave the matter alone, and when Beate fell ill at eight and a half months he said to her, 'Well, you have me to get married to, I'll look after you.'

Even though Beate had no feelings for Peter, his kindness and sympathy helped her. 'I didn't want to get married just for those reasons. But when you're sick, you have no income, you don't know where to go, where to turn, there's nobody else to help you, of course you think in different ways.'

And so in September 1960, Beate and Peter were married. A month later, after a difficult and painful birth, Beate's first son was born.

At the dawn of this new decade she was married, living in a society that was becoming less grim, more affluent and bounding with enthusiasm about a future that would bring so many social and technological advances.

13

Smile, It's the Sixties

In 1961 the contraceptive pill changed sex forever. The chances of Beate's fate befalling women who had the ability to control their reproductive cycle were fading. The traditions of marriage were as strong as ever, but the fact that sex could be fun and relatively risk free in terms of unwanted pregnancy began to change the face of romance.

'Well,' says Ron Palmer, 'you know, you didn't want to run around completely fancy free if you weren't married. The girls got it much tougher than the fellas, that's for sure, but there was this idea about that marriage was the starting line for the whole shebang, so to speak. You know what I mean?'

'Yes, Ron,' I say.

'Yes, well, when the Pill came about it was the sign that the starter's mark was a variable thing. Like you'd have a handicapper onboard. The idea was, you didn't have to wait for marriage for a bit of fun. I think it went both ways, but you know what blokes can be like, all care and no responsibility.'

This was the beginning of what some would call the sexual revolution. And Susan Magarey from pleasant and traditional Adelaide was about to meet that revolution head-on.

Susan's background was extremely conservative: her father was a surgeon and both he and her mother came from the Adelaide establishment. This meant, in Susan's words, 'a specific gender conservatism'. She wasn't expected to go to university, but to a finishing school – not in Switzerland, though, in Melbourne.

She was supposed to get married, which was thwarted by the fact that she gained good enough results in public exams to win a university scholarship. 'This was proof, it seemed, that I was sufficiently serious about continuing to be a student, a high-achieving student.'

A woman of keen wit and intelligence, Susan had been expected to follow a set path to the altar and motherhood, although she thought it was possible to combine a career and her traditional 'duties'. 'Having a family was definitely on the agenda, ultimately. This is what we'd been brought up to believe would mean fulfilment. Would we dream of the possibility of a career as well? At that stage I was heading towards being a schoolteacher. I thought I could possibly be a teacher and a wife and a mother.'

It was at university that Susan Magarey began to spread her wings. She laughs about a particular boyfriend determinedly unhooking her boned bra so he could gain access to her bosom. The boned bra was an article of women's apparel that hooks from your waist to your top and needed the skills of a safebreaker and locksmith combined with the patience of a monk to achieve the desired goal.

'I had a lovely time. My first year at university, I suppose it was my form of rebellion, the dating, but it stayed fairly constrained.'

Susan met her future husband via the campus social life and to her it was another step in embracing a wider world. People were beginning to look outside their own social network of family and friends to find love and a life partner. 'We met because we were both film buffs. We ran the film society. It was a revelation. Seeing the new wave of British films, and European and French films – a world that was just so much bigger and stranger and more exotic than anything we were going to experience in Adelaide.'

This 'exoticism' was part of her attraction to her future husband. 'My husband was English and therefore also represented a part of the wider world. It was part of the appeal that he came from somewhere else.'

Australia must have been a very small country back then.

Susan was charmed and intrigued by him being so different from the boys she was supposed to be drawn to. 'I think slowly I began to love him and there was certainly, eventually, sex. We were both pretty careful about that for quite a long time. I think we were both shy.'

Unlike Beate Hirsch, Susan and her husband took precautions. Even though they were still relatively naive, neither of them wanted a pregnancy at that time in their relationship. When they finally decided to have sex they had to go to the chemist to buy a packet of condoms, which they found deeply embarrassing. 'Remember, this was the sixties, when such a thing was seen as being licentious, not a sign of being sensible and safe.'

Adelaide and the rest of Australia were changing but many things remained the same. A prospective son-in-law was expected to ask the permission of his prospective father-in-law for the hand of his daughter.

'I decided we had to take Dad out to dinner,' says Susan. Her fiancé was old-fashioned enough to take this on so they planned a trip to one of Adelaide's fashionable new restaurants. There was, however, a large amount of fashionable noise and music.

Susan Magarey, 1965.

'I can't hear anything, you'll have to come back and have some coffee,' her father growled, as fathers do when they know something is in the wind.

So over a cup of instant Nescafé, the prospective son-in-law was grilled with all those 'Victorian-style' questions about his ability to keep his daughter 'in the style to which she was accustomed'.

Susan Magarey laughs at the memory of her future husband's face. 'There I was, living in a surgeon's house, and here is this poor bloke, just finishing his Master's thesis, with no prospect of a job. Anyway it worked out all right.'

It worked out all right enough for a conservative and very traditional wedding. 'It was a big party,' says Susan. 'And in spite of the fact I wasn't a virgin I wore a white dress down to the ground, very pretty, made by my mother's dressmaker.' They married in St Peter's Cathedral, then went back to Susan's parents' place, where they'd had a marquee put up on the tennis court, and wined and dined about a hundred people. 'My uncles got red in the face and sang. It was all good fun.'

The fact that she had engaged in premarital sex wasn't a huge concern for Susan, but there was a certain formality she had to play along with. The newlyweds honeymooned in a beach house owned

Susan's wedding day, with her parents.

by her parents and it was here they were supposed to consummate their marriage, in her parents' double bed.

'I had been told about the showing of the sheets in Mediterranean countries so I thought I'd better not leave the sheets on the bed. The only way to wash them in this beach house was to boil them up in the old copper. So I boiled up the sheets so both my parents could maintain the belief that I'd been deflowered that night.'

In this case, marriage can be seen as a way of maintaining social niceties and politeness as much as a coming together of two lives, two hearts. This wasn't lost on Susan Magarey. 'Marriage was about being . . .' She searches for a description that eludes her for a moment. 'Keeping yourself nice,' she settles on.

'We didn't use words like this but I think that's what it amounted to. No – you didn't screw before marriage.'

At the same time that Susan was supposed to be keeping herself nice, Beate Hirsch was discovering that her married life was anything but nice. 'My husband,' she sighs, 'my husband Peter had secrets of his own which he never told me. He was, oh how can I say this? He was a person who had problems in the sexual department. And he was very forceful and the whole situation got out of hand a number of times.

'I tried hard to keep the marriage going, tried to stay, because I had a boy now. He did marry me and I thought I should hang in there. But it came to a situation in which he was very forceful and as a result I got pregnant again, through this forceful incident.'

She says it so simply and gently, in such a matter-of-fact way, that it takes a while for the depth of what she means to sink in. Marriage was meant to provide security and safety. Instead it was violence and abuse and a complex idea of commitment. The idea of rape in marriage found no traction at a time in this country when a wife was seen as an extension of the family, not the head of it – that was the male's role.

After investigations carried out by a lawyer on her behalf it was revealed that Beate's husband had a previous conviction of indecent assault on an eleven-year-old boy and had undergone two years of psychiatric treatment.

Fearing for her son's safety as well as her own, Beate sought refuge with her husband's uncle, only to find out that her husband had been re-admitted to hospital for more treatment and would be released to her after this period. 'It was made clear that he should have his family surrounding him, rather than go anywhere else. So I thought, Well, I've got two children now, he might as well come back home again.'

So Beate's role was to remain in an unsatisfactory, unsafe marriage because society expected it – she must support her husband. She didn't know how to apply for welfare or government support and

Beate Hirsch with her first son in 1961.

this problem became more acute when she found that her first son had a developmental disability.

Eventually, however, the idea of 'keeping yourself nice' stopped concerning her. After more threatening behaviour she separated from her husband. For women who didn't want to stay in their marriages, there was still little choice; divorce was expensive and only granted when one of the partners was found to be at fault.

Beate's situation was further complicated by the nature of her husband's mental illness. 'My husband threatened that if I ever went out with another man, or had contact with another man, he would kill me,' she says. 'He made all sorts of threats when we parted. He would never leave me alone and said other things to upset me.'

Trying to hold down several jobs and provide for her children became a stretch. 'To get welfare you had certain excuses, solicitors advised certain legal phrases to use. For a few months, I tried to get help, applying to a lot of different government departments – to get some assistance for my first boy, either have him looked after or some medical care or some finances to get him the appropriate care. One department suggested I put him in an institution, but I thought a mother's love could handle anything.'

Doctors convinced Beate that her boy needed special care, and an education. Her voice trembles and she speaks with a repetitive cadence. 'The first place he was admitted to was an orphanage, where he got sick with measles which developed into double pneumonia. He ended up in hospital – I nearly lost him.'

A mother's love can handle anything, she had thought. Life as a New Australian had thrown her a few hurdles, but somehow she managed to struggle along. Three years later, she instigated proceedings against her husband for a divorce on the grounds of his behaviour, but he counter-sued the action on the grounds of *her* adultery.

While recuperating from what virtually amounted to a nervous breakdown, Beate had become friendly with another man. She says the friendship was never sexually consummated but it gave an avenue for Peter to proceed with his own course of action.

'He had employed these investigators, two big burly guys to find me out, and of course it went to court. To save costs, money I didn't have, I agreed to the adultery charges. I had no way of ever putting my accusations before the court, of what he had done, how my second child came about.'

Freed from her marriage, Beate decided to aim for what was considered to be the Australian dream, to own her own home. But to some, a single mother, a divorced woman to boot, with two children, one disabled, wasn't a safe bet. She had saved up all the money she could to buy a house she had found and needed a bank loan. 'I went from bank to bank, institution to institution, trying to get a loan, but nobody at that time wanted to give a single woman, let alone someone like me, the money to buy that house. Females just weren't counted in.'

Beate Hirsch, however, wasn't going to let it lie. 'I was fighting for our survival. I went to the last bank – all the others had treated me like a second-class citizen – and finally the manager said, "Here's your application, you can have your loan." And thanks to them I seemed to be the first single woman or single mother who ever got a loan for a house.'

Though she had managed to wrestle the system for a certain amount of independence, she felt compelled by other responsibilities, other than her heart, to enter into marriage again. She tries to explain why she married her friend Frank, who promised to protect her from the looming threat of her ex-husband Peter and to help with raising her children.

'Well, if you marry for one child and it doesn't work out, and you do it again for two children, that's what I call foolhardiness, the wrong reason. To me, marriage should mean love and companionship and a partnership, in which one cares for the other. You don't go and get married because you want safety for your children. But my children were my life and that was all I could think of – the children would have a man figure in the family so in the end reluctantly I said yes.'

As Beate Hirsch embarked upon another marriage, Susan Magarey's was coming apart. She, like Beate, was finding that in many cases a woman became an extension of her husband.

Marriage for women in the sixties meant losing all the benefits that came with their work. 'Well,' says Susan, 'I had thought I would go on teaching, but as a married woman in the mid to late sixties I immediately lost all the tenure and holiday pay, sick leave and so on. Everything I would have been entitled to had I remained single.'

But in the end it didn't matter too much because her husband got a job at the Australian National University in Canberra and, says Susan incredulously, 'I said to myself, now that I am married my husband must be my priority, so I will not take a teaching job again.' She then adds archly, 'So I got a job in the bureaucracy instead, which meant I had all that time to pay attention to him.'

Susan took up further study in the ACT and it was during this period that she met the new movements that were quickly growing around the country. 'It was 1967, and I came across the growing counterculture – the youth movement and of course the anti-war movement.'

In time, as their the interests and beliefs changed, Susan and her husband went their separate ways. 'He wasn't terribly interested in any of those things so from that point on our paths began to move slightly apart. I was trying to be a good wife – doing the cleaning, washing and shopping. Then I'd go out to parties and he'd stay home and watch television.'

Around this time, the counterculture movement was looking for freedoms in all areas of Australian life, especially in sexual relationships. New censorship laws meant films and television were awash with boobs and bums. It seemed everyone who engaged in the counterculture was talking about or having sex.

As for people such as Susan's husband, he could stay at home and watch it on television while his wife engaged with the world. 'I had flirtations and more than a couple of one-night stands, which I found extremely unsatisfactory. Even though the Pill, of course, made one believe everything was safe. I didn't enjoy these experiences because I felt guilty – I was cheating on my husband. I was quite relieved when I realised that sexual liberation was just another excuse for blokes to pressure women into coming across.'

So, as Ron Palmer had put it, you didn't have to wait until marriage anymore for the whole shebang, and it was all care and no responsibility for the lads. Sex now stood outside the confines of marriage as a celebration of independence and rebellion, a political act as well as a biological one.

For Susan, it was not simply a sexual revolution, but also a revolution of ideas. 'What was changing for me were the ideas, the politics. The sense of belonging to something bigger, something outrageous. Making better sense of the world than I had before that.'

She wasn't alone. The radicalism of the student campuses in the late sixties was exemplified by the opposition to the Vietnam War, and it followed that many student and like-minded Australians began to question all forms of political power and institutions, including marriage.

The photographs from the marriage of Sue Sheridan and her husband show a young couple smiling together, she laughingly down at the cake they are cutting and he, with his black, horn-rimmed glasses and hair neatly parted, beams happily.

They look like a poster couple for 'What to Wear at Your Wedding', but in reality theirs was a union that was anything but traditional. 'We decided,' says Sue Sheridan carefully, 'that ours wasn't going to be a conventional marriage; eventually we lived

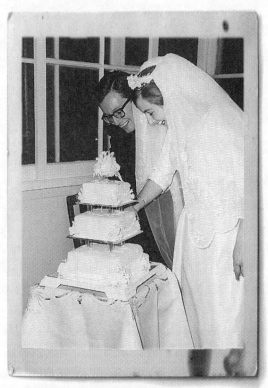

Sue Sheridan's wedding day, 1965.

in a mixed collective household for some four years before we decided to call it quits. After that I didn't want to have anything like marriage again.'

It was around 1970 that I went with my mother for a walk down to Suttons Beach in Redcliffe to get fish and chips for a Sunday night dinner. I wouldn't have been anything more than six and as we waited for our order to be cooked, we stepped outside the fish shop and looked at the gardens of Sutton House, which stood next door.

Sutton House was a reception centre I considered very grand, and in the darkening evening it was, I suppose. Its white walls were gleaming from the garden lights, with a palm tree and eucalypts draping the wide verandahs. In the daytime it was a large and rambling fibro palace. Tonight it was hosting a wedding.

The bride and groom looked not unlike Sue Sheridan and her husband from the photographs. Posing for their own wedding photos next to a Holden Brougham sedan, their wedding car, they were having a bit of trouble with the veil, which kept floating back over the face of the bride in the sea breeze. It looked a little like the beekeeper's hat that the old man in Duffield Road would wear when he tended his beehives.

Suddenly a little black-suited figure ran up to where we stood and called my name. It was my friend Malcolm Parish and after I had said hello and asked him why he was at Sutton House, he told me that he was a pageboy for his cousin's wedding.

He ran back to do what tiny pageboys do at their cousin's wedding and I turned to my mother and asked why he was dressed like Dean Martin. That is, what Dean Martin wore on all his record covers in my mother's collection. She explained that was what people wore at weddings and that it was a very important night and you must look smart and dress like Dean Martin.

I asked my mother if I would wear a Dean Martin suit when I got married and she said yes. Then I asked her if my sisters would wear the white dress with the beekeeper's gauze when they got married. 'They will if they ever get married but who's to know – if they keep reading that book by the woman with the big jaw.'

The woman with the big jaw was Germaine Greer and her book was *The Female Eunuch*. As women's liberation emerged as a powerful international movement in the late sixties and early seventies, Australian women were at the forefront of demanding changes to their public and private lives.

My father said Germaine Greer was good because she put Australia on the map. 'She's a bit like Margaret Court, only she writes. And thinks.'

'She's nothing like Margaret Court. Margaret Court is married and has kids,' said my mother. 'And I'm sure she thinks,' she added.

'Well, yes,' said my father, 'but old Germaine thinks a bit . . . harder.'

'Yes, she certainly does.'

Greer's book renounced the idea that women could only find fulfilment through childbearing. There is footage of her being interviewed for TV, leaning against a brick wall, conjuring up an idea of inner-city intelligentsia. Greer stares down at the interviewer and in an almost bored and preoccupied manner explains a few home truths to the journalist.

'I think what men mistake for happiness is in fact resignation and patience and now women are beginning to feel that patience isn't the answer.'

I remember at primary school doing a picture project on Australia and saw that a smart girl in my class had used a photo of a beauty queen with the label 'Miss Australia' and next to that she had pasted a sheep and a cow, with appropriate labels added.

I followed suit, putting a photo of a sheep and a cow in my project but I couldn't find any beauty queens. Instead I pasted a photo of a fierce-looking Germaine Greer from a *Life* magazine and called her Miss Australia. The teacher, who wore a purple rinse through her hair, just stared at me, and the smart girl giggled.

I always thought Germaine was all right and I wasn't the only one, for what she wrote struck a chord. For Susan Magarey and like-minded women there was joy and a sense of fun in what they now pursued. 'There was this absolutely wonderful exhilaration about breaking all the rules. It was immensely exciting being a part of the redressing of those gender roles, of changing,' she says.

Street demonstrators carried placards with slogans such as, 'The State Does Not Own My Womb' and 'Abortion on Demand' and 'If Men Got Pregnant Abortion Would Be a Sacrament'.

Women demanded equal rights in work and domestic relationships, and financial support for single mothers. While not everyone agreed with women's libbers, or 'bra burners' as my Aunty Rita called them, they were an irresistible force that swept through Australia in the early seventies, changing how the Australian Heart followed its dreams.

14

It's About Time

The Whitlam Labor government has become almost mythic in its perceived impact upon Australian society. It all depends on who you talk to; opinion is divided on the pros and cons of those turbulent three years under the leadership of Gough Whitlam.

There's the glow of Whitlam's aura of high intelligence and reformist zeal mixed with an economic naivety and a management illiteracy that twenty years in opposition breeds. And while it's true that certain Australians can go all misty-eyed at the mention of the great man's name, a little bit of reality doesn't go astray.

Lots of people like to bang on about the 'It's Time' campaign of 1972 as the beginning of some utopian Australia, but they forget the images of a somewhat awkward Gough Whitlam and a gyrating Bob Hawke – who else? – applauding as they are surrounded by high-kicking, high-heeled, black-stockinged dancing girls smiling and strutting their stuff for Gough and the Labor Party.

What is fact is that the Whitlam government did enact an incredible amount of social reform, including single mother welfare payments and legislation such as the 1975 *Family Law Act*, which allowed either spouse to call off a marriage simply and inexpensively. In the wider community, marriage was no longer seen as being for life. The divorce rate soared.

Beate Hirsch was one woman who took advantage of the liberal new laws. She'd married against her better judgement for the sake of her children. At first life went well. Beate gave in to her husband's wish to have his own child, a boy, who was also born with complications. However, her husband started favouring his own son, and rejected Beate's two boys. Many arguments and separations followed and eventually her husband left her for good.

Beate Hirsch.

Struggling on with her three boys, Beate moved to Queensland to begin a new life. In her own words, she says, 'Ever since I moved to Queensland I have made a new beginning. I found a sheltered workshop for my disabled son, and at last I could have him with me. He's been in so many institutions, which didn't do him any good, but now I can look after him myself. I have learned a lot, the hard way, and I'm not the naive young woman I was when I first came to Australia.'

There is resignation in her voice. 'I have learned a lot. I found that I'm not suitable for marriage or a lasting relationship. I'm too trusting and people take advantage of me. I always wanted somebody to belong to, who would love me a little, but I don't wish for that anymore. But look for a new man? No, definitely not.'

A door closed for Beate Hirsch, but her love for her children has opened others. 'I've always had the children in the background, but I am there for them now. My life is totally devoted to my disabled boy. He's got nowhere to go and I'm there for him. I'm his carer as well as his mother. And we do things together. That's my life.'

There is a pause and she adds a phrase that echoes a dignity and strength in all she has endured. The young woman who entered the Australian embassy in Bonn wanting to see the world and learn about as many people as she could has travelled all over Europe, but she says she chose the best country to make her home. She has seen much, and accepted all that life has given. The lies and uncertainty. The doubts and struggles. Her brown eyes stare ahead with a level gaze that shows she wants to make one thing perfectly clear.

'But I don't regret it.'

A mother's love, after all, can handle anything.

Australia is a work in progress and, like every society, trends and fashions can change quickly with the passing of each generation. In the mid seventies, while many women were demanding equality in affairs of the heart and mind, other Australians were beginning to demonstrate for their rights to follow their hearts.

It's one thing to talk to people and listen to their descriptions of how life has changed through the years, it is another to step back and note the changes that have taken place in your own lifetime. That's when you recognise the extent of the evolving nature of a moderate and relatively open society such as ours.

I can remember my father marching in from the garden one Sunday afternoon in late 1979 as I watched the ABC music show *Countdown*.

'That's the song about the navy,' he said approvingly as he walked through the double doors. 'It's a bloody good song, better than that punk rubbish.'

My father was, as the saying goes, a returned man, and approved of a pop song extolling the benefits of a life in the military, even if the force celebrated happened to be the navy. And the American one at that.

He stood in front of the television and gazed a while at the group performing the song, the Village People.

'Jesus Christ.' That was all he could say. He watched the Village People gyrate their way round a bare-looking warship anchored in San Francisco Bay. My brother and I giggled.

'Jesus Christ,' my father repeated. 'Look at what they're bloody wearing. I might have known.' He felt ripped off, we could tell, that a gay group had sucked him in.

'At least bloody Oscar Wilde dressed properly when they locked him up,' he muttered. He then clapped his hands and said, 'Well, it's a free country, good luck to them.' With that he disappeared back out into the depths of the Queensland subtropical garden to wrestle with banana trees and rubber plants and occasionally mutter to himself, 'Bloody navy, bloody yanks.'

Homosexuality, and the right to express it openly, led to marches and demonstrations in the streets of Sydney, with protesters often clashing with police, and little wonder, for it is easy to forget that in 1978 homosexuality was illegal in some Australian states.

And even though it would take many years before it became illegal to discriminate against someone on the basis of their sexuality or living in a same-sex relationship, an opening up of Australian society allowed gay people to follow their hearts more openly than in previous generations.

Yianni Zinonos is a first-generation Australian from a Greek immigrant family who made their home in Sydney's eastern suburbs.

Yianni Zinonos (left), aged fourteen, with his family.

His parents ran a milk bar in Randwick, next door to the old Odeon Picture Theatre, and growing up he saw all the latest movies for free, although he enjoyed his parents' milkshakes much more than the famed ones of the Odeon. 'My parents made really good milkshakes,' he says rather proudly. He also recalls a certain film. 'I remember watching Barbra Streisand and Ryan O'Neal in *What's Up, Doc?*, and from the very beginning, after seeing Ryan O'Neal, I wished I was Barbra.'

That must have told somebody something. Yianni went on enjoying the beachside atmosphere of the eastern suburbs and he had an enjoyable childhood. And of course there were the milkshakes.

'Where I lived was a great mix, culturally; there were boys and girls and lots of Greeks and lots of Aussies and then, later, there was the Asian influx, so it was multicultural.'

Even though he was labelled by his ethnicity he was never made to feel an outsider. 'I've always been proud to be an ethnic. So that's fine. There were too many Greeks to be outnumbered. And it was really good maintaining the culture.'

He was thriving in a community that excited and embraced him, and he immersed himself in both his parents' professions. 'Skill-wise, my mother was a dressmaker and my father a chef, so in a way I'm an incarnation of both of them professionally – I had a cooking show on television and was also a fashion designer.'

Such an all-embracing upbringing brought with it an expectation. Yianni's parents thought he would be a good Greek boy and get married and have kids; that was the path he was expected to follow. But his heart led him in a different direction.

'I was hanging out with this girl called Jenny who had some gay friends, and she was always on my back, saying I was gay.' She based this theory on the fact that Yianni wouldn't make a move on her.

Yianni enjoys recounting her defining argument. 'She said, "You won't put your hand up my legs!" and I'm like, "Whoaa!"' and he holds up both hands in protest and perhaps delight at the salaciousness of it all.

He admits he wasn't sure. He knew he enjoyed checking guys out, and had begun to realise that although he was interested in girls he felt himself veering towards 'the guys'.

After a date that didn't work out, Jenny was at her wits' end so decided to prove herself correct by dropping Yianni at the Midnight Shift nightclub on Oxford Street, the epicentre of Sydney's gay culture. If he was going to find out what he wanted, then it was a fair bet that he would find it there.

'Walking up that staircase to get into that club was the longest, hardest – it was like walking up Mount Everest.' He carried the expectations of his parents and family on his back, but something within Yianni forced him on.

'I knew I had to do it and I did. I walked in there and found this whole new world, a new community. I was incredibly nervous.'

A realisation struck Yianni – that he had found a common land. 'There were other people like me – maybe who were just as nervous? I still go to the Midnight Shift. Twenty-five years later and I'm still going there.'

That night Yianni met someone he thought was 'really nice', who worked in the same suburb Yianni lived in. They started dating. Yianni may have found his handsome prince, but it took some time before he could tell his parents.

Despairing of not confiding in them, and playing a role he believed was only meant to satisfy their expectations, he felt he was 'living a lie'. So he 'sort of came out'. This led to confrontations.

'The screaming and the shouting and the hissy-fits – it was all about being treated like a child and being made to feel you don't have your own choices and other people know best.' It was at this point that Yianni's upbringing began to encroach upon his understanding of what he was and how he defined himself.

'I think the problem with being Greek Orthodox is that it's a religion living in the Middle Ages; they haven't kept up with the times – so the doctrine just won't change. There is an enormous amount of religious pressure. That becomes a part of the culture.'

While Yianni maintains links to his past, he has become part of a new culture, the gay culture. And he hasn't been alone.

After she completed her studies at university Susan Magarey was coming to terms with the nature of her marriage and her under-standing of what she sought from life. She became heavily involved in women's liberation groups and the women's movement in general, but tried to maintain her marriage.

'I stayed in my marriage and my husband got rather good at cooking spag bol, though he really wasn't going to try to learn anything else and we were obviously not going to have any children. We did go off and build a cement house, though.' She laughs with an appreciation of the irony. 'You've heard the term cement babies? Where people have babies to cement a marriage? Well, we had a cement house.'

It didn't cement anything in the marriage because Susan found there was no longer anything meaningful in the union. 'We'd grown too far apart. I had flings with other people that meant a great deal more than the one-night stands I'd had before, but in the end I left the marriage because we had become so separate and so antagonistic. I'd become a radical left-wing feminist – I was no longer the person he'd married; he'd married a mouse from the suburbs of Adelaide.'

He had also married a mouse from the suburbs who'd had a few 'very closeted' relationships with women before her marriage. It was through following this part of herself that Susan found a lasting and loving union.

At a women's studies conference in 1981 she met up with another academic. A woman by the name of Sue Sheridan. 'It turned out that Sue had been teaching at Adelaide University with a fellow member of staff, who was my uncle and so we were talking about the family connections and,' she pauses and smiles at Sue, 'and I think you should tell the next bit.'

Sue continues the story. 'I knew Susan's uncle and I told her he was really nice and she looks at me and says, "All Magareys are sexy!" So I thought, Right, okay how's that for an invitation!'

Even though both women describe themselves as 'anti-romantic', the following year they became a couple and have been together ever since. By the time Susan Magarey's parents had any inkling of the nature of their domestic and sexual relationship, as Susan explains, 'They already knew how lovely she was and so I think they just engaged in that kind of double-think – which is, We just won't think about that!'

Sue Sheridan can't help herself and jumps in. 'We did catch your father referring to us as "bachelor girls" and we thought, Oh, right, that's how he explains us to himself.'

But Susan, although politically active and committed to the advancement of her cause, demonstrates a peculiarly Australian ability to compromise when it's necessary. 'My parents weren't going to be particularly pleased if I made one of those scenes and said you have to recognise I am a lesbian. Besides, they had accepted Sue, accepted that we lived together and I think my mother was sometimes slightly envious of our independence. They were happy

Susan Magarey and Sue Sheridan in 1985.

for us to join them at Christmas and they were very happy, I think, for me in the end. They were happy I was happier.'

Which is what all parents want for their children.

The couple have been together for twenty-eight years and in a moment of reflection, Sue echoes the thoughts of the lady in the Balnarring op-shop and the elastic nature of time upon matters of the heart. 'When I say twenty-eight years, it's difficult to believe that . . . it's just rushed up, you know!'

Time flies when you're having fun, as the saying goes, and Yianni Zinonos is flying along at breakneck speed. He'd found his tribe and was beginning to embrace the idea of being out and about. Still exploring his sexuality, he travelled to his parents' homeland of Greece, as many first-generation Australians did at that time.

'I feel as Australian as anyone else, but my genetic roots have come from somewhere else and you can't erase that in one generation.' But Yianni, being Yianni, wasn't in Greece just to get in touch with the family roots. He laughs with an infectious glee and joy at the memory of cutting the rug under the Mediterranean sun. 'The island of Mykonos was the Gay Greek Disneyland . . . I was kind of hot, if I can say it. I didn't realise it at the time but you always think you're hot when you look back at the photos . . .'

And what photos they are. Yianni wearing nothing but the grains of sand that snuck past the blue towel he was lying on. Well, he didn't really lie on it; it was more like a series of poses that any young, happy person would strike for their partner.

He smiles a lot in the photos, does Yianni, and it's obvious that fun is what he had on his mind. He giggles. 'I mean, you don't have relationships on holidays, let's be realistic. It was romance. It was liberation, it was partying and enjoyment and also it was a lot of fun because of the lack of responsibility.'

Like so many young Australians, both heterosexual and homosexual, Yianni was engaging in ideas of romance and love that had very little connection to the idea of commitment that Rae and Graham Stevens had forty years before.

There are more photos of Yianni with his eighties mini mullet, his pastel clothes and jumpsuit-type trousers, beaming merrily from kitchens, backyards and parties, and various embraces. 'I was partying and eternally single and eternally egotistical. Out there, a bit social, a bit flighty, a bit sexual. I was in my twenties and it was the era of being independent, that was the big thing, a feeling of really not needing anyone.'

Yianni Zinonos on the beach at Mykonos in 1994.

That pretty much sums up a generation right across the board, romance and love, independent of a single commitment. That was the eighties. The words gay and straight entered the modern vocabulary; sex was at the forefront of recreation, as it never had been before.

But something else spread across the globe that brought the party to a grinding halt. AIDS. At first, acquired immune deficiency syndrome was seen as a gay disease, affecting only homosexuals, but like most assumptions born of prejudice and not commonsense, this proved false all too quickly.

AIDS could affect everybody, gay or straight. And Australia became a world leader in combatting the HIV AIDS virus through a vast public education campaign that sought both to jolt and inform.

If there is one television image that conjures up this time it must be the commercial made in the late eighties of the Grim Reaper. Through a misty bowling alley, a deep, sinister voice-over intones that it was not only gays and IV drug users who would be affected by AIDS, now it could touch all of us.

And the Grim Reaper, complete with a scythe held jauntily over his shoulder, rolled a bowling ball to wipe out a collection of the art director's idea of average, everyday Australians in their eighties fashion mistakes. Pleated trousers, sports shirts and citrus colours. The lone blonde mother cradles her baby to protect it from the approaching ball of death.

You could look at it now and call it corny overkill. I mean, the voice-over guy ended up selling televisions and white goods with the same doom-laden voice, but it worked.

Yianni Zinonos is evidence of this. 'Look, I believe in safe sex, otherwise I wouldn't be alive. I was lucky, I came out as the safe sex message really got out there, so I'm grateful to be around.' He turns away briefly, as if in that moment he is remembering some of his friends who never had that chance to feel grateful.

It was Australia's all-encompassing approach of accepting that its citizens come in many shapes, sizes, colours and sexual choices that was a high point of the campaign, especially as paranoia was also rife in the community.

The examples are almost endless. You could catch AIDS via blood transfusions, sharing sweat on the sporting field, using crockery and drinking glasses from certain pubs and cafés, even going to the dentist – so some believed. Reverend Fred Nile of the Festival of Light, upper house member in the New South Wales Parliament and moral crusader, was outraged that gay people were using a public pool.

The scaremongering about AIDS 'caused a lot of fear and it reinstalled a lot of homophobia in people', remembers Yianni. 'On one hand, we had gay liberation. All of a sudden it wasn't illegal anymore and people were finding themselves. But on the other hand there was the AIDS plague and the homophobia – it was terrible.'

Yianni has a theory that he thinks reflects the ultimately moderate view of Australian society. 'It's called the Mardi Gras effect. You look at our society and even with my family, for example, where there is something so deep in our culture, especially in Sydney, where gay people and the gay community went from being trodden and trampled on and abused and bashed and even murdered and being made to feel illegal – we've gone to the extreme of being celebrated, through the Mardi Gras and all these legal changes. Not only that, but also dramatic changes in attitudes towards gay people.' He pauses and smiles his happy smile, the one you can see in all the photos from his childhood backyard with the Hills hoist in the background, to the beach of Mykonos. 'Now if you're a gay you're pretty much celebrated. You know, every gay person is a bit of a diva in a way.'

That tolerance might not always seem to be there; Australians may well forget it occasionally, but as our society has increased in size and become more affluent, so too has its imagination and acceptance of people's romantic lives. And thank you very much to the gay and women's liberation movements because in their wake straight men decided it was okay to explore their feminine side. A new Sunday newspaper headline and talkback radio term was born: the Sensitive New Age Guy.

Getting in touch with your feminine side was open to all and sundry, if they were interested. It was as simple as allowing men to be more demonstrative of their emotions in public. 'Oh brother,' howls Ron Palmer, 'when Hawkie cried at that press conference about his daughter, I thought, Here comes a gutser here. This is no good. A prime minister bawling like a school kid who's had his lunch pinched, but strike me, people loved it. They thought he cared.' He shakes his head. 'Bugger me, it was strange.'

There was a procession of cross-dressing, gender-bending pop stars and celebrities who weren't shy in flaunting their so-called feminine side for a bit of coin, but the fact was there was a movement out there in the land of men. And we aren't just talking about a novelty night at a football club where for some reason if you didn't put boot-black on your face and mime 'My Boomerang Won't Come Back', you were expected to dress up in drag.

Once when I was researching for a film role, I wandered down to a hotel that held a drag show on a Saturday night. I was expected to play a transsexual in this film and on the advice of the director, who happened to be my wife, I was sent to the pub in the name of research.

There, among the regular punters, were men wearing dresses, wigs, eyelashes and heels. I ordered a beer, sat at the bar and watched. Then I heard a voice that was quite familiar, calling my name.

'Will, Will McInnes, how are you?'

I turned to see a man as big as me, maybe even bigger with the high heels he was wearing, smiling at me through make-up, false eyelashes, over-accentuated lipstick and the smell of perfume wafting around him.

I stared at him, then suddenly recognised him as a fellow I had packed down next to in a rugby scrum for a season or two. 'Jesus Christ,' I said, sounding a little bit too much like my father. 'Chris, how are you?'

He laughed and said, 'I'm good, I'm great, all dressed up for a bit of fun.' My fellow second-rower told me he'd discovered he enjoyed dressing in women's clothes and going out to nights like this not too long after he'd thrown on a dress at a rugby talent night.

We talked a bit over a couple of beers and he said he wished his wife wasn't away on business so she could have come along that night. 'So she could have said hello to you again.'

It turned out he was still married to the girl he had become engaged to when we played rugby together more than twenty years ago. His wife, he said, quite liked coming to these dos.

Then he asked if I came here often. I had to admit I didn't. No, he said, it's a long way over from the other side of town.

'Well,' I said, 'I've never come here before.'

'Your first time?' He smiled.

'My wife told me I should come,' I said, and of all things, I blushed.

He raised a beautifully made-up eyebrow. 'Really, your wife?'

'Mate, it's for work.' I blushed even more and then we both burst out laughing.

We made a date to meet up for another drink at the next Bledisloe Cup match in Melbourne.

Many men, it seems, had these feelings of wanting to get in touch with their feminine side. Peter McCarthy was one. 'I grew up having those sorts of feelings, and wants, maybe, not in a gay sense, but just the feminine side of it.'

Peter had always been attracted to 'feminine' things; he certainly considered cross-dressing so. But he kept this attraction a big secret throughout his life. He was, after all, an everyday, knockabout bloke. He played rugby league.

'Started off in the under-thirteens and when I left school and started work, I joined the army reserve and played football as well. I was in the assault pioneers and we blew stuff up, which was a lot of fun. It's who I am.' As he says this he stands in a red evening dress before a mirror, adding make-up touches to his face. He checks a spot on his cheek, and then brushes it away.

Peter McCarthy in the Army Reserve, 1978.

It was in the army reserve that he met his wife, and as their relationship progressed he decided to make a few adjustments to his life. 'I wanted to throw everything away, the entire cross-dressing stuff. I thought, That's the end of that. It's that part of my life gone, I'm getting married to someone and I'm the happiest man in the world. I don't need that anymore.'

They appear happy in their wedding photos, although in a broad moustache and brown tuxedo Peter looks disconcertingly like Saddam Hussein. But that was the least of his troubles. 'So now I've got a wife with a wardrobe full of stuff and one thing led to another.' He shrugs a little and sighs. It wasn't long before things were noticed and it wasn't a happy time.

Peter still finds it difficult and painful to remember the sadness it caused his wife. 'I didn't want, well, I didn't know how to explain. I wanted to explain it but our communication skills weren't good enough to enable us to sit down and discuss what was happening at that point in our lives.' He smiles sadly and it's pleasing to note that he doesn't look like Saddam anymore.

The couple, with two young daughters, divorced. Peter then discovered the Seahorse Society, a discovery that was to change his life.

At my high school in 1980, during a Citizenship Education lesson – only in Queensland would there be an area of study called Citizenship Education – I learned about the Seahorse Society from a chapter in our textbook about what it meant to be a man. There were giggles and jokes in the class and when I told my parents about it that night over dinner, I didn't get the rise I expected.

'Well, it takes all sorts,' said my mother.

'Yeah, as long as they pay their taxes and behave themselves, who cares what they wear,' said my father, sitting in his T-shirt and Stubbies work shorts. It was another example of the growing breadth of Australian society.

For Peter McCarthy it was a difficult step. 'I was a member for six years before I even went to a meeting. I was very reluctant because it was my little secret. Even with a group like that I still found it difficult to come out and be there. But I did and found there was a whole bunch of people very much like myself.'

He was romantically alone, though. Life went by and his daughters became comfortable with their dad, but he went without a serious relationship for seven years. He still felt uncomfortable about being honest with a woman. 'I didn't want to put anyone through that ever again. I'd come to a certain realisation about myself, that this wasn't going away. At the end of the day, I thought, I'll just be happy with the cross-dressing and get on with it.'

Getting on with it didn't involve a long-term relationship, but life has a habit of not really caring about what people plan. Peter met a woman who had also been single for a while since her own divorce, and as a romance novelist would put it, he fell for her.

The woman he fell for wasn't expecting a relationship either; she was too busy succeeding at her chosen career. Her name was Sandra Ellis.

Sandra was a bride in the mid seventies. 'I got married young and I thought I was in love back then. I found married life wasn't that pleasant, though.' She doesn't elaborate, but she clearly didn't see marriage as the be-all and end-all of her worth as a person. 'I wanted to go to university and my husband found every excuse under the sun as to why I couldn't go.'

So once the couple split she wanted nothing to do with men. 'I was going to be the independent, self-supporting female. I used to hang out with a gay friend when I needed a partner so I wouldn't be picked up or anything.' She smiles and adds, 'I started uni a week after I left my ex-husband and from then on my career has moved on very nicely.'

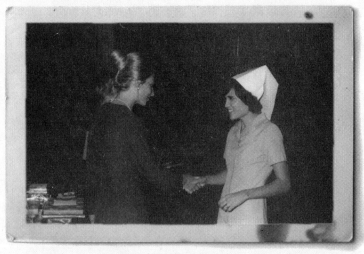

Sandra Ellis at her graduation in 1978.

When she met Peter she changed her mind about men.

Peter thought he was really falling in love, so decided he would tell her about his cross-dressing and if she didn't like it, then the couple would go their separate ways.

It was surprising news to Sandra, as it would be to most people. One day Peter showed her what he was talking about. 'I had a shower,' says Sandra, 'and as I walked out of the bathroom there's this strange woman sitting in the lounge room. I nearly died, thinking, Oh my god, who's this come to visit?'

After she had a little time to come to terms with the 'visitor', she managed to put things in some kind of perspective. 'If anyone's going to have a fault, it could be alcoholism, it could be gambling, it could be violence. I have seen all these things in my life, in other people's lives. Cross-dressing is such a minor one.

Peter and Sandra share a kiss on their wedding day in 2003.

Peter McCarthy dressed as a woman.

'The silly thing is that if I went to someone with one of those other complaints they'd say, "Oh you poor thing." But if I say to someone my husband cross-dresses they look at me and say, "You weirdo."'

Peter and Sandra wouldn't be the first couple to realise that compromise and openness only come with a bit of maturity. 'If we'd met each other earlier, we may not have liked each other. But apart from being a wife, a partner and a lover, Sandra's just a great friend,' says Peter. The couple has been together for nine years and married for five.

Every year the Seahorse Society holds a transgender ball and both Sandra and Peter are enthusiastic attendees. They cluck and fuss over final adjustments as any couple does when they head off for a night out. There is pouting for lipstick and the flicking of hair and the mutual questions 'How do I look?' Then there is a peck on the cheek, out the door they go and on with the night. And their life together.

15

Forever and Ever

Peter and Sandra's marriage, like one-third of all marriages at the turn of the century, was a remarriage. The rate of first-time marriage at the start of the twenty-first century had reached an all-time low. But marriage is still out there in Australian society and it occurs between people who might never have met in the past. More wealth and travel mean demographically odd couples are now falling in love.

Committing to a long-term relationship is becoming increasingly complicated, as Fiona Collins, a city girl with a career in philanthropy, and Stuart Higgins, a cotton farmer from southeast Queensland, found out. They met at an ethics symposium in Melbourne while they were both trying to find their name-tags at the registration desk.

'This rough, tanned, rural hand reached over mine and grabbed the name-tag "Stuart Higgins". I looked up to the face belonging to the hand and there he was,' says Fiona. As they chatted it's a fair bet to say they had forgotten all about ethics and were more interested in each other.

Fiona Collins and Stuart Higgins.

Fiona Collins, though, was not really interested in a long-term relationship, certainly not marriage. Focused on her career, she wasn't keen on leaving her comfortable city life for the cotton country of southeast Queensland. However, there's no stopping a romantic, even a rough, rural one. After six weeks of a long-distance relationship Stuart decided to send her something special to lure her to his side.

Some men would send a sweet letter. Some a bunch of flowers. Others might punt on a bit of jewellery. Still others would try the odd phone call. Not Stuart. He sent a pair of his old work boots.

'I decided to send her something that had been a part of me for the whole time I had been farming. So I put these original work boots in a post pack, along with a love letter, and sent them off to Sydney,' he says proudly.

He was sending her a little bit of his world. The boots were dirty and stinking, and if that was the bit of the world he wanted her to have, Fiona got it. But whether it was the boots, or the first line of his letter, 'Fiona, I'm in love with you', she found it thrilling and terrifying at the same time.

Impressed by the courage, the honesty and the emotion he had expressed, Fiona was attracted enough to engage in a long-distance relationship with Stuart for two years.

Stuart Higgins is a man with a great deal of patience, almost all farmers have it, but even the most patient and stubborn farmers will eventually give up on a crop that doesn't produce a yield. 'Fiona was certainly returning my feelings, but there was this little part that couldn't get tipped over,' he says. 'I made the call and it wasn't going to happen. It wasn't going to tip. So I tipped off. I was an angry man, big time. Angry and confused.'

He cut off all contact with Fiona and spent his time prowling around his cotton farm, refusing to answer any of her calls.

He may have sent her his original work boots when he proclaimed his love for her, but later on Fiona went the whole hog and sent herself. She packed her bags and landed on his doorstep in Queensland. It's a sure bet that she smelled better than the boots.

'I realised Stuart was the person I wanted to spend the rest of my life with and that I had to make sacrifices. It was going to challenge me and push my buttons in all kinds of ways – but I had to have faith that the love would see us through and make it all worth it. It was a massive gamble and I was scared.' Then she smiles.

Stuart proposed. He says now, 'If you'd have said no that would have been it!' They both laugh together. 'I would have walked off and you could have had the farm.'

'Obviously,' says Fiona, 'I said yes.' She loved being a farmer's wife and was falling in love with rural Australia, especially the cotton farm and the surrounding district. But as Stuart had shown before, once his mind is set on a course of action, it's set.

'Stu went away with his dad and had a bit of a boys' weekend. He came back and said he'd decided to sell the farm.'

Fiona is still for a moment; the shock of the news is apparent even now. Stuart Higgins had grown tired of the drought. 'I wasn't surprised, I suppose, but on some level I was shocked and gutted. I think I really wanted to stay,' she says quietly.

But they didn't. Stuart and Fiona Higgins now live in the city with their first child and Fiona dreams that they may one day return to the land. 'I hope that Stu's future path might involve farming again. But wherever it takes us, I'm prepared to go with him.'

These are almost words from another era, but then again, Fiona is bucking the trend. Australians today are marrying less and marrying later, and it's easier than ever to jump ship: forty-three per cent of all marriages in Australia end in divorce.

To some people marriage is an arcane and out-of-date notion enforced upon them by society; to others it is simply the way things are done even if the introduction and courtship are of the twenty-first century.

To Len Masson, marriage was for life, but after nearly forty years together and five grown children, Len's wife left him. The dating game is a bit daunting at the best of times, but try it when you're Len's age and see what happens.

He went to a singles group and to dinners in Wagga Wagga, in country New South Wales, but couldn't find anyone he was attracted to. 'It's very difficult in country towns to find another partner. That's not to say if I'd have been in the city I would have found somebody compatible, but there are certainly more people in the city.'

Len Masson and Ma Sujie on their wedding day.

Ma Sujie and Len Masson, 2005.

He didn't have to try his luck in the big smoke, because he decided, like my friend Mal, from the café in Balnarring, to have a crack at romance on the internet. They are both part of the one million Australians who search the websites of this nation and the world for love.

And for Len, China was his jackpot. He found Sujie by way of an online dating service and packed up his bags to travel to China to meet her. Was it love at first sight?

When she first saw Len, Sujie says he looked skinnier and older than she expected, and she wasn't happy about that. Len attempts to nudge her in the right direction, asking her if she's changed her mind since then. Sujie remains diplomatic and it's nice to know the art of compromise is well and truly alive.

'I have not changed my thinking but the importance is not the outside, it's the heart and the mind.'

That is enough for Len and it's worked so far. He and Sujie are now married and have a three-year-old child. Len couldn't be happier. 'I think the option I followed is wonderful; a fantastic option for the older Australian man to marry such a wonderful wife. Women today in Australia just aren't interested in it anymore,' he says, smiling. Well, he's speaking for himself there, I think.

Women in Australia are interested in lots of things. Robyn Taylor is single, a divorced mother of three, and she's been, by her own admission, falling in and out of love since she was seventeen.

Relationships take a lot of work and sometimes they take a lot of hard work. They can also lend themselves to an ongoing self-assessment. Robyn says, 'When you've got an imbalance in a relationship, like I did with my previous partner, where you put a lot in and get little in return, it's something that affects you. It leaves you with those questions about yourself: Why did this relationship fail? Was it my fault? Was it me?'

Her daughter Katie has witnessed many of Robyn's relationships and her mother's experience has left its mark. Her views are a refrain women have been echoing from generation to generation. 'I want to be successful in my own right and know I got there myself, that I didn't have to rely on a man to get me there. That's a big part of it for me. I don't want somebody who's going to repress me.' She thinks about that for a bit. 'Maybe repress is too strong a word, but I don't want somebody who's going to make me feel I can't do it. Somebody who doesn't support my choices, especially when it comes to something like my career.'

Her mother nods in agreement and as they set out to enjoy a night on the town together, it's Katie's words that underscore the idea of what romance and love and commitment mean. 'I wouldn't mind finding just one person to settle down with, but it doesn't mean I'm going to marry them. These days it's just a big white dress and a bit of paper. Everyone knows if it doesn't work out you can just get a divorce.'

These are words that resonate with Yianni Zinonos. He laughs when he thinks of the efforts he's made to find someone he can be with. His stories make you think he and Len Masson should sit down and have a chat about the success rate of the internet in the course of romance.

'I've had so many internet disasters it's not funny.' And he laughs so much that you know it is very funny. But Yianni is realistic. 'I can't afford to be too fussy nowadays, so I think, Yeah, not bad, and then you meet up with them and it's just a nightmare.'

Those days of the blue towel on the sands of Mykonos, the Gay Greek Disneyland, are long gone, it seems. He shrugs slightly and smiles his smile. Fatalistic and realistic and as always optimistic. He's off to the Midnight Shift in Oxford Street. 'I'm on the market, I guess I'm dating and seeing a few people. You know what?' he asks rhetorically, 'you can't get everything out of one person. That's one thing I've learned. I have to find the fabulous Mr Average and there are so many Mr Averages out there.' It's probably a safe bet to assume that Yianni will do his best to find his own Mr Average.

And in a way, that's what all Australians do. Some of us may not find what we want. Some of us may think we've found what we want and see that love go south, sometimes gradually drifting apart, sometimes suddenly and without any warning.

I look at my friends as we share coffee together. For some Australians the romantic path of the heart is one we tread frequently, and some only once. Marriage is no longer the bedrock of financial and emotional security. We are free to follow our Australian Hearts with few restrictions, but we still hold tight to the dreams and promises of romantic love.

There is nothing quite like that delightful feeling of falling and being in love with another person. I still remember the day I saw my wife for the first time. There was a knock at the door and I opened it to see her standing before me. She stood in a green dress and black boots, Ray Ban sunglasses perched on her head, jingling the keys of her S series Valiant in her hand.

We stared at each other for what seemed like a very long time, but was probably only a few seconds, until she said 'Hello' with a smile. I have often heard her saying that 'Hello' since, and it has always made me happy; it has never ceased to make me soar a little.

That is what can happen to an Australian Heart when it finds love, and who among us has the right to say that is not a good thing to pursue?

I hope we all might.

The
Australian
Dream

16

At the End of the Street

At the end of the street in which I live there are some rail yards. The trains have come and gone ever since I've lived in this area, and like any part of your own neighbourhood, after a time objects begin to take on certain characteristics as they become more familiar to you.

The silver commuter trains slide through rather aimlessly and almost all are invariably late. The big, droning, work-dirty diesel freight trains hum with long, low blasts on their air horns, pushing through the Jeffrey Smart landscape with their multicoloured shipping containers daubed with romantic names like South China Seas and Four Winds Transport. And down by the area where the small railway houses give way to a grassy open field, the Sydney to Melbourne XPT – Express Passenger Train – service, which had once sounded so modern but now looks vaguely like a model from the old *Thunderbirds* television show, pulls up panting while a line is changed further down the track.

Alongside the tracks is some vacant land. Many of the people living around here walk their dogs there, kick the occasional football

---

Page 267: *Olive and Roger Robbins' dream house under construction by hand in 1948.*

and dump the odd bit of unwanted rubbish – usually couches, broken computers and huge televisions.

There is an old woman who walks her dogs; she has three. One of them is a Weimaraner. My aunt used to have a Weimaraner called Bruno and she loved him beyond all reason. Bruno was a heroically stupid dog, endlessly bounding about and leaping with ill-timed enthusiasm, all the while dragging my Aunty Rita this way and that as she bellowed commands he duly ignored, and then she'd be hooting with laughter.

The woman with her dog reminds me of my aunt, who I was very fond of, so I've always enjoyed seeing her and her equally wayward hounds. The other afternoon as I walked along with my daughter and what passes as our dog, I greeted her. She nodded and as she pushed on with her walking frame I noticed that her big Weimaraner wasn't by her side.

When I asked after the dog she stopped and smiled a little, which told me all I needed to know, but she went on and told me the story.

'Oh, the poor old fellow, he got crook and we had to let him go. Go to sleep.'

I said I was sorry.

She nodded. 'Mad as a March hare, but a good dog. Lovely. Oh well.'

There was a television, one of those great big ones, lying out by a telephone pole. She jabbed at it with her walker. 'These people, from the flats. They'll dump anything. Have for years. Couldn't give a fig about anybody else around here.'

I didn't say anything, for if truth be told I have put the odd thing out on the nature strip and waited till the rubbish fairies came and took it away. But the old woman wasn't quite finished.

'That poor bloke keeps his bits and belongings tidier.' She pointed over towards the train tracks and moved off with her walking frame.

My daughter said she was sorry about the dog, and the old lady waved back as she rolled down the footpath.

'He was a good old dog, that's for sure,' the woman said with a half turn.

I looked down by the tracks where she had pointed. In between a small clump of trees a couch and chairs had been carefully placed around a fire and grill. They'd probably been dragged over from the footpath where they'd been dumped at some point.

This place was occupied by a homeless man who had been there for a long time. Long enough, I thought, to be witness to the jumping Weimaraner as he ploughed around the grassy area. I remember the homeless man laughing his head off as the big grey dog went silly as a wheel – and that was when my daughter was barely walking. So perhaps ten years ago.

He had fed the dog treats occasionally and the old woman had sometimes given the man packets of Scotch Finger biscuits as a gift.

'Does he miss the big grey dog?' my daughter asked.

'I guess he does,' I replied. I could see that the man was holding a packet. 'But he still gets his bickies.' It was a packet of Scotch Fingers; I supposed that the old lady had given it to him.

As we walked towards our home my daughter said, 'Doesn't that man get cold at night?'

'Yes,' I said, 'I guess he does.'

'Why does he live there?'

'I don't know. He's been there a long time.'

We walked along our street. It was changing. Weatherboard bungalows were giving way to nests of townhouses. Flats were being renovated with stucco and render replacing the bare brick, but rubbish was still stuck out on the nature strips and the man still lived among the trees with his couches.

Almost all of the homes were renovated, or were in the middle of renovation. In the front windows of some there were signs proclaiming: 'No Freeway for West Footscray' or 'No Freeway Through Our Home'. There are rumours throughout the suburb that the grassy area will make way for a raised freeway, so some residents have formed a protest committee against its construction.

Since the present state government proclaimed the freeway a top priority for their future infrastructure developments, there has been a slight feeling of unease in the neighbourhood. The Minister for Roads and Ports confirmed as long ago as 2008 that properties in the West Footscray area would be acquired, but he could not say where or how many, so it's no wonder people have been whispering conspiracy theories over their coffees at the Jelly Bread Café up on Barkly Street.

As my daughter and I continued walking along our road, she asked another question. 'What's the difference between a house and a home?'

'What?' I ask.

'Is a house a home or is a home something else?'

Well, now there's a question. What is a home? What is an Australian home?

Back in the late 1940s, after the end of the Second World War, a trend began that exists to this day: Australians by and large became obsessed with owning their own home. This, they were told, was the beginning of the Great Australian Dream. Owning your own home was evidence of a better life; home ownership meant success and security.

House ownership makes some sort of sense in the context of the Great Depression that ravaged the world throughout the 1930s, and then the Second World War, when security took on an even more literal meaning. To own a home gave people a sense of permanency; the fragility of life had been all too obvious for the generation that lived through both these social and economic catastrophes.

After the Second World War most of Australia's seven and a half million people lived in suburbs clustered around the major cities. There was such a shortage of housing that many servicemen moved back in with their parents when they returned. Most average houses were small and, more often than not, already crowded. With years of economic deprivation and the fact that the war effort had made building materials hard to come by, this situation was exacerbated by the wartime rationing measures kept up by the Chifley Labor government. So if you were going to set out on your own, you had to be patient.

Roger Robbins, a returning veteran, had to bide his time in uniform before finding a place of his own. A points system was introduced to manage the influx of ex-servicemen into the civilian population – to get out of the army when the war ended, men were allotted points. As Roger recalls, 'If you were married you got points. If you were overseas you got points, and your age, the younger you were the less points you got.

'They kept us in the army because the people who had the most points got out first. You know, I wasn't married and I was young so I didn't get out till six or nine months after the war finished.'

Roger had started going out with Olive, a friend of his twin sisters, and it was at a beach party organised by the twins that Roger and Olive started talking about acquiring some land on which to build a home.

'We were talking about the future, about getting married, and these blocks of land came up with the local council. There were

Olive and Roger on their honeymoon in Lorne, Victoria, in 1949.

about five blocks of land and I went in a ballot. I drew it out and that's how it started.'

And how it went is evidenced by Roger and Olive Robbins, sitting together, finishing each other's sentences, in the living room of the house they built and made their home sixty years ago.

They were both born in Hampton, in Melbourne, and the block of land Roger drew in the ballot was in Black Rock, Melbourne.

'Haven't moved very far, have we? Born, married and lived in Black Rock,' Roger says simply.

The land was set on an old golf course. 'We started building it in about nineteen . . .' and he searches for only a tiny moment before Olive answers.

'Forty-seven.'

'Yeah, that'd be about the time,' says Roger.

Having served in the Engineers in the Second World War, Roger had enough experience to design and build the house. There was a chronic shortage of materials due to the sheer number of houses being built, so the size of their house was in keeping with what was available. Olive remembers the design had to be changed because of the lack of copper.

'At first the bathroom was between the two bedrooms, but water piping was hard to get so we changed the plan – to make the bathroom, laundry and kitchen closer together.

'You were allowed to build twelve and a half squares only, which meant you had to squeeze in three small bedrooms, or sacrifice a third bedroom, which we did – we just built two to have slightly bigger rooms,' says Olive. 'It took three years to build the house.'

'That's because it was all using hand tools. Hand saws. There were no electric saws or drills or anything. If there was an electric drill I couldn't afford it at the time. So we did it all by hand,' remembers Roger.

The couple moved in early because they were afraid of the fittings being stolen. 'Well, they were so hard to buy – we probably waited fourteen or sixteen months for our bath and it wasn't a lot of trouble for someone to come along and take it,' says Olive.

It was a matter of making do with what they could find and also using whatever connections friends and family might have. 'The doors,' explains Roger. 'Olive's father knew someone in one of the big hardware stores in the city and the door handles were the same. That's how we got them – solid doors! It was who you knew, really.'

'The asbestos,' says Olive with a shake of her head. 'The asbestos, the stuff that's causing all the trouble now – we knew someone

The bricks arrive at last for the Robbins' house, 1948.

there who could get it for us. But you had to use it quickly because it would harden in the weather.'

Asbestos was used in almost every building of the time, both private and public – from the Robbins' small two-bedroom home to the local school and library.

There is a pause and then Roger winces with a few memories of his experiences. 'The lining boards I did on my own, and that was hard work because they were such long lengths to be put up. I fell off scaffolds and that sort of thing.' Then he almost giggles. He recalls painting the front of his house with a one-gallon can of paint and the scaffolding collapsed under him. 'I was left hanging on the fascia – we got a concealed spout so the fascia was strong. I had one hand on the fascia and the other on the paint pot and I was swinging there. There was a chap who lived up the road who had polio and he couldn't move very fast, but he saw me hanging and he hurried as quick as he could and told the lady next door. She came out with Olive and a step ladder.'

The pair of them stare ahead for a few seconds.

'But I was hanging there for a long time.'

Olive nods, then smiles. 'He didn't drop the paint!'

'No, no paint dropped,' affirms Roger.

It's amazing the house didn't take longer to build. But finished it was, for a grand total of two thousand, two hundred pounds.

Roger and Olive consider themselves lucky, they were both savers, Roger had already saved eighty pounds from farm work before he joined the army, and they continued saving their army pay of nine shillings a day. They were also able to hold onto a deferred pay on discharge of about six hundred pounds, making a total of one thousand pounds saved.

War service loans were available but, according to Olive, 'It was so difficult to apply for a loan because everyone was coming back and there was a long delay. It wasn't easy getting a war loan.'

Roger sighs a bit. 'Oh well, I didn't think that was the case, I thought because we could finance it ourselves we'd be better off – but if I'd had any brains we could have been much better off. Saw in the paper the other day that you can still get insurance if you are eligible, from war service.'

He shrugs his shoulders a little and Olive smiles. If you were casting for a contented couple from Australian suburbia you wouldn't have to look very far, yet there was a time when Roger wasn't so content. Their home cost two thousand, two hundred pounds. They had saved two thousand, leaving a shortfall of two hundred.

It's at this memory that Roger looks slightly agitated. 'We were a bit short and I had to go to the bank and borrow two hundred pounds. It seemed a very large amount of money and I was worried, wasn't I, Olive?'

'You were worried,' says Olive, smiling gently.

The fact that the land itself cost one hundred and fifty-nine pounds puts the loan into perspective. Money and costs were always on the minds of Roger and Olive – they kept a small black account book and neatly entered into it a record of every expense. It starts with the entry of one hundred and fifty-nine pounds and continues until one quite startling entry: a Silent Night refrigerator for the sum of sixty pounds.

It's startling because it shows that a kitchen appliance – which Roger Robbins thought was broken because it made no noise when he turned it on – cost just under half the price of the land. Quite an investment.

The final cost of the Robbins' house represented three times what Roger earned in a year. The yearning for the security of ownership came at a high price, but Roger and Olive saved on building costs because Roger did most of it himself.

Olive and Roger's grandson, Scott, outside their house in 1983.

'I think other people were paying about four thousand pounds because they got a builder to do it but, as Olive says, we missed out a bit down the track because it took us longer to build.'

Both of them hold the account book. To anybody else the entries are just numbers written in their appropriate columns, but to these two, the figures are touchstones in their lives.

The final entry is for spirits; Olive takes a little breath and then smiles. 'That was for cleaning the brickwork. That was the final thing. A happy day.'

Roger sees another entry in the book and stares in thought. He looks at a door. 'See these doors, seventeen pounds. Well, I just wouldn't like to say what a door like that would cost today.'

He nods his head. And Olive nods hers.

But that was the building, the house. As my daughter asked, 'What is the difference between a home and a house?'

What made this house their home? In part it was the effort that went into building it, Roger riding on his bike with building tools balanced on his handlebars. It was the first time the couple lit a fire in their hearth and warmed themselves under the roof; it was the first Christmas and the decorations Olive put up around the kitchen, the only room that was really finished.

'A few sprigs of tinsel, that was fun,' she says.

'We used to have both families visit us for years, a lot of family, that was good,' Roger says, nodding.

17

One Room at a Time

Roger and Olive Robbins' home was one of the 300,000 built in Australia in the ten years following the end of the Second World War. The idea of home ownership became more than just a need for security, as it had been for previous generations. Instead it became an aspirational concept of self-worth and success. It became the Great Australian Dream. And as the number of houses grew, so did institutional support for this concept.

This postwar period coincided with the rise of the Cold War and Robert Menzies saw private home ownership as an important weapon in the fight against communism. Home was, he argued, a sacred place 'into which no stranger may come against our will'.

These Great Australian Dreams were fairly modest: usually freestanding houses on a quarter-acre block, about one thousand square metres, big enough for the house, the garden, a vegetable patch and a place for the kids to play. Inside there were four small rooms with a separate kitchen and bathroom, and electricity was available in every room.

Over the next ten years a vast immigration scheme fed the growing economy's hunger for labour. In that first decade more than 200,000 of these immigrants came from Italy. And of those, two were Angelo and Lina De Rossi, farm workers from Treviso in Italy's north.

Lina tells their story. 'We wanted to come here because after Italy was destroyed we had no chance to find a job. That's why my husband said, "Try another way." That's why we came to Australia.'

Angelo had attempted to find a job in the Belgian mines but the work was dangerous and erratic, so he came to Australia. Nine months later his wife and young son Franco joined him, and the family settled in the New South Wales town of Yenda, near Griffith.

Lina's first impressions weren't very positive. 'I cried all day long. I didn't want to stay in Australia . . . Even the Australians never liked us. They called us dagos, we are dagos. I don't know – what does it mean, "dago"?'

It's an open question that is asked quite innocently.

A woman who had worked all her life, from the farms of her homeland to Australia, from hacking out minerals in a mine 'like a man with a shovel and wheelbarrow during the Second World War', Lina only wanted a place of security for herself and her family. She still wonders now as she did when she first arrived, what does dago mean?

She shrugs her shoulders. 'But after, slowly, slowly we started work.'

Lina's cousin owned a farm, so she and Angelo worked there, picking vegetables, saving money all the time. The temptation to leave was great.

Lina and Franco's boat ticket, 1953.

Lina, Franco and Angelo at one of the first homes they lived in at Yenda.

The couple shared a small farmhouse with another family – Lina and Angelo had the lounge room and half of the kitchen with no electricity. Angelo had to fashion a fridge out of a burlap sack dunked in water and placed in a hole in the ground to keep their milk, butter and meat cold.

Having travelled across the world and working for nearly three long and hard years on the farm – sometimes six and seven days a week – Lina and Angelo decided to buy a small farmhouse of their own. Not surprisingly, their decision was based solely on security.

'The farmer, he can kick us away, because he had many people to pick the grapes. This house, it belongs to us. Nobody can kick us out anymore.'

In 1955 they bought a small weatherboard house on a two-acre farm in Leaver Street, Yenda. 'Cash money. Yeah, we paid straight away. Cash money, one thousand pounds,' says Lina.

One thousand pounds for a fifty-year-old, two-bedroom weatherboard. It needed a lot of work, or in real estate parlance, it was your classic fixer-upper.

Lina chuckles and explains, 'There was no bath there, no bath, no hot water. It doesn't matter, you do it one at a time. When you build the money, you fix one room after the other. The house had power with only one light. No power points, just one light and switch.' One room at a time, the house was renovated and repaired.

Angelo rolls his eyes and rubs his nose as Lina claps her hands and laughs. 'First thing I bought was a fridge, a kerosene fridge, because we had no electricity down there. Then I bought a bicycle. I said to my husband we should buy a bicycle so I could go to work. And we got money for another fridge – first a kerosene, then we bought the new one, electric. I like to buy,' Lina says.

The house in Leaver Street, as it was when the De Rossis bought it in 1955.

Frank De Rossi, aged four, on his bike at his family's home in Yenda.

Like Roger and Olive, it was security that drove Angelo and Lina to buy and build their house; and like Roger and Olive, it was what they invested in that house that made it a home.

'My house is my home; my home is good for me because my home is my husband, my children. That's my home,' says Lina.

In time, Lina and Angelo subdivided their land and built another home on the property. Lina and her son Franco dug the foundations of the new house in 1975. Franco and Angelo then helped the builder to complete the job and, just so she was sure it was done in the way she liked, Lina took on the task of painting it.

'When they finished, I painted the whole house by myself. I gave it three coats!'

For Lina and her husband, creating a home wasn't just for their own security. 'We work and we want to build something for our family, for our children,' says Lina.

Lina and Angelo have passed this strong feeling that the home is for the whole family down to Franco and to their grandchildren.

A sign hanging above the stove in the De Rossi kitchen reads: 'Nana's kitchen – kids eat free here.' Lina smiles. 'Yeah, we are all together for birthdays, Christmas.'

This is her home. Even though she may wonder why she was called a dago, this is her home. 'I know. I know I am Australian now. Well, I know I'm Italian, but I am Australian.'

She knew this most of all when she returned to the land of her birth twenty-three years after settling in Australia. 'I arrived there and said to Angelo, "What are we doing here? I feel like a fish out of water." I feel like that – I don't feel like it was my home. I am Italy, I am my country, but I never say Italy is my home anymore.'

Lina doesn't cry anymore either. She is too busy in her garden, or in her kitchen. She is home.

The same year Lina and her son Franco came to Australia, another immigrant stepped ashore with her family. Carol Berling emigrated from England at the age of four, travelling on the assisted immigration scheme for English nationals, known as 'ten-pound Poms'. They settled in Narrabeen, a northern beachside suburb in Sydney.

The Menzies government encouraged migrants to build. And with cheap secured loans and large areas of land on offer in the early 1950s, when Carol arrived, many people started to build their own homes. As the economy gathered pace, better availability of building materials and an influx of skilled labour fuelled the boom.

The most popular material was a substance called Fibrolite, an asbestos cement sheet that was hardy and fireproof. Most of the new estate houses were built of weatherboard or fibro, or a combination of both.

Carol Berling, a woman with a keen eye for property, remembers her first home in Narrabeen. There was a row of these little fibro houses in her street. Inside the house it was pretty basic – a lounge, three bedrooms and a verandah at the back. But it was the garden that caught her and her mother's eye.

'A good-sized back garden, I remember that. My mother had an apple tree and she used to grow vegetables at that house – yeah, that was fun. Coming from England, it was a lot of space for her to have. It was unlike anywhere she had lived before.'

There is a photo of Carol in the backyard wearing thongs, shorts and a singlet. In her summer outfit it's hard to imagine that she could have come from anywhere else but Australia, and her face is beaming with optimism. Carol would go on to buy and sell, renovate and create many homes as an adult, and when you look at the photo of her as a joyful young girl you are not surprised that

Carol Berling (left) *with friends Lyn and Sue.*

she achieved so much, but you can also see quite clearly that the house is made of fibro.

'Well,' says Carol in her matter-of-fact way, 'fibro was a very viable product, very inexpensive, and it did the job.'

It was extremely popular, and as the intense building program continued at a pace, sometimes things were left a little unfinished. There were always bits and pieces of building materials left around – for youngsters to play with.

Carol is thoughtful and chooses her words carefully. She gives a half-smile, then says, 'The street I lived in was not a very tidy one, so there was rubble left over and mounds of dirt, on which pieces of fibro lay around, different sizes, and we played with them. We used these pieces like chalk.'

She would write her name, make patterns and draw pictures with her chalk. She would mark out the squares for a game of hopscotch on the pavement. Perhaps even draw her home and what she saw around her. The fibro was just lying around.

The Australian Dream may have been modest for many, and in some cases the fact that it was realised at all made it even sweeter. Kevin Duncan was born in 1937 in the northern New South Wales town of Moree, the son of a railway worker, a member of the Gomilaroi mob, and his mother came from Tingha, nearby. While his elder brother followed his father into the railways, Kevin, on the advice of an Aboriginal welfare officer, became an apprentice to a builder in Moree. This builder wanted to find an apprentice to become the first Aboriginal tradesman.

'I left school on the Friday and had the nail bag and the hammer on the Monday. I didn't have much of a holiday from school –

and the first house I ever built was just up the road here, for a schoolteacher, one of the teachers from my school.'

Kevin has lived in Moree all his life, and fell in love and married a local girl, Coral Joy Binge. Three years later they bought a piece of Crown Land.

All by way of a friendly cab driver named Wilbur.

As Wilbur was driving Kevin and Joy to the mission one day, the conversation came round to the topic of where Kevin might like to build a house, seeing as he was a builder. Kevin said perhaps on the mission, but that he also liked the town life in Moree. Wilbur the cabby had an idea.

'He said, "I'll tell you where this block of land is, I'll show you,"' explains Kevin in his quiet way of speaking. 'He turned the meter

Kevin Duncan, aged eighteen, in 1955.

off and took us up there and showed us the land. Then old Wilbur pointed next door and said, "I'm building a house over there, see?" He told us we should get onto it, and that he'd tell us what to do.'

Wilbur the cabby told Kevin to contact the then Department of Crown Lands.

'And I did, I applied for this block of land and I got her. And it cost me six pounds ten. A block of land for seven dollars! Just as well, too – you can't live with the in-laws forever,' he says with a mischievous glint in his eyes.

The building itself was made possible because Kevin applied for a loan through the Aboriginal Welfare Scheme. 'Oh yeah, I was the first Aborigine to apply for a loan and then it was only two thousand pounds.' He shakes his head. 'Two thousand pounds. You couldn't build a house for two thousand pounds. It might buy the materials, it's only a nine-square home. But not build it and paint it and all.'

So what did Kevin do? He wrote away and asked for more. He got in touch with a welfare officer and put forward the proposition that if he could get four thousand pounds he could buy the materials and build it himself.

He and Joy were living with Joy's parents when there was a knock on the door one day. It was the welfare officer. He wanted to know if Kevin had written a letter to Sydney for a loan to build a house. 'I said, "Yeah, I thought I might build a house there for me and Joy before she had too many kids." She ended up having eight, anyway,' he says. 'I told the officer I wrote away to Sydney for the loan.'

The welfare officer stared at Kevin, didn't say anything for a while, then held out his hand. 'I want to congratulate you, you've got the loan, and you've got the extra money to build yourself a house. I've been with the Welfare for a long time and you're the first Aborigine I've known to get a loan like that.'

Coral Joy Binge (top) *with her friends Edlo Craigie* (middle) *and Joyce Wright.*

They shook hands. And Kevin built his home.

It was home not only for his wife and children, but also his grandchildren and great-grandchildren. This house he built has the same sense of home and of family as the homes of the De Rossis and Olive and Roger Robbins.

It only took Kevin about three weeks to build the house because it wasn't very large. Soon, their new home became so busy with family members coming and going that Joy Duncan called it Pitt Street. Kevin and Joy and their eight children had friends, cousins and other relations living there on and off.

Kevin sits with his son Kevin junior and daughter Cindy at the dinner table. 'You'll find that in all Aboriginal families, they have big mobs of family living in one house. You'd probably have up to fourteen people living in a three-bedroom cottage. And that was how we were here,' Kevin says with a smile.

Cindy lets out a raucous laugh. 'Oh, it was happy, it was always happy with laughter. Everyone was happy. Mum would call it Pitt Street all right, because everyone would be in and out. And there were friends and the kids' friends and their friends. It was just a happy house. There was music and laughter and Mum and Dad would be rock and rolling when they were younger. I can still see them in the lounge, Mum would go through Dad's legs, you know, the rock'n'roll.'

And Kevin looks towards a photo of his wife, with long, flowing hair, smiling away from the camera. It is a while since she died, he says, but he always has a drink for her on their wedding anniversary. He still believes Joy should be here bossing him around.

His eyes dwell on her photo. 'She was a good dancer,' he says softly, then finishes, 'great mother, great mother to the kids. They loved her, all of them.'

Kevin Duncan's granddaughters, Kiaya (left) and Anita, eating an orange, with their friends, 1989.

'I wouldn't know what to do if anything happened to this house,' says Cindy.

'No, you lose your house, you lose all your memories, too, I reckon, everything goes,' her brother Kevin adds.

For Kevin, Cindy and their father, their home holds the memories of their family members who have lived and died there. They understand the idea that the house is a backbone of stability and strength. Of certainty. This is a belief that runs through many families.

The fact that Kevin Duncan built the house in the days when Indigenous Australians did not have full citizenship rights counts in the pride the family take in their home. It's a remarkable story, especially when you consider the state even in today's Australia of Indigenous housing.

In parts of this nation, the overcrowding, lack of services and the standards of health were one of the factors that led to the Federal government's polarising Northern Territory National Emergency Response into Indigenous life in the Northern Territory in 2007. The program, more widely known as The Intervention, has continued over two Australian governments with no likely end in sight.

Against this background Kevin and his family seemed to have enjoyed a remarkably warm, happy and inclusive life in Moree. 'I was lucky, you know, I moved alongside good neighbours, fellas like Wilbur. And I'm one of those blokes, I just click on real well with anyone. I've still got hundreds of friends in town here. Good mates. I don't care who they are.'

To Cindy the question of racism is in every town, but she didn't experienced it here in the street where she grew up. 'I never had racism until my thirties. Late thirties and I thought, "Oh God!" But growing up here, our friends were all little whitefellas and we loved them.'

'Oh,' says Kevin, 'I must have worked on about sixty homes east of Moree and about fifty out in Moree and lots of those commission homes.' He smiles a little and you get the sense that he hasn't just made one happy house, he has added a little bit of himself to many homes. And Moree is the better for the youngest Duncan boy not following his dad and big brother in joining the railway, but instead picking up a hammer and carpentry belt.

18

It Looked Like Hollywood

The federal and state governments, in the late fifties and early sixties, focused their attention on the cities. The rapid rise in the population put pressure on the inner urban areas where the houses were small and often crammed into narrow streets and laneways.

Dolly Wilson lived in the inner Sydney suburb of Waterloo, in a small street, called Mary Street, lined with about twenty or so houses, little two-bedroom cottages with small backyards. They were old, and sometimes the sewage would overflow into the yards.

'Well, they were slums, but it was home – it was a place to live,' says Dolly. 'So you never complained. We had a ninety-nine-year lease with the government and then the Housing Department bought the whole block up. One day a Welfare woman came around and very quietly said that they had a new place for us to go.'

The new place was touted to be a bold new social experiment. The state's Housing Commission was building high-rise, high-density apartment blocks and the spiffy looking New South Wales Housing Minister Abram Landa assured journalists that, 'The block of flats to be erected on this block of land will be very much like a lot of apartment houses I saw in Stockholm, Sweden. It will be very beautiful indeed.'

The development, which became known as Northcott, was unlike any other. Certainly Dolly and her husband, Ronnie Wilson, were impressed.

'Oh,' says Dolly, 'it looked like Hollywood when we came in here, we never had a place like it in our lives. We both liked it – we, Ronnie, me, and my daughter Marcia, moved in the next day. Two bedrooms, a bathroom and a kitchen – you couldn't ask for more.'

The trio moved in 1960 – they were Northcott's first residents – and by 1963 it was home to more than five hundred low-income families. Regarded as a showpiece of public housing, it was the scene of a royal visit by Queen Elizabeth II and Prince Philip during their trip to Australia in 1963.

Dolly didn't catch the Queen; she was busy working as a barmaid and didn't see her, although she did have a bit of trouble getting home because of her. The roads were all blocked and Northcott was 'all secured up', in Dolly's words. 'There was this policeman and he said, "You can't come in because the Queen is still here."

'I said, "I can't help that, I want to get home because my young daughter's down there." So he let me through. I didn't see the Queen, though. I think she popped up to the fourteenth floor and dropped in on some people up in Block B.'

Dolly thinks about it and nods her head, 'Yeah, Block B.'

She is still for a while and then carries on, a perfect example of someone who is chock-full of character, as my father would say.

'You know, a lot of people said the Queen came to open Northcott because it was the highest building in the southern hemisphere, but that's not right. She only stopped for a half-hour. The band was still here when I came down and the little scout boy opened the door for her, but I didn't see that. They tell me she only stopped for half an hour.'

Dolly lets out a sniff and then a roar of laughter. 'I opened it. Me. Yeah, I cut the ribbon in 1960 when Northcott was officially opened, because this was the only block that was built. No Block B back then. And Sir Robin Askin and Sir John Northcott held the yellow ribbon and I cut it with scissors. And he said, "I declare Northcott open." Sir John Northcott said that.'

On the question of who Sir John was, Dolly is nothing if not honest.

'I don't know, to be truthful.' And she gives a deadpan look.

He was, in fact, the Governor of New South Wales at the time and a highly decorated former Second World War senior military officer.

Dolly nods her head. 'Well, whoever he was, he was there. And he had a wooden leg. Or, ah, a stiff leg, and he had a walking stick. They called me up to speak, to ask me where I was from. I got up there and they gave me some flowers and, well, wouldn't you know, I tripped over Sir John's walking stick. Fell over the walking stick.'

When Dolly sat down with her husband Ronnie, she asked him where her flowers were. 'I don't know, love,' he said, 'couldn't tell you. They went that way last time I saw them.' And he pointed with his hand and just waved his fingers.

She has a great laugh, Dolly Wilson. No doubt she has had good reason to use it over the fifty years she has lived at Northcott. It has been her home.

When she first moved in almost all of her weekly wage of three pounds, ten shillings paid the rent, and the couple would live off Ronnie's wage. She has paid rent for all that time and has always felt at home.

'No, I never think of owning my own home. Never think of that, I'm happy here. I'd never have enough money to buy one. I live here and I love it. I'd never move out.'

As those years went by the tenants of Northcott changed. At first they were all low-income families. There has been an influx of immigrants, Germans and Russians, says Dolly, over in Block B. She sees them on the bus and they seem quite nice, she says.

There have been Africans and Chinese and Aboriginal people. 'I speak to them to say hello and if they see me out the front they always say hello. But I don't have anything to do with them. Nearly all of them live in Block B.

'There's people with problems and drug addicts, and that's been happening in the last fifteen or so years. When I see them coming I know they are not all there, so I just keep, well I walk a bit faster and go the opposite way. It's not the Housing Commission's fault, they don't put them in here. Doctors give them letters to come here and they have to give them a room.'

She has seen much in her life, has Dolly Wilson. 'Oh, some sad things. Terrible things. People jumping off balconies. I've got a friend, she's in Housing, who got moved to a little cottage. She was talking to a woman, then this woman went upstairs and my friend heard this terrible bang. So she went up to her verandah and the woman had jumped straight over the balcony and landed down at the bottom. In pieces. And my friend rang me straight away.

'She told me it was the woman she was just talking to. "She must have been a dill." That's all she said.' There's a pause and Dolly continues slowly, 'but there's plenty jumping off this building here. They don't tell you anymore, they don't make it public. There's people with problems.'

And still it's her home. Showing off her rooms proudly it's clear Dolly keeps her flat with a great deal of pride. Photos of children and grandchildren dot the walls. It's her home. She has seen some terrible things but she has also seen glorious things.

One night when her husband Ronnie sat down to dinner, a beer can was thrown through the window, narrowly missing his head. Dolly never said anything but the building's manager, a Mr Hilton, was alerted, so the next day he came to inspect the breakage and Ronnie told him what had happened. Mr Hilton brought the boy who had thrown the beer can, along with the boy's mother, down from Block B.

'Well,' says Dolly, 'Mr Hilton says, "Mr Wilson, do you want to charge this boy?"'

Dolly's voice changes and it's evident she speaks with a great deal of pride. 'Ronnie stood there and the boy's mother was upset, very upset. My Ronnie said, "No, I don't want him charged."

'"Are you sure, Mr Wilson?" asked the manager.

'"He's only thirteen or fourteen," Ronnie says, "and if he gets charged he'll get a police record and he'll never get a job. I don't want that. I don't want him charged,"' recounts Dolly.

Years later, long after the death of her Ronnie, Dolly was walking down Crown Street in Surry Hills, weaving through the crowds of workers and commuters, when she suddenly heard her name being called.

'Dolly! Dolly Wilson!' It was a voice she didn't know. She looked this way and that, and was approached by someone she had never seen before, or so she thought.

'I turned around and there was this young man, a young man in a suit and tie, holding a briefcase, and he was very polite and well spoken. He said, "Excuse me, you don't remember me, do you?"

'And I said, "No I don't, son."

'And he said, "I'm the mad boy who broke your window. I'd like to just thank you. And thank your husband for not prosecuting me."

Dolly Wilson at home at Northcott, Surry Hills, Sydney.

'Turned out he's a managing director of some big paper place down in Foveaux Street. He says, "I'd never be here if it weren't for your husband. I've got two boys and every night I try to teach them about what's right and wrong and I tell them about your husband." My Ronnie. That's what he said.'

Every time she walks up the hill to Northcott, a hill that's steeper and harder to climb as she grows older, she always feels happy, for she knows she is home.

On the bus she is not ashamed to say she lives in 'housing'.

'As soon as you mention "housing", that you're in housing, people don't want to seem to know you. I don't know why. Makes no difference to me.'

Ronnie Wilson has died and so too has Marcia, Dolly's daughter, suffering a brain aneurism at the age of twenty-eight.

'Home. My home. The reason I don't want to go from here, the reason it's my home is that I had them here. They were always with me; I can't leave here because of them.'

For Dolly Wilson, a home isn't about walls. 'I think of all the love in this place. That's why I like it so much. All the love that was here. Is here. I can always talk to them, you know?'

19

Different Dreams

Sydney was a developer's dreamland. High-rise apartment towers grew everywhere in the 1960s, creating an updated version of the Australian Dream. And the people who have made a living out of selling things to other people did what they have done since time began: they talked it up big.

There is a priceless piece of ABC television footage from the early seventies showing a hard-hat-wearing project manager in a suit and tie spruiking for a harbourside apartment tower. 'Double oven stoves, intercom systems, dishwashing machines and garbage disposal units! This is the marble we're using in the kitchen, it's a travertine. It's the same type of marble as used in the Colosseum.' And he gives a conspiratorial nod of his head, as if to say of course you knew it was travertine!

Only a real estate salesman could connect a harbourside kitchen with its dishwasher and garbage disposal unit with ancient Rome. With that other well-known, high-rise development, the Colosseum. The project manager was so sincere and off-hand when making the comment that he made it sound as if the Colosseum was somewhere around the corner, at Cremorne or Mosman.

In one form or another the idea of home ownership had travelled quite a way, and by the end of the sixties just over seventy per cent of Australians owned or were in the process of owning the houses they lived in.

It wasn't just this high-rise version of the Dream with its touch of Ancient Rome that was being sold to Australians and prospective Australian citizens overseas. In a series of films made by the Commonwealth Film Unit to encourage immigration from targeted countries with a surplus of skilled workers, Australia as a bountiful playground with affordable and comfortable housing was a major selling point.

In glorious colour, happy 'new settlers', who looked generically European enough to be perceived by any number of nationalities as their own – Germans, Swedes, Dutch – could be seen water-skiing and enjoying the healthy, fun-loving life that Australia specialised in.

In one version of the film, a narrator extols life Down Under as a smiling couple soars over a water-ski jump pulled at great pace by a rocketing powerboat. Then there was the deal-clincher: 'Australia has a lot of different housing styles to choose from, and many new settlers do so well that after only a few years [here a happy family chomps summer fruit on the verandah, and you know the father is a 'new settler' because he wears a cravat], they own their own home.'

It was this idea of home ownership that caught the attention of a young engineer who saw the Swedish version of the film. Bertil Klintfalt, who immigrated from Sweden in 1968, recalls the film's message. 'I'd thought about going to Canada, the States, South Africa or Australia. Now, Australia, they showed that everybody lived in a house – the great Australian Dream – not in a small apartment like everybody else. And that played a huge part in me coming to Australia.'

It didn't take Bertil long to settle into life here: within a year and a half he had met and married an attractive young woman who used to play hopscotch on the footpaths of Narrabeen, and who now worked in the central business district of Sydney refurbishing nightclubs and hotels. Her name was Carol Berling. She had an eye for style and she liked what she saw.

They sit together in their home and she laughs. 'Oh, I can even remember what he wore at the time, the black jacket and the grey pants and, yeah, the blue shirt. He looked good!'

Bertil and Carol on their wedding day.

Good enough to keep. And after their marriage they decided to buy their first place. A unit on the Pacific Highway in the lower north shore suburb of Artarmon was the start of their adventures in property.

After the birth of their first child, a daughter, they decided to renovate. 'We put in a wardrobe, and a kitchen nook and built a cradle and a cot and then we started to look around for other places to buy,' says Carol.

Carol and Bertil speak about the acquisition of property with an enthusiasm that is akin almost to that of a fishing enthusiast or a hunter. Every new property they would buy was to be an experience, even if they struggled a bit at the time. For Carol and Bertil it was, in fact, this struggle that made the creation of a home fun.

'We saw a house in Chatswood, and it was lovely,' says Carol. 'It was probably a jump too soon, maybe – but the man who owned the property helped us with the finance.'

Bertil nods and takes over the story, which is quite an incredible one for young homebuyers. It was a private sale and what happened was, as Bertil recounts, 'The fellow had two blocks and he had built a new house on the spare block, and moved into it, he then sold the older house to us. And he provided finance, so we didn't have to go to the bank. It was vendor finance. And that was attractive to us because we didn't have a lot of money. We thought, Oh great!'

It was the first house they owned, and they were the first among their group of friends to own a home. And they were rightly proud of this accomplishment.

Bertil felt a sense of achievement in owning his home primarily because of what he, himself, put into the house. 'I enjoy working with my hands and I always changed something, be it knocking a wall down or painting or tiling or whatever. And I got great satisfaction both from the finished product and actually doing it.'

A Christmas family gathering at Carol and Bertil's home in Chatswood, Sydney.

They obviously enjoyed their house. 'We ended up doing a lot of entertaining there. It was an older house so the rooms were big, it had a huge lounge room,' says Carol.

'It even had a swimming pool,' adds Bertil. 'Oh yeah, you really felt like you were the king of the castle!'

The couple have super-eight film footage of their life in that house, Bertil in the pool with their daughter in a swimming ring, splashing and waving to the camera. It wasn't to be home for long, however. Just after fitting out a room for their newborn baby boy, Bertil received a job offer too good to refuse, which meant relocating to New Zealand.

So after three years the couple left a home that many people would be happy to live in for a lifetime. It wasn't that the Australian Dream was finished for Bertil and Carol, it was just that it wasn't contained to one property, one home.

In the sixties and seventies the idea of the dream home was evolving. Anyone who grew up in Brisbane during this time would have an instant pang of recognition at the words 'Mater Prize Home'. The homes were part of the fundraising drive for the Mater Hospitals and Children Foundation, and for twenty cents you could buy a ticket in a lottery to win a 'Brand New Architecturally Designed Dream Home'.

These houses had great billboards – each year they popped up all over Brisbane. And while the house was open for display over a season of weekends, thousands of people would travel from various suburbs to walk through and view this 'dream home', a home that was only available to most people through luck, through the magic of a lottery draw.

In 2009, Nigel Harris from the Mater Hospital Brisbane told a television interviewer with a great deal of pride that, 'Visiting

Brochure for the Mater Prize Home, at Aspley Heights.

a Mater Prize Home on the weekend was the third most popular thing to do in Brisbane in the 1960s.'

Wherever he got that statistic from, it is still amazing to think that the third most popular thing to do was to traipse through a Mater Prize Home. Well, that was Brisbane then.

There were some enticements – usually a Mr Whippy van or a local radio station Mini Moke with a couple of radio personalities handing out station stickers and the odd balloon. When you heard them speaking as they handed out their '4IP good guys giveaways!', their voices bore no relation to what they actually looked like – which was like the bloke at the bus stop.

Slowly you would join the throng milling through the carpeted house, stepping across the lounge room like the respectful hordes you would see on the television news filing past the embalmed body of Lenin as he lay in state in Red Square.

'On a Saturday, there'd be a queue a mile long outside the house,' says Les Smith, a builder responsible for building five of the homes. 'And no wonder, 'cause all the materials we used in 'em were top-shelf. There was no second stuff in 'em or anything like that.'

One wonders what builders would use in other, lesser homes. One afternoon my father came bursting into the house, yelling for my mother. 'Ris! Ris! Iris! Ris! Where are you?'

My mother appeared from the kitchen where she was trying to de-clog the chimney.

'What?'

My father exploded with the news. It was if the government had fallen. 'Ris! They're building a Mater Prize Home – on the Peninsula!'

My mother stared.

'Yes, love, here on the Peninsula!'

'They're not!' my mother said in disbelief.

'They are,' said my father.

'A Mater Prize Home?'

'In bloody Kippa-bloody-Ring! It's double brick. Double brick, up by the Drive-in.' My father looked at me and said, 'The Peninsula may well never be the same.'

When the house was built we dutifully went and did the Lenin traipse through it.

'Double bloody brick,' my father muttered as he patted walls here and there.

My mother and Aunty Rita were aghast at the colour of the carpet. 'Why cream? How would you keep it clean? And it's so big. So big.'

There was no pool. I told my father that it wasn't a real Mater Prize Home because there was no pool.

'Double bloody brick,' was all he said. 'It's a Mater Home, all right.'

My father bought five tickets, one for each of his children.

We didn't win.

Bertil and Carol, meanwhile, had returned to Australia and bought another house, this time in Wahroonga, one of Sydney's northern suburbs. They renovated and again enjoyed what they created. 'The front of the house was brick and the back was fibro,' recalls Carol.

'We painted up the kitchen, the bedrooms, re-did the bathroom. Cubby house and above-ground pool,' says Bertil. 'A little canvas above-ground pool and there was lots of space.'

'It was a large block of land, very child friendly,' says Carol. 'And there was an old shed. The fibro shed – I remember it had a fair few cracked sheets. I remember us buying more and re-doing the shed and repainting it. The garden was a big part of the house, and we spent a lot of time there, with a lot of friends.'

After making another home, the couple moved to Norfolk Island and then to Sweden. They felt it was important that the children had a sense of where their father had come from, and for a number of years the family travelled around Scandinavia every second weekend.

They returned to Australia in 1986, but this time it was a vastly different place. The age of full employment was over, but the standard of living had risen. There was money flooding in and the idea of the global economy was taking shape. In 1985 changes were made to the practice of negative gearing. And the Hawke–Keating Labor government had initiated economic reforms, floating the dollar and slowly deregulating the economy. These changes had a huge impact on the housing supply in Australia.

With the deregulation of the banking system, buyers had access to loans with more favourable interest rates. The housing industry boomed. Around the country more land was being put on the market and developed. This created satellite suburbs that soon outstripped the ability of governments and communities to provide infrastructure for the new residents.

The government cut back on the kinds of negative gearing interest that could be claimed and from this point on, interest could only be claimed against rental income, no other forms of income. This change made property portfolios more and more attractive. Where once a couple would have been happy to stop at one house, a layered ownership of property began.

By the end of the 1980s, Australia's population had grown to seventeen million, a serious shortage in housing had been exposed and the high demand pushed prices to record levels. Seduced by the idea of profit, hundreds of thousands of people became investors. The Australian Dream was, more than ever, up for sale.

This was the Australia to which Bertil and Carol returned. 'We got left behind in the property market. That was the main thing. Everything had gone up and up and up,' Carol says, ticking off the points of the dilemma the family faced on their return.

Bertil nods as he speaks, sometimes adding a 'yep' here and there. 'We had bought and sold and as you do. You go up the ladder quite well, and we had.'

The couple found that in relation to their friends, who had stayed in Australia and slowly built up a property portfolio, they had slipped down the ladder.

'I had to go back to work because I was forty and I didn't feel secure,' says Carol. 'Renting was not a secure feeling, so it gets back to the old feeling about owning your own home that is in your mind. I needed to have the security of owning my own property again.'

As Carol crystallises the need for that security Bertil nods slowly in agreement. 'No matter what it took,' she continues, 'no matter how hard it was – and it was hard, because we basically had to start all over again at the ages we were, and that was not easy.'

There is a little pause and Bertil says simply, 'Yep.'

There are about nine words that are certain to send a shiver up the spine of a generation of homebuyers, showing just how hard the task would be for Carol and Bertil.

'This is the recession that Australia had to have,' said the then federal treasurer, Paul Keating, in sombre tones, with his hands clasped in front of his chin like a grim but thoughtful doctor about to give advice on how to treat a nasty illness. The illness was an overheating economy and the bitterest of all pills for so many was the slowdown. The brakes needed to be applied and that meant interest rates soared to eighteen per cent.

Whatever the economic merits of the decision to firewall the economy, prospective homebuyers like Carol and Bertil suffered, but they were nothing if not determined.

'We couldn't afford to buy a house, so we thought we should buy a block of land and build,' says Bertil.

Carol saw an ad for some land in the upper north shore suburb of Hornsby. 'I went up with my daughter because Bertil wasn't keen. I remember standing on the kerbside and looking at the view.' Carol pauses, gently sweeping her hand across her face, and you can almost see her standing on the kerbside. 'And I said to myself, "I can see it. I can see it."'

Bertil may not have been keen but the deal was as good as done.

The couple share a look and then Carol says with a grin, 'Anyway, we got it.'

For a while they considered the possibility of kit or project homes, until Bertil thought, just like Roger Robbins had all those years before, 'Perhaps I should design and build it myself.' There is a crafty look in his eyes and it's obvious that, although he knew it would be hard, it would be the most enjoyable of all the houses he had worked on.

'I basically built it myself. I had help putting in the poles, which needed a crane, and the big bearers, of course. A lot of work, oh, a lot of work. I stayed here on the weekends. Came up on the Friday and slept in the car.' He smiles his crafty smile and finishes with, 'But it was fun, in a way.'

Images of the pole house being constructed in Hornsby show Bertil's immense determination. Huge poles swing through the air, lifted by a giant crane. The scaffolding and structure of the three-storey house built into the slope of an acute hill slowly take shape.

Bertil and a friend putting up the cedar cladding on the Klintfalts' home.

The floors are on, then some walls, windows are being fitted. And finally the house was finished.

This was a special house, just how special they would find out in the years to come.

20

What's a Home?

During the recession of the early 1990s, thousands of people were forced to sell their properties. But millions more did not – showing the lengths to which the Australian people would go to keep the Dream alive.

And despite cycles of boom and bust or smaller hiccups since, it's an ideal that continues to this day. Australians are among the highest proportion of homeowners in the world. We have an abiding fondness for almost anything remotely connected to the idea of homes and housing. This became more than apparent in the last couple of decades of the twentieth century, and well into the first decade of the new millennium, with the cult of do-it-yourself, or DIY, home building and renovation. Television shows, radio programs and a whole new service industry sprang up as an adjunct to the trade and building industry.

The earlier generations of homebuilders and buyers, such as Roger Robbins, had often built their small homes themselves because it was more economical. Subsequent generations, the Baby Boomers and the rest, wanted more.

The search for the perfect renovation can lead Australians to the most bizarre of adventures. My own history of renovations is chequered. With the first, largely homemade effort, the highlight was pulling a chimney down on top of myself. Another memorable moment was witnessing my eight-month's pregnant wife and her old school friend putting a beam into the roof of the house. I had returned from work to see a seriously large chunk of timber propped up by a car jack on a series of tables.

I asked the worst possible question. 'Is that thing safe?'

I wore most of the contents of the cups of tea my wife and her friend were enjoying up until that point in celebration of their efforts.

But the most perplexing renovation experience I had ended with ten millimetres.

He looked at me and I looked at him. 'Ten millimetres,' he said.

'Ten millimetres,' I repeated.

He nodded his head in the direction of his yellow tape measure. 'Ten millimetres,' he said again, then snapped the recoil on his tape. He was a building inspector. I was a man who had just renovated my house. A man who looked at the building inspector, who wasn't going to give me a certificate for the work I had done.

An interior step was too deep by ten millimetres. Now, what at the time had seemed like a good idea had come to this. Two grown men staring at each other, saying nothing.

Just a small renovation this time. Nothing too big, just an extra room and a verandah. Why not? The rest of Australia was doing it. People at barbecues talk about their tradesmen or architects the way people used to talk about their hobbies or their pets. Whatever happened to hobbies or pets?

William's father and sister at the McInnes family home, in the 1970s.

At such a barbecue a friend of mine, Neil, who happens to be an architect, said that people turn their focus to their own homes in times of uncertainty in the world, because it's in their homes that they can have some order and control. The homes can be made safer with more order; everything has its role and place. Neil, by way of example, pointed with a very expensive imported beer at the home next door, which was being renovated.

There are so many reasons why my friend Neil the architect is wrong on this matter. If you want order and control in your house you do not renovate, especially if you have children and dogs and chooks and whatever new pets have been acquired. Renovations are a nightmare. You live through them, just. People are not renovating homes because of the threat and uncertainty of modern life. They do it because property values are going up, interest rates are low and reinvesting in your home is financially prudent.

Friendly Neil the architect laughed when I pointed this out to him. 'Whatever you reckon, old mate,' he said, 'but my clients love that sort of guff.'

Neil finished his beer then went to admire the sausages on the barbie, one of which promptly spat at and burned him. Who says there's no justice?

Renovations drive people insane. You suddenly find yourself moving in a new circle of people, 'Hardware People'. These are other renovating folk whose paths you cross at the local Bunnings or whatever other DIY hardware shop you choose to loiter at. People who all nod sagely as the aproned shop assistants point to this knob and that fitting then go and hide in another aisle.

I saw one man at my local Bunnings five times in a single day. We almost hugged as we staggered out the last time.

Well, this renovation was going to be different. I had tradespeople I knew and they liked doing the work and, what's more, I was going to help out. At least I dared to dream.

To use a phrase of my father's, I am 'not a tradesman's arsehole'. I had little or no idea of what to do but I did what I did with a great deal of enthusiasm. I broke panes of glass and put holes in walls, doors and frames . . . and that was just making the coffee.

As I mentioned, I knew all the people who did the work on the renovation. Nick the builder, who liked the same music I liked, could build, was honest and enjoyed a joke. The only thing wrong with him was the fact that there was only one of him. Bitter Kevin was an electrician. A bitter one. Nothing was right. And everything about the job reminded him of his ex-wife. First it was the floorboards, 'She liked spotted gum.' Then the nails, 'She used to crucify me, mate.' The way I made coffee, 'You make it too strong, like her. She hated instant.' He looked at the instant coffee with smouldering hatred, snarling, 'I loved International Roast.'

My long-suffering friend Adrian the Good Bloke helped out on weekends. We listened to the football and had a few beers. I would break things and he would mend them. It was very pleasant.

Adrian is the type of man who just turns up to help. No questions, no fuss. He helped all his friends with their renovations. I asked him why. 'Dunno. You're my friends and it's a good thing to build a good home. Good thing to be a part of.'

Adrian hates lifestyle shows on television. He thinks they are for people with no imagination. 'People who think they've got more money than they have and more time than they have. I don't know why they just don't pick rubbish off the streets. We'd all be happier. Instead they want to live in a house that's exactly the same as the one next door, which is exactly the same as the one on the telly.'

Maybe we live in a time when people don't look outside their houses. Don't look outside – you might find something really important to renovate, like a community, a way of life, a social fabric. No, just put a new bathroom in, a new parents' retreat. Build up the walls in your house to shut out the outside.

What could bridge that gap? That gap between the lifestyle renovation and the world outside, our new uncertain world? Ten millimetres can.

I looked at the building inspector. 'Why does it matter?' I asked him.

He looked at me. 'It's ten too high, someone might trip. Trip and sue the council.'

I looked at him. 'No one has ever tripped on that step. It's been there four years.'

He looked at me. 'I may believe you. That could be true. But, matey, who would have thought that people would drive jet planes into big tall buildings?'

I blinked.

To stand in my house with a step ten millimetres too high and invoke the awful day when people 'drove' planes into 'big tall buildings' was too much. If he had just said that regulations are regulations that would have been okay. But to play the big fear card all for the sake of ten millimetres was too much.

This is the world we live in. I looked at him, he looked at me.

'What if I fixed a strip of carpet on the floorboards at the bottom of the step?' I said slowly.

He looked at me. 'Yep, I can live with that,' he said.

Well, good for him. I guess we all have to live with something. I've got to live with paisley carpet on the floorboards. Until the next renovation, which may be four years down the track.

· It is evident from this trend of reinvesting in the family home that the purpose is no longer to provide a source of security and protection. Instead, it becomes the cornerstone upon which wealth can be created and self-worth assessed. Family homes provide equity with which funds can be raised to buy more properties, and in many cases this has enabled new generations to benefit.

Franco (Frank) De Rossi is the son of Angelo and Lina, and since buying into the family farm he has continued the family appreciation of property as a method of wealth creation. 'We've been able to go outside the square and invest, and the kids have been following in our footsteps,' he says with a hint of pride.

For Frank's daughter, Amanda De Rossi, it's clear what drives her parents. 'Dad just wants to make sure everyone's got somewhere

Lucy De Rossi with her children, Daniel, Amanda and Renee, at home, 1982.

to live. You know, it's your security, you've got somewhere to go,' she says as she drives down the street of a housing estate in Griffith. It's a familiar sight to many, only a few trees here and there, more are yet to grow, and the houses sit on easements dotted with bits of lawn, for the landscaping is yet to be done.

Amanda pulls to a stop and smiles. 'So this is the first unit I purchased; when I came back from holidays Dad saw this in the papers and thought it would be a good thing to work towards. It was bought off the plan and I've never lived in it. It's been rented ever since.' She smiles again.

'The kids have had to rent – at times,' says Frank as he sits beside his wife Lucy in the house they have renovated and enlarged and used as the base to build the family's security.

Lucy adds quietly, 'Only Renee.'

There is a pause and Frank, a pretty jolly man with a hearty outlook on life, almost seems a bit embarrassed at the thought that someone in his family would rent. 'Only for short periods,' he says. 'Then we quickly worked out the sums and said it's not worth it, you're . . .' He corrects himself and almost smiles as Lucy shoots him a look. 'We're better off buying something for you. And that's what we did.'

Renee De Rossi, who had been renting for about seven years, laughs with a humour she shares with her father. 'My parents couldn't fathom the idea of paying rent to somebody else. So Dad said he would buy a place that I could move into.'

Renee thinks for a bit. 'When I thought about it, I knew it would be better for me if I could contribute towards it. It's not an apartment I could have afforded on my own, so we came to an agreement where we were both owners of the property.' She smiles and says, 'That made me feel much better.'

For Frank and Lucy the concept is quite simple. 'Why pay rent for the rest of your life? All you're doing is giving the money to somebody else. It's always better to pay interest than to pay tax.' His eyes twinkle.

Lucy finishes for him, 'And eventually own it yourself.' She looks away a little shyly.

Frank, though, has no qualms. 'Well, that's my philosophy.'

'That's right,' says Lucy quietly.

Renee is acutely aware of how lucky she is, for at a time when the average home in Sydney is worth more than nine times the average annual salary, people are increasingly discovering that the Australian Dream has actually become unaffordable.

And in some cases chasing the dream can end in bitter disappointment.

Left to right: *Sandra, Lina, Genoveffa and Francesco (Angelo's parents visiting from Italy), Angelo and Frank De Rossi, 1973.*

Sophia Helene was renting when she first met Joe Doueihi in 1996. Together they were soon pursuing the Dream in northern New South Wales and married six years later in 2002.

Their first step was a modest but modern three-bedroom house north of Coffs Harbour. Sophia and Joe owned and lived in their first home for three years until 2001, when they sold it to purchase their favourite property in Emerald Beach.

'I was really, really excited to have my own home – to have a place to do something with,' says Sophia. 'We renovated it, we didn't do any major structural work but we got it to the point where it was just lovely.

'It was four bedrooms, two bathrooms, a three-quarter-acre block. A couple of minutes to the beach and anybody who came there felt the peace, the love in the place. It was a beautiful home,' says Sophia, almost wistfully.

Joe can't help but agree. 'The house in Emerald Beach was probably as close to my dream home as I came because it was a big old place on a bit of land. I love land. Three-quarters of an acre to me was like ten or twenty acres to most other people, because I just loved it.'

Joe and Sophia's love affair with their home didn't stop there. Sophia explains. 'Joe's idea of the dream was to expand and to use the available equity in our home, as a financial base to feed the rest of his dream – owning multiple properties.'

Joe's grand plan was to 'amass a property portfolio of about, possibly, say ten properties'. As he says it he shifts a little in his seat. 'My plan was to start off with one.'

Sophia stares blankly ahead and somehow as soon as you hear the word 'amass' you have a feeling that this story won't end happily. 'He always said, "I know how you can make money from property,"' she says.

Joe considers this for a bit and comes up with a thought. 'Probably ten properties may have been a bit too big. I was being ambitious. But it's very hard to explain, I used to drive past and say, "Well, I own this one and I own that one." Yeah.'

It was a dream and Joe and Sophia were living it. The couple had no superannuation, so this portfolio was going to be the means by which they could enjoy their old age together. It was a dream.

'I knew a little bit, I had been studying property investment strategies for some time,' says Sophia and she pauses, trying to find the right words to express Joe's understanding of the realities of a property portfolio. 'And he didn't really know anything, so when we did buy an investment property it was the wrong property because I let him follow his dream.'

'Now, I didn't do a hell of a lot of research,' says Joe. 'I relied on the buyer's agent. He seemed like a fairly nice person.' Joe smiles a little, then says with a bit of effort, 'But at the end of the day he's a businessperson.'

The couple bought some flats and again did all the renovations themselves to keep costs down. There is a picture of Sophia smiling beneath a facemask giving the thumbs-up sign.

In the end the flats couldn't be rented out with a consistent return, and with a series of upkeep repairs requiring more funds, the strains of paying off these properties in addition to running a small business began to show.

'The dream turns into the nightmare,' says Sophia.

When their business failed they moved into rental accommodation and let out their dream home by the beach. Joe's idea was to get employment in Sydney, maintain the payments on the properties using the rental income, and then save enough to buy another property in Sydney.

When Sophia and Joe looked through their financial situation, however, they came to the awful realisation that even with the income from rent, their outgoings were too great. Each month they were two and a half thousand dollars in debt.

'You probably could have exploded an atomic bomb in front of me and I'd still have been sitting there. I would have to say that was the lowest point in my life,' says Joe. He is so open in his acceptance of his dream falling apart that it's painful to hear.

'I was simply relieved to see the truth in black and white,' says Sophia.

The couple have since separated and now Sophia lives in a three-bedroom apartment in the outer Sydney suburb of Bankstown. 'I'm in rented accommodation that somebody else owns and I am the happiest I have ever been – with no debt. Not even credit card debt, and I own my own car. My life is simple and I am happy.'

Joe shares a house owned by his brother with some other people. It's a nice, comfortable house. 'My housemates are all very lovely people but I miss having my own home and my privacy.'

Despite all he has gone through, despite all he has lost, Joe can't help himself. 'At one stage there I thought, No, this is crazy, this dream I have is not going to work, it's ludicrous. Um . . .' He looks away, embarrassed almost, until he confides with a sad smile, 'it's still there, it won't go away.'

The idea of home is a powerful one to Australians. Roger and Olive Robbins sought safety, security and stability in their home in Hampton. They bought in a street where many other returned servicemen had bought houses and raised their families. But as time has come and gone those families have become fewer and the street has changed, as Australia itself has changed.

'What Australia is like now to what it was when we were building is so different. You know, we have good Italian friends and they have been out here for a long time but they won't believe me when I tell them what things were like here just after the war,' says Olive.

'I mean, the food you can buy now and the refrigerators and the air conditioners – there was none of that. The cars, now everyone can just about have a new car if they want it – my old Humber, I think I pushed it more than I drove it. People won't believe you when you say how much this place has changed.'

Perhaps that is because to be completely honest about recognising and accepting change, a person has to accept their own mortality. We, all of us, are temporary and perhaps that urge to rise above our finite nature leads us to pursue the Australian Dream. In a world where all is impermanent, a sense of security can be attained and can hold us for a little while.

After a lifetime of creating and making houses into homes, from Narrabeen to Wellington, New Zealand, to Norfolk Island to Sweden and now to the hill in Hornsby, Carol Berling sits in her home. After all her adventures and the things she has done, she was diagnosed with mesothelioma. Asbestos cancer.

'I'd never heard of it. I didn't know what it was but I have become an expert on it now. There is no cure, it's terminal.'

She speaks in her measured, thoughtful tone, and Bertil flicks her a look now and then.

'The average time from diagnosis to dying is 153 days. So what am I still doing here three years later? Goodness knows, but I'm living and I'm not living to fight cancer, I'm living to live.'

Bertil gives a proud nod of his head.

How she was exposed to the asbestos dust has occupied her thoughts, but not her whole life. 'Playing hopscotch, there were fibres everywhere, some of our renovations, some of our houses were covered in asbestos. Perhaps some of the nightclubs and restaurants I helped refurbish. It's criminal, absolutely criminal that the companies who made it knew about the dangers. It doesn't need a lot of exposure, so it can get anyone.'

But she is home.

'When it's a day like today and the sun is out and I'm in my own place. Yeah, it's good; it's good to be alive. I think this place has done a lot for my wellbeing. I find it a very soothing house.'

The idea of home to Carol is simple. 'Security. I think that is a very important thing to me and to gain security you've got to have love. And love is warmth. Safe, safety.'

Along the street where I live, I walk with my daughter. What is the difference between a house and a home, she asked me. I haven't been able to give her an answer. Down the other end of the street, where an old tyre factory with the glorious name of South Pacific Tyres once stood, a new housing estate is being built. It's been given a name that a marketing genius has, with great pride no doubt, thought up: Banbury Village. It sounds like something out of an Agatha Christie novel. No, that is being unfair to Agatha Christie. It sounds like something from a would-be Agatha Christie novel. Something twee and neat and homely.

The houses are being built. The gossip in the Jelly Bread Café is that some of the houses have been bought off the plan for over a million dollars.

One million dollars. I wonder in a vague way how much a Mater Prize Home, that home attainable only through the luck of a draw, would now cost. Should you put a cost on a dream? Well, everybody seems to today.

Those houses had seemed so big to my mother and aunt as we shuffled through them. So big. But that was a long time ago. Today, new Australian homes on average are the biggest in the world. Outstripping America and Europe and New Zealand. The Australian Bureau of Statistics released data showing that the typical size of a new Australian home is 215 square metres.

Those who could afford, and perhaps those who thought they could afford it, bought a dream that was swollen in terms of price paid and of living spaces available.

I look at my daughter and wonder whether she will ever be able to own her home. Her own home. I cannot imagine my home without her and her brother in it, but then I suppose that is how all parents feel.

For almost fifty years after the Second World War the average Australian home could be bought for three times the average household's annual income. Today in Melbourne, Adelaide and Brisbane it is six times the average annual income, and in Perth and Sydney it is eight times that.

There is a fair chance that many low and middle income earners will never realise that Great Australian Dream. They will be lifetime renters.

Or perhaps some will be like the man under the trees; they may well become part of the nation's homeless. On Census night in 2006, according to the Australian Bureau of Statistics, the homeless population numbered 105,000 people.

Our street is changing. Time slips by. My daughter holds my hand and I do something that I should have done as soon as she asked me her question. I admit that I don't exactly know what makes a home different from a house.

'Perhaps,' I suggest, 'perhaps you might be able to tell me?'

She smiles and says simply, 'A house is a house but a home is where I live. With the people I love.' And she waves her arms in a circle, a circle that seems to cover the whole street and the sky and beyond.

There's an answer that Olive and Roger, Kevin and his mob, the De Rossi family and Dolly Wilson and her Ronnie, and brave Carol and Bertil, and Joe and Sophia would be happy with, I think.

An answer for us all.

Australia Day

It's muggy and moist and it's morning. It's Sydney. And it's Australia Day. The noise that wakes me is a voice over a loudspeaker telling the fishermen on McMahons Point wharf to vacate for the day's ferry service, which begins at eight o'clock.

I lean up in my bed and look outside. Framed in the window is the birthplace of European Australia: Sydney Harbour. I glance down and see a lone fisherman packing up his gear. The scene is like a moving postcard, with all the icons sandwiched neatly into the frame. Luna Park, the Bridge, Sydney Opera House, Circular Quay, and behind and above, the city of Sydney.

The harbour is quiet. I get up and start the day.

I am staying in an old sixties high-rise block of flats, like the ones that sprang up at the time – when Sydney was beginning to be a developer's paradise. Further around the bay is a Harry Seidler box.

The block I'm in is somehow reassuring and cosy. I ponder vaguely if there's any marble anywhere and whether it's travertine – the same stuff as they used in the Colosseum. I wonder what happened to that real estate salesman. But then I doubt there's any travertine: this block of flats doesn't seem to have changed much since it was first built. The families who bought the flats back then have kept them.

The place is constantly filled with folk from the country, as most of the apartments were bought as town homes by people from out west and beyond. There are always lots of families in the building, which is nice, always someone about who's up for a chat.

The night before, mucking around in the apartments' pool, which is separated from Sydney Harbour by a few metres of landscaping and stonework, I chatted to a man about the same age as me. His grandfather had bought a flat in the block when it was built and every January since the family has holidayed there.

He looked at the kids, both his and mine, playing in the pool and said, 'You know, I've grown up in this pool. And that's no bad thing – it's not a bad little pond to play in.' Then he gave a nod to the vast harbour dotted with lights. 'It's changed a bit, but it's not a bad spot.'

That was last night. Now I head out, up a couple of floors to where my mother-in-law is staying. I stomp up the stairs, serenaded by a woman walking down, singing 'Que Sera Sera', the old Doris Day song. I don't see her before I leave the stairwell, but as is so often the case, when you hear a song in the morning, it stays with you for the rest of the day.

I have a couple of jobs to do this Australia Day. One is hosting an Australia Day concert in Sydney's outdoor venue the Domain; the other, and far more important, job is to wipe my mother-in-law's windows. She wants a clearer view of the harbour's traffic and can't reach out there herself. There's next to nothing happening on the harbour at the moment, but as the day draws on it will teem with vessels of all shapes, sizes and forms.

I reach around and clean away the salty film on the window. As soon as I lean outside, it's as if I've entered the day proper. It's hot, and the skies are clear. My mother-in-law says there is talk of a storm brewing later in the day.

I have breakfast with my wife, our children and my mother-in-law, watching as the harbour begins to fill with craft. Black military helicopters scoot this way and that like giant locusts. Tall ships and ferries gather. A huge Sea King helicopter chugs through the sky, towing a massive Australian flag.

We sit and watch until it's time for my next job. When I reach the wharf, to catch the ferry from McMahons Point to Circular Quay, I wave up to the apartment, and my family wave back. Even at this distance I can see my wife and daughter smiling. Then I look a little closer and realise I am waving at the wrong people. Nevertheless, it's a beautiful day. The blue of the sky is matched by the harbour's water.

There are Australian flags everywhere: on the wharf, on boats, in the windows of units and homes. On a bus parked by the wharf and as tattoos stuck on the cheeks of a little boy waiting with his parents for the ferry.

We travel across the harbour. As we go past Luna Park a mother in an oversized windcheater, carrying an Australian flag almost as big as the one towed beneath the Sea King helicopter, bellows at her children to stand still and smile.

'Bigger, I'm just trying to get the big mouth behind you. Smile, SMILE, it's Australia Day!'

The kids grimace and the mother snaps, holding the camera in front of her to check the screen, and then nods. 'That's a beauty.'

The kids turn and look at the water churning as the ferry makes its way to Circular Quay. 'Can we sit in the shade, Mum?'

But Mum is sitting, smiling at the camera. 'What a beauty.'

She chuckles and shows an elderly American couple the image. They nod and smile along with her.

'That sure is a big set of teeth,' says the elderly American man.

'Yeah, very LA!' laughs his wife.

I walk through Circular Quay, past all the people milling about, past the buskers – some didgeridoo players and frozen statues who move a little too much for a small boy, who bursts into tears when a statue suddenly waves to him. His parents laugh and pick up the boy to comfort him.

A busker sits cross-legged in his spot near the waterside railing and slowly wipes his didgeridoo with a cloth. He's talking with a man who looks European, German maybe. This man, dressed in khaki trek-style clothing, is festooned with cameras.

'But it's not your day? This day?' the camera man asks.

'Well, matey, it's called Australia Day but whether it's a day where my people feel like they can have a party is a bit of a question.'

'You are not Australian?' asks the man with the cameras.

''Course I am. Come on, mate, we're the original mob. I'll have a good day. I don't mind people having a party, just hope people think a bit about things.'

The man with the cameras stares and then asks if he can take the busker's photo.

The busker finishes wiping his didgeridoo and laughs. 'Yeah, why not?'

I walk past last night's leftover drunks and street people, staring at the mass of people who smile and take photos, the families and friends and those who stand alone.

This is Australia Day, faces change and come and go, faces of all ages and colours and shapes.

Vintage double-decker buses parade around; once they ruled the streets of this city along with trams, but that was years ago. Years. The Opera House seems to have been here forever, but really it's only middle-aged. It used to be a tram depot. Things change quickly.

Up in Macquarie Street I find an assembly of vintage cars parked bumper to bumper. I notice that vintage cars no longer just include Model Ts and the like but also the cars of my youth. I look around and see touchstones of my life.

Holdens in which I used to go to drive-ins with my family; a Morris Minor like my mother's, and a panel van, the same as the one the toughs on the corner by the shop would clean and polish to prowl the streets in search of cheap thrills.

An old Kingswood. I kissed a girl in a car like that, hoped for a bit more and then nearly wet myself when her father banged on the roof and yelled through the window at me, 'A kiss is all right, but you should have kept both hands on the wheel!'

I'd borrowed the car from a mate because it was the only car I knew of that worked. He never forgave me for the dent in the roof.

Someone laughs; it's a woman, laughing at a man who is almost beside himself as he strokes a green car.

'Oh, Ross,' she guffaws, 'for goodness' sake, it's a just a car.'

'It's not just a car, it's not. It's a Charger!'

Then there is an S Series Valiant, the car my wife was driving when we first met. I look at the flowing lines and the fins and remember the day I met her. And I smile.

I see a tall, middle-aged man reflected in the gleaming windows. He looks a little rumpled, a little thick around the middle, a little barrel-chested. And I see he's smiling. In a way, he looks a little like my father. Only a little.

It's me. I'm getting older. It's pretty obvious when I think about it, but that's not a bad thing. Then a man interrupts me, asking me about the car I'm looking at. I tell him it's an S Series Valiant.

'Is it yours?' he asks.

'No,' I say, 'but someone I know owned one once.'

'They don't make cars like this now,' he says.

He is dressed well, in a suit and tie. In fact, what I take to be his family are all dressed up.

'The cars these days, they look much the same. It's hard to believe they all used to look so different.'

I nod. 'Things change, I guess.'

The man nods. Then he laughs. 'They do,' he says. He has a big smile. He is very tall. He's African, I think. But I'm wrong.

'They do,' he says again. 'Today I became Australian! My wife and I, my children, we are Aussies!"

The man who was drooling over the Charger looks over and says, 'Congratulations!'

His laughing wife says, 'Welcome aboard!'

'Thank you,' replies the man.

I walk around the Domain, to where the stage for the concert is set. As I walk I think about how Australians are like those old cars in Macquarie Street. We come in all shapes and sizes and colours. All types. New and old, good and bad. We may share characteristics but we are all our own stories.

Living in a place like Australia, it's good to remind ourselves to listen and ask and learn about each other's stories. When that happens we share each other's experiences. That's what is making modern Australia – all our stories.

Then I try to whistle a little of the song I heard on the stairwell that morning, 'Whatever will be, will be.'

Endnotes

Chapter 1

Page

22   'The Minister thinks' quote: National Archives of Australia, A 461, A 3490/1/7 Part 1 Immigration Child, Immigration General, Guide to Records; Coldrey, Barry, *Good British Stock: Child and Youth Migration To Australia*, 1999.

29   Horne, Donald, *The Lucky Country*, Penguin Australia, first published 1964.

34   'A bodgie is' quote: National Film and Sound Archive collection, 84244, *Menace – or Just Another Craze: Bodgies and the Widgies*, 1951.

Chapter 3

65   'A mother's primary' quote: Santamaria, B.A., National Film and Sound Archive collection: 18928, *Point of View. P.V. 404*, 1974.

Chapter 7

97   'What sort of' quote: Lenin, Vladimir Ilyich, 'V.I. Lenin: In Australia', Marxists Internet Archive www.marxists.org/archive/lenin/works/1913/jun/13.htm

98   'the maintenance of' quote: Deakin, quoted in Frank Parsons, 'Australasian Methods of Dealing with Immigration', *Annals of the American Academy of Political and Social Science* no. 431 (July 1904), Immigration Restriction League Papers, Houghton Library, Ms Am 2245 (1111).
      Source for the above: Lake, Marilyn and Reynolds, Henry, *Drawing the Global Colour Line: White Men's Countries and the Question of Racial Equality*, Melbourne University Press, 2008.

116 'The threat of' quote: Menzies, Robert, National Film and Sound Archive collection, 17314, *Menace*, 1952.

122 'My basic opposition' quote: Santamaria, B.A., National Film and Sound Archive collection, 18955, *Point of View. P.V. 435*, 1974.

Chapter 8

132 'I didn't come' quote: Graham, Billy, ABC Library Sales: 218587, *This Day Tonight – Program – Dr Billy Graham*.

Chapter 9

146 Catholic experience: Noone, Val, *Disturbing the War: Melbourne Catholics and Vietnam*, Spectrum Publications, 1993, page 189.

167   'The council thinks' quote: Rashid Raashed in interview with Lyn Gallacher, *The Religion Report: Mosques and Priests*, 4 November 1998: Radio National Transcripts, www.abc.net.au/rn/talks/8.30/relrpt/trr9845.htm

Chapter 10

171   Senescall, Rebecca and Narushima, Yuko, 'Backlash over new Islamic school', *Sydney Morning Herald*, 6 November 2007.

172   'Churches united against Camden Islamic school', *CathNews*, 21 May 2009.

178   World Youth Day figures: Lee, Julian and Saulwick, Jacob, 'Doubts raised over economic benefits', *Sydney Morning Herald*, 9 July 2008.

179   'Australian support for' quote: Nicholls, David, 'Australia – Guilty by Supportive Association', Atheist Foundation of Australia, 5 May, 2008.

180   'The promotion of' quote: Keane, Bernard, 'Kevin and Mary: a match made in Heaven', *Crikey*, 14 December 2009.

Chapter 13

234   'I think what' quote: Greer, Germaine, ABC Library Sales: 299225, *This Day Tonight – Program – Germaine Greer*, 1972.

Chapter 16

280   'into which no stranger' quote: Menzies, Robert, 1942, 'The forgotten people: a broadcast address delivered Friday, May 22, 1942 through 2UE Sydney, 3AW Melbourne', Robertson and Mullens, Melbourne, 1942.

Chapter 18

296–97   'The block of flats to be erected' quote: Abram Landa, NSW Housing Minister, 1958, in 'Sticky Bricks play wows Sydney Arts Festival', *The 7.30 Report*, Australian Broadcasting Corporation, January 2006.

Chapter 19

303   'double oven stove' quote: *Home Sweet Home*, Australian Broadcasting Corporation, 1968.

304   Immigration encouragement: Essential Media and Entertainment, Episode 'The Australian Dream', 2010.

308–09   'Visiting a Mater' quote: Harris, Nigel, www.materprizehome.com.au/

Chapter 20

329   Housing figures: Martin, Peter, 'Home truths: Australia trumps US when it comes to McMansions', *Sydney Morning Herald*, 30 November 2009.

Acknowledgements

Thank you to Ron and Marjorie Palmer and the many contributors to *The Making of Modern Australia* – the book and the documentary series – who so generously shared their personal stories. From 'The Australian Child': Les Dixon; Helen Huynh; Rose Kruger; Karen Lawrence; Ben and Jo Madsen; Donna Meehan; Bob and Loretta Moore; and Geoff, Polly and Paedor Stirling.

From 'The Australian Soul': Abu Ahmed; Makiz Ansari; Susan Balint; Bruce Ballantine-Jones; Margaret Bennett; Beryl Carmichael; Judy and Father John Cottier; Graeme Dunstan; Chris Gresham-Britt; Sister Vianney Hatton; Maureen McLoughlin; and Val Noone, whose advice was invaluable.

From 'The Australian Heart': Marta and Tony Bárány; Fiona and Stuart Higgins, whose story first appeared in Fiona's memoir, *Love in the Age of Drought*; Beate Hirsch, who is also a writer; Katie Jones; Susan Magarey and Sue Sheridan; Peter and Sandra McCarthy; Len Masson and Ma Sujie; Graham and Rae Stevens; Robyn Taylor; and Yianni Zinonos.

Acknowledgements

From 'The Australian Dream': the De Rossi family – Lina, Angelo, Frank, Lucy, Amanda and Renee; Joe Doueihi; the Duncan family – Kevin Snr, Cindy, and Kevin Jnr; Sophia Helene; Carol and Bertil Klintfalt; Olive and Roger Robbins; and Dolly Wilson.

Thank you for helping to bring alive the story of modern Australia.

Thank you also to the hard working team at Essential Media and Entertainment: Ian Collie, Jay Court, Susan Lambert, Elissa McKeand, and Steve Westh, who produced *The Making of Modern Australia* television series and provided research, interview transcripts and photographs for this book. Thank you also to Peter Cochran, for his historical background material.

We are grateful to Jackie Chamberlin from the Mater Archives and Heritage Centre, and Mater Prize Homes for their assistance sourcing archive material.

William McInnes and Hachette Australia

Photography credits

The photographs in this book are sourced from the participants' private collections and are reproduced with their permission, with the exception of the following:

Page 34, *The West Australian*
Page 156, Yong Ah Chot
Pages 168 and 170, Kathryn Milliss, Essential Media and Entertainment
Page 193, Clem McInnes
Page 308, Mater Archives and Heritage Centre

The Making of Modern Australia
Readers' Notes

INTRODUCTION

'History, like that bird, will always try to talk to you. The least we can do is listen.' (p. 4)

With this opening gambit, the author of this book, acclaimed writer and actor William McInnes, declares his hand. This is *not* a book that repeats the stories that have been well-documented and we've all heard a thousand times before. Instead it unearths the stories the history books generally don't tell us, about ordinary Australians and how their lives reveal aspects of the Australian culture and experience that are often overlooked.

'Listening to our history' has been made possible via this book and its companions:

- The website (www.makingaustralia.com.au) allows any Australian to tell his or her story for posterity.
- The television documentary series.

This is a collection of stories about the lives and experiences of some regular people in Australia since World War Two, told in their own words. William McInnes' narrative returns to these people at various stages in time and shows how their early decisions and circumstances have affected their later lives as well. He also inserts his own childhood stories into these chapters, making this a rich amalgam of memoir, biography, oral history, and political and cultural history during the post-World War Two era in Australia.

'That is all. Nothing more, nothing less.' (p. 4)

CHAPTER NOTES AND KEY QUOTES

The following notes relate to each part and to the chapters within them, and highlight in italics key quotes that can stimulate discussions in reading groups or classrooms.

History as a Caged Cockatoo (p. 1)

'History is many things.' (p. 2)

Discussion point: As this book so richly points out, history is in the eyes of the beholder. Consider all the various 'partners' in the practice of creating history. Which versions are represented in this book?

THE AUSTRALIAN CHILD

The theme here is the changing nature and changing views of Australian childhood in the years since World War Two.

1 Just Come Back by the Time it's Dark (p. 7)

'It's like an afternoon stretching forever. Being a kid is like that. It's great.' (p. 9)

'Childhood should be like that. It's great to live and think that things just go on. It's a shame that it ends, but it does, and childhood's a beautiful thing.' (p. 9)

'. . . *you could walk anywhere in the bush.*' (p. 17)

'*The bush was as big as your dreams . . .*' (p. 18)

Discussion point: The title of this chapter is a statement most 'Baby Boomers' recall well. The years from the 1950s to the '70s were a halcyon period in which kids explored local creeks, paths and surrounding neighbourhoods, on bikes or on foot, and when parents felt a sense of assurance that their offspring would be safe. Kids felt that the world was 'a never-ending backyard' (p. 18). The quotes above about childhood are tinged with nostalgia and regret for the simple things that such a childhood represents. Does adulthood inevitably deny us these freedoms and privileges? Does today's child have access to much less freedom?

'*We were the "lucky country"*' (p. 29)

Discussion point: Donald Horne was being ironic (p. 29) when he described us as a 'lucky country' in 1964. Many believe this was a celebratory or optimistic statement about the nature of Australians, but it actually referred to our over-reliance on abundant mineral resources to the detriment of developing skills and inventing new products. Discuss.

2 Hillbilly Cats (p. 33)

'. . . *there is nothing that makes people forget the past like a booming economy.*' (p. 33)

'. . . *teenagers had become prime targets for economic growth.*' (p. 33)

'*This was the beginning of the commercialisation of childhood. And teenagers were the first target.*' (p. 39)

'*It was a new direction in culture and expression. It was music and a way of life based solely around youth.*' (p. 35)

Discussion point: The 1950s and early '60s was the era of 'rock and roll', when teenagers were first identified as such, and when they discovered music and started dressing as bodgies and widgies (p. 33) to distinguish themselves from their parents. Les Dixon in Perth in 1956 was a fan of the new music and listened to and played like the great 'hillbilly cat', Elvis Presley. He watched shows like *Six O'clock Rock* with Johnny O'Keefe and *Bandstand*. Even Rose Kruger would sneak out of the orphanage to visit the Snake Pit. Before that time teenagers didn't nominally exist; children became adults, not adolescents. These new trends developed a whole new market. Teenagers wanted new clothes, music, places to 'hang out' and new forms of transport, too. So was this as much an economic as a social revolution? Discuss.

'. . . out on the fringes of society there was a group of children whose presence and status remained unrecognised . . .' (p. 40)

'It's a horrible irony that at the time of this removal, the 1960s, the family was seen as the core element of society.' (p. 46)

Discussion point: Donna Meehan grew up in an Aboriginal camp in Coonamble, New South Wales (p. 40) and she and her brothers were taken by the state in 1960 (p. 43). As one of the Stolen Generations (p. 46) she spent her life without a birth mother or father, without a family network, and without access to her own culture. She shared with her German migrant adoptive parents a sense of isolation in society. Did you know about the forced removals and displacement of so many Aboriginal children? Discuss it further.

3 Family Nights (p. 56)

'The adult world can't discuss sex sensibly.' (p. 60)

'. . . in 1973, when teenage pregnancies accounted for nearly eight per cent of the babies born in Australia.' (p. 63)

Discussion point: Until the 1960s, sexual behaviour among teenagers and young adults was very restricted. Bob and Loretta Moore speak about the expectation to be a virgin when one was married. Les Dixon and Rose Kruger married young (to other partners) (p. 58) as a result of teenage pregnancy. Abortions and STDs were rife (p. 59) due to a lack of sex education, and there was a prurient attitude to sex education, which only began in the 1960s (p. 60). Even today fathers still find it awkward to explain sex, as William admits (pp. 60–61). What should be done to make teenagers more aware of the issue of sex and its consequences?

4 A Kid's Job (p. 72)

'. . . childminding became a major industry.' (p. 78)

Discussion point: The issue of double-parent incomes, working families and childcare (pp. 78–79) is raised in Jo Madsen's story; the daughter of Bob and Loretta Moore, she and her husband Ben Madsen have a baby daughter Georgina (pp. 79–81). Jo has a full-time job and a full-time nanny, and her toddler takes classes every day, and is not yet in pre-school. Discuss the possible impacts of this change in our lifestyles (for and against) in a debate, drawing on research and others' personal experiences.

'Why'd you give us away?' (p. 81)

'An apology costs you nothing, and if you don't mean it then it's worth less than that. But if you mean what you say, then, brother, there's not the richest man's treasure that's worth more.' (p. 83)

'One of the greatest crimes humans can commit is to steal a person's childhood.' (p. 83)

Discussion point: Reconciliation between the aggrieved victims of past injustice and those who instituted such policies is a suggested theme in this section of the book, which tells of how Donna Meehan's mother found her (p. 81) and refers to the National Apology to the Stolen Generations in 2008 (Donna Meehan) and Forgotten Generation in 2010 (Rose Kruger) (pp. 82–83). Discuss some of the situations suggested in this chapter, regarding both the Stolen and Forgotten generations. Read some memoir, fiction and non-fiction on the former, such as *Home* (2004) by Larissa Behrendt and *Rabbit-proof Fence* (2002) by Doris Pilkington, or the latter, such as *The Forgotten Children* (2007) by David Hill.

THE AUSTRALIAN SOUL

The theme of this part is religious and spiritual belief, and the decline of organised Christianity in Australia, as well as the growth of multi-denominational religions.

6 My Front Doorbell (p. 91)

'Well, you're something.' (p. 96)

Discussion point: McInnes describes the series of people who come to his door either selling or seeking help; some are wasted, mentally ill or vagrants. But Ron Palmer (p. 93) is a sort of symbol of all we are as Australians; all that is good and decent and honest. He is 'Mr Footscray', ex RAAF, 84 years old and still loving life. Do you agree with this idea that Australians are basically solid and decent and that everyone has something in them that demands respect?

7 Postwar Prophets (p. 97)

'Nobody knew what was going to happen, so going off to church was a part of holding on to your routine.' (p. 101)

Discussion point: The postwar period, although founded on a democratic system, was nevertheless also divided by the White Australia Policy (p. 97) and religious sectarianism dominated by Catholics and Protestants. Ron Palmer returned from war to his beloved Footscray and a society still very conscious of religious difference, post nuclear bombs and a looming Cold War. Linda Visman was Catholic and grew up loving rituals such as Catholic sodalities (p. 104). Graeme Dunstan was a Baptist (p. 101) and there were strict rules about mixing with other religions, although he found that Presbyterian dances were where he could meet girls! Maureen McLoughlin was from a staunch Labor Catholic family (p. 104) and was not allowed to attend Protestant ceremonies, even weddings. There were businesses that wouldn't employ Catholics and vice versa. Margaret McLoughlin married Gordon Bennett (p. 108) in a Presbyterian church which 'became her life'. John Cottier discovered religion (p. 110) and says that 'over a long time it came to me' (p. 111), and he became a minister. Vianney Hatton (p. 111) joined a strict order of Catholic nuns. If you interviewed a range of people today would you find that the majority would profess to observing a religion? Or would they be in a minority? Test your assumptions.

> 'Too much religion is never much chop in the end. You can't think straight.' (p. 122)

Discussion point: The 1950s was a time of religious and political divisiveness and not the calm and secure period that it's often described. Discuss.

8 Spreading the Word (p. 124)

> 'There were more and more enticements to lure Australians away from indulging in too much religion — and it wasn't just the beach.' (p. 130)

Discussion point: The 1950s and '60s were a more secular time because of prosperity, a growing middle class and new interests, and the word 'teenager' became common. Churches fought the new temptations by supporting the four-month rally tour conducted by US evangelist Billy Graham (p. 131) in 1959, which was attended by three million out of the 10-million-strong population of Australia at the time (DVD). Bruce Ballantine-Jones and Graeme Dunstan were both at the rallies, but where Bruce embraced them and became a preacher, Graeme never visited a Baptist church again, and the two went on separate paths (pp. 132–35). What were some of the enticements and obstacles that lured people like Bruce into the fold and yet encouraged people like Graeme to reject Christianity?

10 Just Wait Until the Fireworks (p. 171)

'Here on this night, with these people, that seems to be a pretty good circle to be in. The Australian Soul.' (p. 184)

Discussion Point: The annual Carols by Candlelight in Footscray is painted as a quietly multi-faith and diverse event with warmth and humour. Do you agree with McInnes that such events reveal the real 'soul' of Australia?

THE AUSTRALIAN HEART

The theme of this part is relationships, sex and love, and how the sexual revolution, women's liberation, gay liberation and other such movements have affected marriage and partnerships.

11 Coffee at Balnarring (p. 187)

'Fifty and never a cross word!' (p. 190)

'It was just a natural progression, wasn't it?' (p. 197)

Discussion point: Some marriages work and some don't. Some older couples have been married for decades; some last only a few years. William McInnes reflects on his and his two friends' differing experiences. (One chooses to visit an RSVP site for online dating.) Rae Peters and Graham Stevens married in 1947 (p. 193), having met as family friends in childhood. Graeme went to war and came back to her; they simply expected to marry when the time was right. They enjoyed a model postwar marriage; he was never out of work and she never worked in the paid workforce. Their era saw an enormous boom in births, too (p. 200). Is this sort of marriage less likely today? (The divorce statistics would seem to indicate that it is less likely.)

12 Love in a Distant Land (p. 201)

'The country needed more young, single women to marry these men.'
(p. 209)

Discussion point: Like Marta, Beate Hirsch was a single woman who arrived in Australia, tempted by a new life proposed by Immigration Minister Arthur Calwell's subsidy to bring women here for at least two years (p. 209). However, she didn't realise that the policy's aim was to provide potential partners for the many skilled workers who'd been recruited. Unfortunately, her story wasn't as happy as Marta's. In 1959 she met Eric, became pregnant and the latter left her (p. 219); she considered suicide but battled on and eventually married Peter, another seemingly protective man, and had her son. Read this immigrant's story in the context of works of literature such as Richard Flanagan's *The Sound of One Hand Clapping* and non-fiction analysis of the times. The policy had some positive and negative outcomes. Discuss.

13 Smile, It's the Sixties (p. 221)

'In 1961 the contraceptive pill changed sex forever.' (p. 221)

Discussion point: Access to contraceptives, and to the rights which the women's liberation movement would bring, was all ahead of the women who matured into adulthood in this era. Susan Magarey was educated and liberated, but she was still expected to marry and to keep a home, and not particularly encouraged to become better-educated. However, sexual freedom meant individual choice and gave women and men more options. How did the introduction of contraception alter the social strata of society? Discuss.

'If Men Got Pregnant Abortion Would Be a Sacrament.' (p. 235)

Discussion point: This witty slogan highlights the inequity in a situation where men and patriarchal institutions such as the Catholic Church can dictate to a woman what she should do with her body. Debate this argument.

14 It's About Time (p. 236)

'At least bloody Oscar Wilde dressed properly when they locked him up . . .' (p. 239)

Discussion point: Gay liberation has changed attitudes to homosexuality, and despite Australia's overtly 'ocker' male culture, we've been a country that has allowed gay rights to flourish. Yianni Zinonos wished he was Barbra Streisand (p. 241) when he watched the film *What's Up, Doc?*, and he later found his family's homeland, Greece, to be excitingly free. But for many gay Australians, an open lifestyle is still restricted. Discuss.

'A new . . . term was born: the Sensitive New Age Guy.' (p. 249)

Discussion point: Recently, tolerance for men who behave in ways perceived to be more 'feminine' has grown, reflecting a change in Australian attitudes. Bob Hawke's famous tears about his daughter's addiction were a public statement of that, and it's evinced in general fashion and lifestyle too. (For example, men now have facials, and wear clothes which are more stylish than they once were.) Discuss gender roles and how they might be differently played out in a relationship. For example, Peter McCarthy isn't interested in becoming a woman, just in dressing like one. As a cross-dresser (p. 251) he attends 'Seahorse Society' (p. 253) meetings with his wife. Are there limits to how a man can behave in public? How tolerant are your friends and family?

15 Forever and Ever (p. 257)

'Marriage is no longer the bedrock of financial and emotional security.' (p. 265)

Discussion point: Romance survives despite these many social changes, as William indicates in his feelings about his wife (p. 265). Has sexual liberation made people more careful to preserve their romances, rather than less so?

THE AUSTRALIAN DREAM

The theme of this part is 'home' and the evolution of the 'great Australian dream' of owning a house/home.

16 At the End of the Street (p. 269)

'It was changing.' (p. 271)

Discussion point: McInnes observes a familiar homeless man (pp. 270–1) while walking with his daughter. He reflects on how his suburb in Melbourne and all our capital cities are undergoing a transformation which many find unsettling. Gentrification and high-density inner city dwellings are necessitating government investment in infrastructure such as roads, bridges and tunnels. Renovation is a national pastime. Is this a sustainable trend? Does this development obscure from our attention the many homeless people who also populate the nation and who have no hope of participating in this pattern of renewal and growth?

17 One Room at a Time (p. 280)

'Instead it became an aspirational concept of self-worth and success.'
(p. 280)

Discussion point: In the postwar period, a busy time of building began, albeit of fairly modest homes compared to today's. Angelo and Lina De Rossi (p. 281) were Italian migrants who worked very hard to acquire a home so that they could pass on a better life to their children. Carol Berling (p. 287) was four when her parents, who were 'ten-pound Poms', emigrated from England. She grew up in a fibro home in a street full of rubble as others created their dreams around them. Kevin Duncan, one of the Moree Gomilaroi mob, was the first Aboriginal tradesman as a builder, married Coral Joy Binge, and they had a happy home which he built himself. He was granted the first Aboriginal loan, and can feel proud of what he's contributed to Moree. (And yet Indigenous housing is still short, and the NT intervention (p. 295) is stark evidence of what is still to be achieved nationally.) The title of this chapter is descriptive of the slow growth in people's fortunes in this era. Compare this to the pattern in contemporary life where young couples purchase huge 'McMansions' and furnish them in the latest style, before discarding them.

18 It Looked Like Hollywood (p. 296)

'. . . the reason it's my home is that I had them here.' (p. 302)

'. . . there's plenty jumping off this building here.' (p. 299)

Discussion point: Dolly and Ronnie Wilson moved to Northcutt (p. 297) when it was built as a pioneering high-rise public housing development in 1960. They'd never owned a house and were happy to have a home there. (Although for many people such developments are not happy.) There's a story about a boy throwing a beer can (pp. 300–2) at Dolly's window which speaks volumes about neighbourly kindness. Dolly lost both her husband and daughter Marcie but has fond memories of making a home with them there. What messages did you take from Dolly Wilson's story? Discuss the fact that such seemingly isolating, even dangerous, places can be considered 'home' by those who've always lived there.

19 Different Dreams (p. 303)

'It's the same type of marble as used in the Colosseum.' (p. 303)

Discussion point: Australians have fallen in love with the idea of the 'dream home', epitomised by the Mater Prize Homes of the 1960s and '70s. But is the dream real? Has Australia fallen too heavily for hyperbole and spin? Discuss.

20 What's a Home? (p. 315)

'Don't look outside – you might find something really important to renovate, like a community, a way of life, a social fabric.' (p. 320)

'Instead, it becomes the cornerstone upon which wealth can be created and self-worth assessed.' (p. 321)

'You're my friends and it's a good thing to build a good home.' (p. 319)

Discussion point: The home renovation team *chez* McInnes is hilarious (p. 319) but the message here is that it's not about the improvement, but about the process of sharing (with family and friends) in the house's development. In contrast to McInnes' fond memories of his shambolic 'renos', he suggests that today many people's renovations have become seriously flawed pretences to betterment and social and economic superiority. How does this differ from postwar families desperate to secure themselves with an edifice symbolic of their prosperity? Discuss.

Australia Day (p. 331)

'We come in all shapes and sizes . . .' (p. 336)

Discussion point: Is tolerance the central message of this book and series? Does it have an underlying ideal cloaked in its colloquial, tangential and wry humour? Do Australians need to be reminded of their innate egalitarianism? Or of their ability to survive as a small country in an ocean of global competitors? Is this approach more powerful than issuing a rallying call for action, fierce criticisms of our failures as a nation, or a dire message about potential outcomes of the flaws in the Australian character which are outlined here? Discuss.

CONCLUSION

Reading this book is like walking down a memory lane inhabited by both McInnes' loved ones and by many others whose lives have touched him. It may also remind you of history books you've read, which outline the trends and influences that have determined the development of Australia over the last 60 years. McInnes cleverly reflects on many of them, but in such a way that the reader is disarmed and made aware, as if in passing, of the major strands of our cultural life and psyche. Moreover, his self-deprecating insertion of his own experiences serves to highlight the fact that each of us is a 'microcosm' of Australia – whether we be a talented actor and writer, or a postwar immigrant or an Aboriginal person denied their status in society until far too recently.

We all have a story, and we all contribute to the grand – and often not so grand – narrative of what Australia is, and more importantly, what it *can* be in the future.

RESOURCES

Fiction, Memoir, Plays

Ballou, Emily 2007, *Aphelion*, Sydney, Picador.

Behrendt, Larissa 2004, *Home*, St Lucia, QLD, UQP.

Behrendt, Larissa 2009, *Legacy*, St Lucia, QLD, UQP.

Bone, Ian 2002, *The Song of an Innocent Bystander*, Ringwood, VIC, Penguin.

Condon, Bill 2009, *Confessions of a Liar Thief and Teenage Sex God*, Sydney, Woolshed Press.

Do, Anh 2010, *The Happiest Refugee*, Crows Nest, NSW, Allen and Unwin.

Drewe, Robert 2000, *The Shark Net*, Sydney, Picador. [Television series available.]

Earls, Nick 1996, *After January*, St Lucia, QLD, UQP. [Play script available.]

Flanagan, Richard 1997, *The Sound of One Hand Clapping*, Ringwood, VIC, Penguin. [Film available.]

Garner, Helen 1996, *Monkey Grip*, Ringwood, VIC, Penguin. [Film available.]

Hartnett, Sonya 2002, *Of a Boy*, Camberwell, VIC, Viking Penguin.

Horniman, Joanne 2008, *My Candlelight Novel*, Crows Nest, NSW, Allen and Unwin.

Lawrinson, Julia 2008, *The Push*, Camberwell, VIC, Penguin.

Lette, Kathy and Gabrielle Carey 2002, *Puberty Blues*, Sydney, Picador. [Film available.]

Malouf, David 2008, *Johnno*, Camberwell, VIC, Penguin.

Marchetta, Melina 1992, *Looking for Alibrandi*, Ringwood, VIC, Penguin. [Film available.]

McCarthy, Maureen 1998, *In Between*, Ringwood VIC, Penguin. [Films available.]

McCarthy, Maureen 1995, *Queen Kat, Carmel and St Jude Get a Life*, Ringwood, VIC, Puffin. [Television series available.]

McInnes, William 2006, *Cricket Kings*, Sydney, Hachette Australia.

Metzenthen, David 2003, *Boys of Blood and Bone*, Camberwell, VIC, Penguin.

Perlman, Eliot 2005, *Three Dollars*, Sydney, Picador. [Film available.]

Pung, Alice 2006, *Unpolished Gem*, Melbourne, VIC, Black Inc.

Pung, Alice 2011, *Her Father's Daughter* Melbourne, VIC, Black Inc.

Rankin, Scott and Purcell, Leah 1999, *Box the Pony,* Sydney, Hodder Headline. [Play script available.]

Roy, James 2007, *Town*, St Lucia, QLD, UQP.

Seymour, Alan 1962, *The One Day of the Year*, Sydney, Angus & Robertson. [Play script.]

Sparrow, Rebecca 2006, *The Year Nick McGowan Came to Stay*, St Lucia, QLD, UQP. [Play script available.]

Wheatley, Nadia 1988, *The Blooding*, Ringwood, VIC, Viking Kestrel.

Williamson, David 1984, *The Removalists*, Sydney, Currency Press. [Play script.]

Winch, Tara June 2006, *Swallow the Air*, St Lucia, QLD, UQP.

Winton, Tim 1991, *Cloudstreet*, Ringwood, VIC, Penguin. [Film available.]

Zusak, Markus 2002, *The Messenger*, Sydney, Pan Macmillan.

Film and DVD

Samson & Delilah 2009, Dir. Warwick Thornton.

Yolngu Boy 2000, Dir. Stephen Johnson, ACTF.

Monkey Grip 1982 Dir. Ken Cameron.

Non-fiction

Anderson, Warrigal 1996, *Warrigal's Way*, UQP, St Lucia, QLD.

Brennan, Frank 1995, *One Land, One Nation: Mabo – Towards 2001* St Lucia, QLD, UQP.

Bringing Them Home: Report of the National Inquiry into the Separation of Aboriginal and Torres Strait Islander Children from Their Families, April 1997. [Commissioner: Ronald Wilson], Human Rights and Equal Opportunity Commission, Sydney.

Brooks, Karen, *Consuming Innocence*, 2008 St Lucia, QLD, UQP.

Buckingham, David 2000, *After the Death of Childhood: Growing Up in the Age of Electronic Media,* Oxford, Polity Press.

Healey, Kaye, ed., 1998, *The Stolen Generation* (Issues in Society Vol. 91), Spinney Press, Balmain, NSW.

Hill, David 2007, *The Forgotten Children: Fairbridge Farm School and its Betrayal of Australia's Child Migrants*, North Sydney, NSW, Random House.

Horton, David 1994, *The Encyclopaedia of Aboriginal Australia* (2 vols.), Canberra, ACT, Aboriginal Studies Press.

Kidd, Rosalind 1997, *The Way We Civilise: Aboriginal Affairs – The Untold Story*, St Lucia, QLD, UQP.

Manne, Robert 2001, *In Denial: The Stolen Generations and the Right* (Quarterly Essay Issue 1), Melbourne, Black Inc.

McInnes, William 2005, *A Man's Got to have a Hobby*, Sydney, Hachette Australia.

McInnes, William 2008, *That'd be Right*, Sydney, Hachette Australia.

McInnes, William and Watt, Sarah 2011, *Worse Things Happen at Sea*, Sydney, Hachette Australia.

McMalcolm, Janet 1993, *Journeyings: the Biography of a Middle-class Generation, 1920–1990, Melbourne,* Melbourne University Press.

Morgan, Sally 1987, *My Place*, Fremantle, WA, FACP.

Postman, Neil 1983, *The Disappearance of Childhood*, London, Allen and Unwin.

Pung, Alice 2006, *Unpolished Gem*, Melbourne, Black Inc.

Ward, Glenyse, 1996, *Wandering Girl*, Broome, WA, Magabala Books.

Websites

The Making of Modern Australia <http://www.abc.net.au/tv/makingaustralia/>

Australian History: Selected Websites National Library of Australia <http://www.nla.gov.au/oz/histsite.html>

Pop Culture Madness <http://www.popculturemadness.com/index.html>

Other Resources

There are several major histories of Australia which you might refer to by Charles Manning Clark, Geoffrey Blainey, Henry Reynolds and others as background to what you read here. See also resources referred to in relation to chapters, in the back of the book.

For a full set of Readers' and Teachers' Notes and other educational resources associated with *The Making of Modern Australia*, visit: www.abc.net.au/tv/makingaustralia/

William McInnes is one of Australia's most popular writers, delighting readers with his memoirs *A Man's Got to Have a Hobby* and *That'd Be Right*, his novel *Cricket Kings*, and his insight into Australian life since the 1940s, written with Essential Media and Entertainment, *The Making of Modern Australia*. In 2011, with his wife Sarah Watt, he co-wrote *Worse Things Happen at Sea*, their celebration of family life in words and photographs. A month after the book's release Sarah lost her battle with cancer.

These works are bestsellers and award winners. In 2006 *A Man's Got to Have a Hobby* was selected as one of the Books Alive 50 Great Reads and William was named Newcomer of the Year at the Australian Book Industry Awards (ABIA). *Worse Things Happen at Sea* was named Non-fiction Book of the Year in the Indie Awards and the ABIA, 2012. As an actor, William received critical and public acclaim for his leading role in the film *Look Both Ways*, written and directed by Sarah Watt. He is the Ambassador of the Year of Reading, 2012, and Chair of the Museum of Australian Democracy Advisory Council, Canberra. William grew up in Queensland and now lives in Melbourne with his two children.

Essential Media and Entertainment is one of Australia's leading television production companies. Based in Sydney, they have produced critically and commercially successful programming for Australian broadcasters and also for some of the world's best, including the BBC, National Geographic, PBS, Discovery, Sundance Channel, Arte France, France Five, and RTE Ireland, to name a few. Their recent credits include *The Time Traveller's Guide*, *Australia on Trial*, *Ten Pound Poms*, *Rogue Nation*, *Voyage to the Planets*, *Solo*, *Miracle on Everest* and *The Floating Brothel*. The ABC TV series *The Making of Modern Australia* was produced by Ian Collie and directed by Susan Lambert and Steve Westh.

For more information see www.essential-media.com and visit http://www.ovationshop.com.au/the-making-of-modern-australia to buy the DVD or download *The Making of Modern Australia*.